CONTEN

D0373677

INTRODUCTION

The purpose of this book is to identify the most common trouble spots for English speakers learning Spanish, to provide a basis for understanding why these trouble spots cause difficulties, and to offer guidance and practice for avoiding potential errors.

Many errors commonly made by speakers and learners of a second language are caused by transferring the patterns of the native language to the language being learned. This happens in all aspects of language, from pronunciation to word formation to sentence structure. Following are some examples of problems English speakers have when learning Spanish.

1. There are only a few sounds in Spanish that do not exist in English. Many sounds common to both languages, however, are represented by different letters in each language. For example, in certain situations the letter *d* in Spanish is pronounced like the "th" in the English "brother." Also, English and Spanish have different pronunciation patterns for vowels, which can cause English speakers to mispronounce many words.

2. Although there are some clues as to whether Spanish nouns are masculine or feminine, many nouns seem to defy regular patterns. English speakers must learn the gender of Spanish nouns and be careful to use the correct corresponding articles and pronouns.

3. Although many Spanish words have cognates in English, there are also many false cognates, aptly called *falsos amigos* in Spanish. One example is *sensible*, an adjective in both languages; it means "levelheaded" in English but "sensitive" in Spanish.

4. In many cases, one word in English has two or more noninterchangeable translations in Spanish. One example of this is the verb "be" in English, whose correspondents in Spanish are *ser* and *estar,* as well as other verbs used idiomatically. Another is the English "for," which has several Spanish translations, among them, *por* and *para*.

5. Particles, such as prepositions and conjunctions, have no one-for-one equivalents in both languages. For example, the Spanish preposition *en* can be translated into English as "in," "on," "at," "of," and

"about." Likewise, the translation of English "on Sunday" is *el domingo*, "the Sunday."

6. A more insidious type of *falso amigo* is encountered in the use of verb tenses. The present tense, for example, can be used identically in both languages for certain functions. It is, therefore, often assumed that the function of the present tense will be the same in all instances. Actually, the Spanish present tense can also be used for functions that are expressed in English in the present progressive, present perfect, past, and future tenses. Every verb tense, in fact, represents a potential trouble spot for English-speaking learners of Spanish.

7. Information can be expressed one way in one language, and in a different way in the other. In English, for example, one says "I am hungry," while in Spanish one says the equivalent of "I have hunger." Likewise, the English "I like ice cream" is stated in Spanish as "Ice cream appeals to me." Expressions of this type present more complications when their individual words are modified; for example, "I am *very* hungry" is the equivalent of "I have *a lot of* hunger." Again, the pitfall is transferring the English pattern to the Spanish.

In this book you will find the reasons behind these and many other common but lesser-known "blunders" through explanations of how regular patterns of Spanish differ from those of English. You will be made aware of potential trouble spots and shown how to break bad habits and correct your own mistakes. Several examples are given for each topic, followed by exercises that test your understanding and help you avoid the pitfalls encountered when translating word for word, structure for structure, from English.

Because individual words of a language are used in connection with other words, you will find that most topics are mentioned in more than one place. This repetition allows for cross-referencing and provides multiple examples of the most problematic structures. You will find that many of the lists are structured for sense and meaning; adverbs are listed in order of *nunca* "never" to *siempre* "always," for example. Nouns are grouped by their endings, and verbs are grouped by usage. In addition, the comprehensive, detailed index at the back of the book serves as a guide to finding all the references to each topic. At the back of the book you will also find the answers to all the exercises. It is hoped that the materials presented here will help you improve your proficiency in Spanish and avoid the most common blunders.

Suggestions for Using This Book

The book is divided into three parts: Pronunciation and Spelling, Grammar, and Vocabulary. The largest section is Grammar, which identifies the various types of words according to traditional terminology. If you are unfamiliar with these terms, or if you find them more confusing than helpful, follow these suggestions:

- First look for the "Avoid the Blunder" headings in each section. Read the examples, then read the related explanation.
- Use the Index, rather than the Contents, to find what you are looking for.
- Check all the cross-references to a topic you are interested in to find more examples.
- Do the exercises on a separate sheet of paper, then check your answers in the Answer Key at the back of the book. If you have made mistakes, reread the pertinent sections, then do the exercises again.

Throughout the book, all blunders are printed in red type and marked by a stylized ✗. These are words, phrases, and sentences that are unacceptable.

The guidelines here are based on current standard usage in all countries where Spanish is the native language. However, be aware that language is constantly changing, that there are many different forms of expression, and that certain items identified here as "blunders" are accepted as standard usage in some areas. The biggest blunder of all would be to correct a native speaker, or to in any way imply that he or she doesn't speak "correct" Spanish. Recognizing the differences you encounter in different places will enrich your Spanish and enable you to identify regional variations. The best way to learn a language is to listen to its native speakers and practice by communicating with them.

Acknowledgments

The author is indebted to her many teachers, colleagues, friends, and students, from whom she continues to learn. She especially appreciates the advice of Ligia Ochoa Sierra, and the help of Jeannette Walters Márquez and Luz Noemi Curet, who read the entire manuscript and provided many insightful comments and suggestions.

PRONUNCIATION AND SPELLING

PRONUNCIATION

ONE-SYLLABLE VOWELS

a   e   i   o   u

ONE-SYLLABLE VOWEL COMBINATIONS

Any combination of **a**, **e**, or **o** with the letter **i** or **u**

ia	ie	io	iu	ua	ue	ui	uo
ya	*yeh*	*yo*	*yu*	*wa*	*weh*	*wee*	*wo*

ai	ei	oi	ui	au	eu	iu
eye	*ay* as in "say"	*oy* as in "boy"	*wee*	*ah-oo*	*eh-oo*	*you*

TWO-SYLLABLE VOWEL COMBINATIONS

Combinations of **a**, **e**, or **o** with accented **I** or **u**

ía	íe	ío	úa	úe	úi	úo
EE-ah	*EE-eh*	*EE-o*	*OO-ah*	*OO-eh*	*OO-ee*	*OO-o*

aí	eí	oí	aú	eú	iú
ah-EE	*eh-EE*	*o-EE*	*ah-OO*	*eh-OO*	*ee-OO*

Combinations that do not contain **i** or **u** and that have no accent mark

ae	ao	ea	ee	eo	oa	oe	oo
ah-eh	*ah-o*	*eh-ah*	*eh-eh*	*eh-o*	*o-ah*	*o-eh*	*o-o*

CONSONANTS	IN INITIAL POSITION similar to:	AFTER VOWEL
b/v	*b* as in "boy"	breathed through almost-closed lips
c before *a, o, u* k qu before *e, i*	*k* as in "skate"	
c before *e, i*	*c* as in "ceiling" (in Latin America) *th* as in "thumb" (in Spain)	
cc		*cc* as in "access"
d	*d* as in "dog"	*th* as in "brother"

3

CONSONANTS	IN INITIAL POSITION similar to:	AFTER VOWEL
f	f as in "find"	
g before a, o, u gu before e, i	g as in "girl"	breathed through almost-closed throat
g before e, i j x	ch as in Scottish "loch" or German "ach"; a voiceless, scratchy sound from the throat	
h	h as in "honest" (silent)	
l	l as in "love"	tl as in "bottle"
ll y	yy as in "say yes" OR j as in "jar"	
m	m as in "man"	
n	n as in "next"	
ñ	ni as in "onion"	
p	p as in "spin"	
r	rolling trill of the tongue	d as in "body"
rr		rolling trill of the tongue
s	s as in "sun"	
t	t as in "stamp"	
w	w as in "wash"	
x	s as in "sun" (in native Mexican words) (see also g, j, x)	x as in "extra"
y	(see ll)	y as in "guy," "way," "boy"
z	s as in "sun" (in Latin America) th as in "thumb" (in Spain)	

Spanish Letters and Sounds

Because the Spanish and English alphabets are so similar, it is important to keep in mind that the sounds represented by most letters in Spanish are different from the sounds they represent in English.

Vowels

Spanish vowel sounds are produced by first positioning the mouth correctly, then uttering the sound without moving the jaw.

AVOID THE *Blunder*

Do not pronounce a single vowel with two vowel sounds.

a   pronounced like the *a* in "father," but cut short: *taco*

    ✗ ta uh co

e   pronounced like the *e* in "bet": *bueno*

    ✗ bwayno

i   pronounced like the *i* in "machine," but cut short: *fino*

o   pronounced like the beginning of *o* in "open"

Do not glide into an /ow/ sound: *fino*.

    ✗ finow   ✗ tacow

u   pronounced like the beginning of *u* in "tuba"

Do not make a /yu/ sound: *Cuba*.

    ✗ kyuwba

Unstressed vowels in English are usually pronounced with the mouth in a relaxed, almost-closed position, making them all sound something like "uh." In Spanish, each vowel is pronounced clearly.

rosas	"ro sas"
buenos días	"bwe nos dee ahs"

AVOID THE *Blunder*

✗ row zuhs
✗ bway nuhz dee uhz

Any combination of the vowels *i* or *u* with *a*, *e*, or *o* is pronounced as one syllable unless there is an accent mark over one of the vowels.

pia no	die ta	Ma rio	viu da
a gua	bue no	rui nas	cuo ta
Jai me	rei na	oi go	cui dar
Lau ra	Eu ro pa		

Any combination of the vowels *i* or *u* with *a*, *e*, or *o* is pronounced as two syllables when there is an accent mark over either vowel.

dí a	rí o	Ma rí a	le í	
grú a	ac tú a	re ú ne	Ra úl	con ti nú e

Any combination of the vowels *a*, *e*, or *o* is pronounced as two syllables. No accent mark is used.

pa e lla	fe o	po e ma	ca os	le er

AVOID THE *Blunder*

✗ Jaíme	✗ oígo	✗ óigo	✗ dia	✗ Raul
✗ paélla	✗ féo	✗ poéma	✗ cáos	✗ leér

When a word ends with a vowel, and the following word starts with the same vowel, the vowel is pronounced only once.

Ana anda al parque	"a nan dal par que"
la casa de Eduardo	"la ca sa de duar do"

AVOID THE *Blunder*

✗ Ana | anda | al parque
✗ la casa de | Eduardo

When a vowel is repeated within a word, however, like *ee* or *oo*, the vowels are pronounced as two syllables that glide together.

leer	"le ER"
coordinar	"co or dee NAR"

AVOID THE *Blunder*

Do not add a /y/ or /w/ sound, as you would in English.

✗ le yer
✗ co wor di nar

Words are connected in a stream of speech, without a break between words.

¿Cómo está usted?	"co mwe stau sted"
Vamos a la piscina a nadar un rato.	"va mo sa la pi si na na da run ra to"

AVOID THE *Blunder*

✗ co mo | está | us ted
✗ va mos | a la pis cina | a na dar | un ra to

Consonants

The sounds /p/, /k/, and /t/ at the beginning of English words are followed by a puff of air. Do not produce this puff of air when pronouncing these sounds in Spanish.

Pepe   papá   taco   capa   Paco   tapas

The sounds of the Spanish letters *b*, *v*, *g*, and *d* are similar to their English equivalents at the beginning of words. However, when these letters fall between two vowels, they are softer and may be lengthened.

b, v   Keep the lips slightly apart and let the air come through.

bebe   habas   tuvo   uva

g   Keep a slight opening at the throat and let the air come through. (This sound is like the French *r*.)

haga   traigo   mago   llegue

d   Place the tongue between the top and bottom teeth, exactly like the *th* in "brother."

cada   dedo   mide   seda

AVOID THE *Blunder*

Do not use the English /d/ sound for the Spanish *d* in the middle or at the end of words. This sound is used for the Spanish *r*.

Say the following words aloud, pronouncing *d* like the English *th*, and *r* like the English *d*.

cada	cara	cedo	cero
todo	toro	dudo	duro
ida	ira	comed	comer
mide	mire	hablad	hablar

Remember that *ll* and *y* are consonants and are pronounced like the doubled *y* in "say yes" or the *j* in "jar." They must be pronounced with force to avoid misunderstanding. For example, if the *ll* is not pronounced forcefully enough, a person might hear you say "I love myself" (*me amo*) rather than "My name is" (*me llamo*).

se llama Yolanda	"se yya ma yyo lan da"
	OR "se ja ma jo lan da"
ya me llamó	"yya me yya mó" OR "ja me ja mó"

AVOID THE *Blunder*

✗ se ama Yolanda   ✗ ya me amó

The sound /r/ in Spanish is very different from the English /r/. To pronounce the English /r/, the lips are rounded, the top teeth are somewhat bared, and the tongue is suspended in the middle of the mouth without touching anything. To pronounce the Spanish /r/, keep your lips in a flat position and tap the tip of your tongue once on the ridge behind your top front teeth. The sound is like the *d* in the English "body."

cara	cero	hora	iré	loro	oro	para

Learn to make the trilled Spanish *r* by placing the tip of your tongue loosely on the ridge behind your top front teeth, then forcing air between the tongue and the ridge, causing it to flap rapidly and automatically. This takes practice, but it's worth learning.

The letter *r* before another consonant requires a half-trill.

carta	embargo	cierto	cerca	forma

The letter *r* at the beginning of a word is fully trilled, as is the *rr* in the middle of a word.

río	rama	rosa	carro	perro	cierra	error

The Spanish *s* is pronounced like the *s* in "sun," even in the middle or at the end of a word. It is never pronounced like the English *z*, as in the second *s* of "Susan" or at the end of a word.

AVOID THE *Blunder*

Pronounce the Spanish *s* (even in the middle or at the end of a word) like the *s* in "sun."

✗ Suzanna   ✗ rozez

In Spanish, the only consonants that are doubled are *l*, *r*, and *c*; all of the doubled consonants represent sounds that are very different from the sounds of the single letters. (See the chart on pages 3–4.)

AVOID THE *Blunder*

Do not use a double consonant in Spanish where it is used in the English cognate.

✗ intelligente ✗ professor ✗ recommendar

SPELLING

Consonants

The sound /k/ is spelled with *c* before the vowels *a, o,* and *u,* and with *qu* before the vowels *e* and *i.*

ca	que	qui	co	cu
casa	queso	quieto	come	cuna

The sound /kw/ is always spelled *cu.*

cua	cue	cui	cuo
cuatro	cueva	cuidar	cuota

The sound /th/ (in Spain) and /s/ (in Latin America) is spelled with *z* before the vowels *a, o,* and *u,* and with *c* before the vowels *e* and *i.*

za	ce	ci	zo	zu
zapato	cero	cinco	zona	zumo

The sound /g/ is spelled with *g* before the vowels *a, o* and *u,* and with *gu* before the vowels *e* and *i.*

ga	gue	gui	go	gu
gala	guerra	guitarra	goza	gusano

The sound /gw/ is spelled *gu* before the vowels *a* and *o,* and *güi* before the vowels *e* and *i.*

gua	güe	güi	guo
guante	güera	pingüino	antiguo

The "stronger than /h/" sound (more guttural—from the throat—than the English *h*) is spelled with a *j* before the vowels *a, e, i, o,* and *u.* It can also be spelled with a *g* before the vowels *e* and *i,* and with an *x* in the words *México* and *mexicano.*

ja	je OR ge OR xe	ji OR gi	jo	ju
jaleo	jerga	jitomate	joya	jugo
	general	gigante		
	México			
	mexicano			

The sound of the letter ñ is similar to that of the *ni* in the English "onion." The ñ represents a combination of the consonants *n + y*. The tilde that distinguishes this letter from *n* may be written as a straight line over the *n*. Always pronounce the /y/ sound clearly after the /n/ sound.

año	"an yo"
baño	"ban yo"
pequeño	"pe ken yo"
niña	"nin ya"

AVOID THE *Blunder*

Do not forget to write the tilde.

✗ ano ✗ bano ✗ pequeno ✗ nina

■ When grammar forces a vowel change, this may affect the consonants described above. This consonant change occurs in the following situations:

■ adding a plural ending to a noun or adjective

un lápiz	dos lápices	(✗ lápizes)
la actriz	las actrices	(✗ actrizes)
el arroz	los arroces	(✗ arrozes)

■ present indicative *yo* forms

recoger	yo recojo	(✗ recogo)
dirigir	yo dirijo	(✗ dirigo)

■ preterite *yo* forms

sacar	yo saqué	(✗ sacé)
jugar	yo jugué	(✗ jugé)
empezar	yo empecé	(✗ empezé)

■ present subjunctive verb forms

sacar	saque	(✗ sace)
rogar	ruegue	(✗ ruege)
recoger	recoja	(✗ recoga)
almorzar	almuerce	(✗ almuerze)

■ making an adjective from a noun

Nicaragua	nicaragüense	(✗ nicaraguense)

■ intensifying an adjective

simpático	simpatiquísimo	(✗ simpaticísimo)
feliz	felicísima	(✗ felizísima)

AVOID THE *Blunder*

✗ lápizes	✗ actrizes	✗ arrozes
✗ recogo	✗ dirigo	
✗ sacé	✗ jugé	✗ empezé
✗ sace	✗ ruege	✗ recoga	✗ almuerze
✗ nicaraguense		
✗ simpaticísimo		
✗ felizísima		

Accent Marks

■ Accent marks are used above both uppercase and lowercase letters.

When writing the accent mark by hand, make a small mark directly over the vowel, slanting upward toward the right. When the accent mark is above a lowercase *i*, do not dot the *i*.

AVOID THE *Blunder*

Do not "float" accent marks above words.

✗ lápiz   ✗ difícil   ✗ saque

■ The following present-tense forms of the verb *estar* require an accent mark.

estás   está   están   estáis

The following present-tense forms of the verb *estar* do not require an accent mark.

estoy   estamos

■ Certain verbs whose infinitive ends in *-iar* require accent marks over the *i* in the *yo, tú, usted/él/ella,* and *ustedes/ellos/ellas* forms of the present tense, but not in the *nosotros(-as)* and *vosotros(-as)* forms.

confiar (*to trust*)	confío	confiamos
	confías	confiáis
	confía	
	confían	

Other verbs of this type include the following.

enviar	*to send*
guiar	*to guide*
variar	*to vary*

Other verbs that end in *-iar* do not have accent marks over the *i* in their conjugated forms.

estudiar (*to study*)	estudio	estudiamos
	estudias	estudiáis
	estudia	
	estudian	

Other verbs of this type include the following.

abreviar	*to abbreviate*
cambiar	*to change*
limpiar	*to clean*

■ The words *quién, cómo, qué, cuál, dónde, cuándo,* and *por qué* have an accent mark when they begin a question, whether direct or indirect. They do not require an accent mark in other contexts.

"Why" is expressed with two words and has an accent mark: *¿Por qué?* "Because" is expressed with one word and does not have an accent mark: *porque*

ACCENT MARK	¿**Quién** es?	*Who is it?*
ACCENT MARK	No sé **quién** es.	*I don't know who it is.*
NO ACCENT MARK	Fui yo **quien** vio el accidente.	*I was the one who saw the accident.*
ACCENT MARK	¿**Cómo** estás?	*How are you?*
ACCENT MARK	No entiendo **cómo** lo haces.	*I don't understand how you do it.*
NO ACCENT MARK	Debes trabajar **como** tu papá.	*You should work like your father does.*
ACCENT MARK	¿**Qué** es esto?	*What's this?*
ACCENT MARK	Él no sabía **qué** hacer.	*He didn't know what to do.*
NO ACCENT MARK	Él me dijo **que** lo haría.	*He told me he would do it.*
ACCENT MARK	¿**Cuál** es su nombre?	*What's your name?*
ACCENT MARK	Quisiera saber **cuál** de los libros es el mejor.	*I would like to know which one is the best book.*
NO ACCENT MARK	He perdido mi tarjeta, sin la **cual** no puedo comprar nada.	*I lost my card, without which I can't buy anything.*

ACCENT MARK	¿**Dónde** estás?	*Where are you?*
ACCENT MARK	Me preguntó **dónde** estaba su mamá.	*He asked me where his mother was.*
NO ACCENT MARK	Vamos al restaurante **donde** comimos ayer.	*Let's go to the restaurant where we ate yesterday.*
ACCENT MARK	¿**Cuándo** es la fiesta?	*When is the party?*
ACCENT MARK	Tengo que averiguar **cuándo** es el examen.	*I have to find out when the exam is.*
NO ACCENT MARK	**Cuando** lo vio, se desmayó.	*When she saw him, she fainted.*
ACCENT MARK	¿**Por qué** no vienes con nosotros?	*Why don't you come with us?*
ACCENT MARK	Me puedo imaginar **por qué** lo hiciste.	*I can imagine why you did it.*
NO ACCENT MARK	Trabaja mucho **porque** quiere ganar más.	*He works hard because he wants to earn more.*

■ The meaning of certain words is distinguished by the use of an accent mark.

aún	*still*	aun	*even*
dé	*give!* (command)	de	*of, from*
él	*he*	el	*the*
más	*more, plus*	mas	*however*
mí	*me*	mi	*my*
sí	*yes*	si	*if*
sólo	*only*	solo	*alone*
té	*tea*	te	*you* (object)
tú	*you*	tu	*your*

■ The following guidelines apply to the use of accent marks with other words.

In order to know where to put an accent mark, you need to know how the word is pronounced and be able to identify the syllable that is stressed or slightly more emphasized.

☐ When the emphasized syllable is the final syllable:

■ there is no accent mark if that syllable ends in a consonant other than -*n* or -*s*.

verd<u>ad</u>   rel<u>oj</u>   ani<u>mal</u>   err<u>or</u>   est<u>oy</u>   arr<u>oz</u>

- an accent mark is required over the vowel of the final syllable if it ends in a vowel, a one-syllable vowel combination (see page 3), -*n*, or -*s*.

habló   comí   comió   comerán   acción   sabrás

☐ When the emphasized syllable is the next-to-last syllable:

- there is no accent mark if the final syllable ends in a vowel, -*n*, or -*s*.

hablo   supe   comen   sabes   aprendemos

- there is no accent mark if the stressed vowel is part of a two-syllable vowel combination (any combination of the vowels *a*, *e*, and *o*).

video   cacao   Corea   poema   paella

- there is no accent mark if the final syllable is a one-syllable vowel combination.

Mario   Colombia   agua   perpetuo   superficie

- there is an accent mark over the stressed vowel if the stressed vowel is part of a normally one-syllable vowel combination (any vowel combination that includes *i* or *u*).

María   día   tío   ríe   Raúl
maíz   país

☐ When the emphasized syllable is the third-, fourth-, or fifth-last syllable, it always has an accent mark.

anímate   propósito   estudiándolo   dígaselo   rápidamente

☐ Adding a syllable can change the need for an accent mark. For example, words that end in -*ión* always have an accent mark, but when they are made plural, they lose it.

acción   acciones
lección   lecciones

Certain other words may not have an accent mark in the singular but may need one in the plural.

examen   exámenes
joven   jóvenes

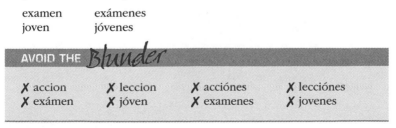

AVOID THE *Blunder*

✗ accion   ✗ leccion   ✗ acciónes   ✗ lecciónes
✗ exámen   ✗ jóven   ✗ examenes   ✗ jovenes

Exercises

A *Fill in the blanks with the consonant or consonants that precede the vowel to produce the sound indicated.*

1. The sound /k/ is spelled: _C_ a   ___ e   ___ i   ___ o   ___ u
2. The sound /g/ is spelled: _g_ a   ___ e   ___ i   ___ o   ___ u
3. The sound /th/ or /s/ is spelled: _z_ a   ___ e   ___ i   ___ o   ___ u
4. The sound /kw/ is spelled: _cu_ a   ___ e   ___ i   ___ o
5. The sound /gw/ is spelled: _gu_ a   ___ e   ___ i   ___ o
6. The sound /h/ is spelled: _j_ a   ___ e/___ e   ___ i/___ i
                                        ___ o   ___ u

B *Write an accent mark where necessary in the underlined words.*

1. <u>Mi</u> hermano no <u>vino</u> a clase <u>porque</u> no <u>hizo</u> la tarea. Ahora <u>esta</u> en casa.
2. ¿<u>Quienes</u> van al cine <u>esta</u> tarde? ¿Vas <u>tu</u>? ¿Va <u>tu</u> hermano?
3. <u>Si</u>, <u>mi</u> hermano va, pero <u>solo</u> <u>si</u> hace la tarea primero.

C *Write the number of syllables in each word on the line next to it.*

1. rápidamente   _____
2. Mario   _____
3. María   _____
4. video   _____
5. aprendemos   _____

CAPITALIZATION

Many conventions used in English are the same in Spanish, but there are some important exceptions.

■ The words *usted, ustedes, señor, señores, señora, señorita, don,* and *doña* are capitalized only in the abbreviated form.

Ud.	*you*	Sra.	*Mrs.*
Uds.	*you all*	Srta.	*Miss*
Sr.	*Mr.*	D. ⎫	friendly term of respect for an older person,
Sres	*Gentlemen*	Da. ⎭	used with his or her first name

AVOID THE *Blunder*

✗ Usted   ✗ Ustedes   ✗ Señor   ✗ Señora   ✗ Don

■ The names of months and days are not capitalized in Spanish.

enero	*January*	lunes	*Monday*
febrero	*February*	martes	*Tuesday*
marzo	*March*	miércoles	*Wednesday*
abril	*April*	jueves	*Thursday*
mayo	*May*	viernes	*Friday*
junio	*June*	sábado	*Saturday*
julio	*July*	domingo	*Sunday*
agosto	*August*		
septiembre	*September*		
octubre	*October*		
noviembre	*November*		
diciembre	*December*		

AVOID THE *Blunder*

✗ Enero   ✗ Mayo   ✗ Lunes   ✗ Domingo

■ The names of languages and nationalities are not capitalized in Spanish.

argentino(-a)	*Argentine*	náhuatl	*Nahuatl*
colombiano(-a)	*Colombian*	panameño(-a)	*Panamanian*
español(a)	*Spanish*	peruano(-a)	*Peruvian*
francés/francesa	*French*	portugués/	*Portuguese*
inglés/inglesa	*English*	portuguesa	
mexicano(-a)	*Mexican*	quechua	*Quechua*

AVOID THE *Blunder*

✗ Español   ✗ Inglés   ✗ Peruano   ✗ Colombiana

■ The names of religions and religious affiliations are typically not capitalized in Spanish.

budista	*Buddhist*	el budismo	*Buddhism*
católico(-a)	*Catholic*	el catolicismo	*Catholicism*
cristiano(-a)	*Christian*	el cristianismo	*Christianity*
hindú	*Hindu*	el hinduismo	*Hinduism*
judío(-a)	*Jew*	el judaísmo	*Judaism*
musulmán/	*Muslim*	BUT el Islam	*Islam*
musulmana			

AVOID THE *Blunder*

✗ Cristiano   ✗ Judía   ✗ Musulmana
✗ Budismo   ✗ Catolicismo   ✗ Hinduismo

■ In the titles of books and articles, only the first word and proper names are capitalized.

Gramática de la lengua española	*Grammar of the Spanish Language*
Don Quijote de la Mancha	*Don Quixote of la Mancha*

AVOID THE *Blunder*

✗ Gramática De La Lengua Española
✗ Gramática de la Lengua Española
✗ Don Quijote De La Mancha

Exercises

A *Write the abbreviated form of the following words.*

1. don _____

2. señora _____

3. usted _____

4. señores _____

B *Circle the words below that have incorrect capitalization.*

1. Septiembre   6. Católico

2. viernes   7. judío

3. español   8. Miércoles

4. Inglés   9. Argentino

5. octubre   10. peruana

PUNCTUATION

■ Two question marks are required for every question: an upside-down question mark at the beginning, and one identical to the English question mark at the end.

¿Adónde vas, papá?	*Where are you going, Dad?*
¿Me compras un juguete?	*Will you buy me a toy?*

Two exclamation points are required for every exclamation: an upside-down exclamation point at the beginning, and one identical to the English exclamation point at the end.

¡Váyanse de aquí!	*Get out of here!*
¡Déjame en paz!	*Leave me alone!*

The first question mark or exclamation point is placed at the beginning of the question or exclamation, which is not necessarily at the beginning of the sentence.

Papá, ¿adónde vas?	*Dad, where are you going?*
Chicos, ¡váyanse de aquí!	*Guys, get out of here!*

■ In writing dialogue, a dash, rather than quotation marks, is used to indicate the spoken word or a change in speakers.

—¿Qué piensa hacer usted, Sr. Rodríguez?	*"What are you planning to do, Mr. Rodriguez?"*
—No sé. Tendré que hablarlo con mi familia.	*"I don't know. I'll have to talk it over with my family."*

■ Quotation marks are used, as in English, to mark someone's exact words within a text. In Spanish the symbols «...» are often used for this purpose. If the end punctuation of the quote is a question mark or exclamation point, it goes before the final quotation mark. In Spanish, unlike English, this is followed by a period. A colon, rather than a comma, is used to introduce the quote.

El director le preguntó: "¿Qué piensa hacer usted, Sr. Rodríguez?".	*The director asked him, "What are you planning to do, Mr. Rodríguez?"*

When a quote ends in a period or is followed by a comma, the period or comma goes after the quotation mark.

El Sr. Rodríguez contestó: "No sé, tendré que hablarlo con mi familia".

"No sé", dijo el Sr. Rodríguez.

Mr. Rodríguez answered, "I don't know. I'll have to talk it over with my family."

"I don't know," said Mr. Rodríguez.

AVOID THE *Blunder*

✗ Adónde vas, papá?
✗ ¿Papa, adónde vas?
✗ Déjame en paz!
✗ "No voy," dijo Juan.

In Spanish, items in a series are separated by commas. No comma is used between the last two items (that is, before *y*).

Luisa, Elena y Dolores están en México este verano.

En el mercado compramos carne, queso, tomates, aguacates y fresas.

Luisa, Elena, and Dolores are in Mexico this summer.

At the market we bought meat, cheese, tomatoes, avocadoes, and strawberries.

AVOID THE *Blunder*

✗ Luisa, Elena, y Dolores
✗ carne, queso, tomates, aguacates, y fresas

Exercise

A *Punctuate the following sentences.*

1. María vas a estudiar conmigo hoy

2. No no puedo

3. Me llamas más tarde

4. Si te llamo a las ocho

5. Te voy a extrañar dijo Paco

6. Fueron a Guatemala El Salvador Honduras y Nicaragua

GRAMMAR

NOUNS

A noun is a word that names a person, an animal, an object, a place, an event, an idea, a quality, an action, a state, or other abstract notion.

Gender

Every noun in Spanish has gender—it is either masculine or feminine.

Generally, words that name male people or animals are masculine, and those that name female people or animals are feminine, but there are exceptions.

Words that name objects, places, events, periods of time, and abstract notions are also either masculine or feminine.

The gender of a noun is indicated by the article that precedes it: *el* indicates a masculine noun; *la* indicates a feminine noun.

AVOID THE *Blunder*

Learn nouns with their articles, as if they were one unit.

Nouns That Name People and Animals

Many nouns end in *-o* for males and *-a* for females.

el chico	*the boy*	el cartero	*the male mail carrier*
la chica	*the girl*		
el hermano	*the brother*	la cartera	*the female mail carrier*
la hermana	*the sister*		
el amigo	*the male friend*	el enfermero	*the male nurse*
la amiga	*the female friend*	la enfermera	*the female nurse*
el esposo	*the husband*		
la esposa	*the wife*		

Both males and females can be named by nouns that end in -e. The article used indicates the gender of the person named, *el* for a male, *la* for a female.

el estudiante ⎱ *the student*
la estudiante ⎰

el paciente ⎱ *the patient*
la paciente ⎰

el gerente ⎱ *the manager*
la gerente ⎰

el ayudante ⎱ *the assistant*
la ayudante ⎰

el hablante ⎱ *the speaker*
la hablante ⎰

el presidente ⎱ *the president*
la presidente* ⎰

La presidenta is used in some countries but not in others.

There are some exceptions.

el jefe   *the male boss*
la jefa   *the female boss*

el monje   *the monk*
la monja   *the nun*

Both males and females can be named by nouns that end in -*ista*. The article used indicates the gender of the person named.

el optimista ⎱ *the optimist*
la optimista ⎰

el protagonista ⎱ *the main character*
la protagonista ⎰

el especialista ⎱ *the specialist*
la especialista ⎰

el periodista ⎱ *the journalist*
la periodista ⎰

Both males and females can be named by several common nouns that end in -*o*.

el modelo ⎱ *the model*
la modelo ⎰

el soprano ⎱ *the soprano*
la soprano ⎰

el piloto ⎱ *the pilot*
la piloto ⎰

el miembro ⎱ *the member*
la miembro ⎰

el testigo ⎱ *the witness*
la testigo ⎰

el médico ⎱ *the doctor*
la médico* ⎰

La médica is used in some countries but not in others.

Both males and females can be named by nouns that end in -*ía*.

el policía	*the male police officer*
la policía	*the female police officer*
el guía	*the male guide*
la guía	*the female guide*

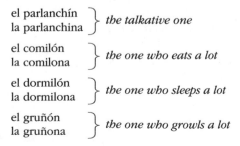

AVOID THE *Blunder*

Do not change the endings of these nouns to -*o* or -*a* in an attempt to make them masculine or feminine. The article is all you need to distinguish them.

✗ la estudianta   ✗ el artisto   ✗ la modela   ✗ el policío

Many nouns that name males end in -*or*. Their counterparts for females end in -*ora*.

el profesor la profesora	*the teacher*
el doctor la doctora	*the doctor*
el ganador la ganadora	*the winner*
el perdedor la perdedora	*the loser*
el contador la contadora	*the accountant*
el encantador la encantadora	*the charmer*

An exception is the feminine equivalent of *el actor*: *la actriz*.

Certain nouns that name males end in -*ín* or -*ón*. The counterparts for females end in -*ina* or -*ona*.

el parlanchín la parlanchina	*the talkative one*
el comilón la comilona	*the one who eats a lot*
el dormilón la dormilona	*the one who sleeps a lot*
el gruñón la gruñona	*the one who growls a lot*

A few nouns that name people do not change gender, regardless of the gender of the person they refer to.

la persona

María es una persona muy simpática.	*María is a very nice person.*
José es una persona muy simpática.	*José is a very nice person.*

la víctima

María es la víctima de una tragedia.	*María is the victim of a tragedy.*
José es la víctima de una tragedia.	*José is the victim of a tragedy.*

la estrella

Verónica es la estrella que le gusta más a Pablo.	*Verónica is the movie star that Pablo likes best.*
Antonio es la estrella que le gusta más a Ana.	*Antonio is the movie star that Ana likes best.*

AVOID THE *Blunder*

Do not try to change the gender of these nouns.

✗ el persona   ✗ el persono   ✗ el víctima
✗ el víctimo   ✗ el estrella

When referring to a group of people, if there is at least one male in the group, the masculine plural noun is used.

dos hermanas	*two sisters*
dos hermanas y un hermano / tres hermanos	*two sisters and one brother / three siblings*

Gender of Other Nouns

For all nouns that do not name people, the gender refers to the word, not to the person the object belongs to.

el brazo (*the arm*)	masculine, whether it is the arm of a male or a female
la pierna (*the leg*)	feminine, whether it is the leg of a male or a female
la corbata (*the necktie*)	feminine, even though it is usually worn by males
el vestido (*the dress*)	masculine, even though it is usually worn by females

Many nouns that end in *-o* are masculine. Many nouns that end in *-a* are feminine.

el carro	*the car*	la casa	*the house*
el año	*the year*	la empresa	*the enterprise*
el ojo	*the eye*	la pulgada	*the inch*

Certain nouns that end in *-ma* are masculine.

el problema	*the problem*	el programa	*the program*
el sistema	*the system*	el aroma	*the aroma*
el clima	*the climate*	el síntoma	*the symptom*
el trauma	*the trauma*	el carisma	*the charisma*
el drama	*the drama*		

Nevertheless, others are feminine.

la trama	*the plot*
la crema	*the cream*
la yema	*the egg yolk*

Nouns that begin with a stressed *a-* or *ha-* may be feminine, but they are preceded by *el* instead of *la* for pronunciation purposes. Adjectives and other determiners that refer to these nouns are feminine. (See pages 55–56.)

el agua	*the water*	el águila	*the eagle*
el hambre	*the hunger*	el asma	*the asthma*
el alma	*the soul*		

El agua está fría.	*The water is cold.*
Tengo mucha hambre.	*I'm really hungry. (I have a lot of hunger.)*
Te amo con toda el alma.	*I love you with all my heart. (I love you with all my soul.)*

Do not use *la* with these words. Do not use masculine adjectives
with these words.

✗ La agua está fría.
✗ El agua está frío.
✗ Tengo mucho hambre.

Certain nouns that end in -*a* are masculine. Certain nouns that end in
-*o* are feminine.

el día	*the day*	el planeta	*the planet*
el mapa	*the map*	la mano	*the hand*
el tranvía	*the streetcar*		

Buenos días. El día está muy
　bonito.
Ella tiene las manos bonitas.

*Good morning. It's a beautiful
　day.*
She has pretty hands.

Unless the noun begins with a stressed *a*- or *ha*-, use the article,
not the noun's ending, as a guide to gender. If the article is *el*, use
masculine adjectives. If the article is *la*, use feminine adjectives.

✗ El día está muy bonita.
✗ Ella tiene las manos bonitos.

Certain nouns that end in -*o* are feminine, and they are really just shortened forms of nouns that end in -*a*.

la foto
la fotografía } *the photograph*

la moto
la motocicleta } *the motorcycle*

✗ el foto　　　✗ el moto

All nouns that end in -*ción*, -*sión*, or -*xión* are feminine.

la nación	*the nation*	la tensión	*the tension*
la evolución	*the evolution*	la conexión	*the connection*

Certain other nouns that end in -*ión* are feminine.

la unión	*the union*
la reunión	*the meeting*
la región	*the region*

Other nouns that end in -*ión* are masculine.

el avión	*the airplane*	el camión	*the truck*
el guión	*the script*	el sarampión	*the measles*

AVOID THE *Blunder*

If an unfamiliar word ends in -*ión* (but not -*ción*, -*sión*, or -*xión*), check the gender before using it.

✗ el nación   ✗ el región   ✗ la avión   ✗ la sarampión

All nouns that end in -*tad*, -*dad*, -*tud*, or -*umbre* are feminine.

la libertad	*the liberty*
la amistad	*the friendship*
la facultad	*the university department*
la ciudad	*the city*
la honestidad	*the honesty*
la nacionalidad	*the nationality*

la virtud	*the virtue*	la costumbre	*the custom*
la gratitud	*the gratitude*	la cumbre	*the summit*
la actitud	*the attitude*	la muchedumbre	*the crowd*

All nouns that end in -*ie* are feminine.

la serie	*the series*
la superficie	*the surface*
la planicie	*the plain*

AVOID THE *Blunder*

✗ el ciudad   ✗ el universidad
✗ el muchedumbre   ✗ el serie

A number of words change in meaning according to their gender. Here are some of the most common.

MASCULINE		FEMININE	
el capital	*the money*	la capital	*the capital city*
el cólera	*the cholera*	la cólera	*the anger*
el coma	*the coma*	la coma	*the comma*
el cometa	*the comet*	la cometa	*the kite*
el corriente	*the current month*	la corriente	*the current*
el corte	*the cut*	la corte	*the court of law*
el cura	*the priest*	la cura	*the cure*
el defensa	*the defensive back in soccer*	la defensa	*the defense*
el editorial	*the editorial*	la editorial	*the publisher*
el escolta	*the male escort*	la escolta	*the group of escorts, the female escort*
el guardia	*the male guard*	la guardia	*guard duty, the guard unit, the female guard*
el guía	*the male guide*	la guía	*the guidebook, the female guide*
el orden	*the arrangement*	la orden	*the command*
el policía	*the male police officer*	la policía	*the police force, the female police officer*
el recluta	*the male recruit*	la recluta	*the recruitment, the female recruit*

AVOID THE *Blunder*

Be aware that as the role of women in society is changing, nouns that refer to females are changing—and changing differently in different parts of the Spanish-speaking world. When in doubt about the gender of a noun, check it in a current dictionary.

Plurals

There are several different conventions for making nouns plural.

- Add *-s* to most nouns that end in a vowel.

casa	*house*	pie	*foot*
casas	*houses*	pies	*feet*
libro	*book*	papá	*father*
libros	*books*	papás	*parents*

| ejercicio | *exercise* | sofá | *sofa* |
| ejercicios | *exercises* | sofás | *sofas* |

- Add -*es* to a noun ending in stressed -*í* or -*ú*.

| rubí | *ruby* | marroquí | *Moroccan* |
| rubíes | *rubies* | marroquíes | *Moroccans* |

| esquí | *ski* | hindú | *Hindu* |
| esquíes | *skis* | hindúes | *Hindus* |

- Add -*es* to a noun ending in a consonant.

| ladrón | *thief* | reloj | *watch* |
| ladrones | *thieves* | relojes | *watches* |

| ciudad | *city* | | |
| ciudades | *cities* | | |

- For nouns ending in -*z*, change the -*z* to -*c* and add -*es* (see page 11).

| lápiz | *pencil* | cruz | *cross* |
| lápices | *pencils* | cruces | *crosses* |

| arroz | *rice* | | |
| arroces | *rice dishes* | | |

When making a noun plural, an accent mark may need to be added or deleted to indicate stress on the same syllable as in the singular form (see pages 14–15).

| crimen | *crime* | ladron | *thief* |
| crímenes | *crimes* | ladrones | *thieves* |

| orden | *order* | reunión | *meeting* |
| órdenes | *orders* | reuniones | *meetings* |

AVOID THE *Blunder*

Double-check the spelling of plurals you use. Keep in mind that accent marks may need to be added or deleted.

| ✗ rubís | ✗ esquís | ✗ relojs | ✗ lápizes |
| ✗ crimenes | ✗ ladrónes | ✗ aviónes | |

A family is referred to by the singular form of its surname.

los Santiago	*the Santiagos*
los Galván	*the Galvans*
los Valdés	*the Valdeses*
los González	*the Gonzalezes*
los Pérez	*the Perezes*

Certain nouns are the same in the singular and the plural.

el lunes	*Monday*	la crisis	*the crisis*
los lunes	*Mondays*	las crisis	*the crises*
el martes	*Tuesday*	el virus	*the virus*
los martes	*Tuesdays*	los virus	*the viruses*
el miércoles	*Wednesday*		
los miércoles	*Wednesdays*		
el jueves	*Thursday*		
los jueves	*Thursdays*		
el viernes	*Friday*		
los viernes	*Fridays*		

AVOID THE *Blunder*

Do not try to pluralize these nouns.

✗ los luneses   ✗ los viruses

Certain nouns are plural in English but singular in Spanish.

la gente	*people*
la ropa	*clothes*

La gente es muy simpática.	*The people are very nice.*
La ropa es cara.	*Clothes are expensive.*

The names of certain school subjects end in *-s* in English, even though they are singular. They do not end in *-s* in Spanish.

la política	*politics*
la economía	*economics*
la física	*physics*

Mi hermana estudia física.	*My sister is studying physics.*

AVOID THE *Blunder*

Do not pluralize these nouns, and do not use plural adjectives and verbs with them.

✗ Las gentes son amables.
✗ Voy a comprar las ropas.

Certain nouns are singular (or noncount) in English but plural in Spanish.

las vacaciones	*the vacation*
los celos	*the jealousy*
los aplausos	*the applause*
las elecciones*	*the election*

*_La elección_ means "the choice."

Buenos días.*	*Good morning.*
Buenas tardes.	*Good afternoon.*
Buenas noches.	*Good evening./Good night.*

*_Buen día_ is used in some places.

AVOID THE *Blunder*

Do not use these nouns in the singular.

✗ Voy a tomar una vacación.
✗ La elección es en noviembre.

AVOID THE *Blunder*

✗ Buena tarde. ✗ Buena noche.
✗ Buen tarde. ✗ Buen noche.

Nouns that are compounds of a verb plus a plural noun are singular, even though they end in *s*.

el cumpleaños	*the birthday (the completion of years)*
el lavaplatos	*the dishwasher (the washer of dishes)*
el abrelatas	*the can opener (the opener of cans)*
el sacacorchos	*the corkscrew (the remover of corks)*
el salvavidas	*the life saver/lifeguard (the saver of lives)*
el quitamanchas	*the spot remover (the remover of spots)*
el paraguas	*the umbrella (the water-stopper)*
el parabrisas	*the windshield (the wind-stopper)*
el parachoques	*the bumper (the accident-stopper/breaker)*

Their plurals have the same form.

Tengo un paraguas.	*I have an umbrella.*
Mi amigo tiene dos paraguas.	*My friend has two umbrellas.*

Hoy es el cumpleaños de mi amigo.	*Today is my friend's birthday.*
En su familia siempre celebran los cumpleaños de los niños con una fiesta.	*In his family they always celebrate the children's birthdays with a party.*

AVOID THE *Blunder*

Do not add -*es* to these nouns to make them plural.

✗ dos paraguases   ✗ los cumpleañoses

Exercises

A *Complete the following chart by adding the male equivalent of the feminine nouns and the female equivalent of the masculine nouns.*

MASCULINE	FEMININE
1. el hermano	_____
2. _____	la profesora
3. el médico	_____
4. _____	la especialista
5. el paciente	_____
6. _____	la amiga
7. el miembro	_____
8. _____	la jefa
9. el hombre	_____

B *Write the article that goes before each noun.*

1. _____ brazo	5. _____ crema	9. _____ cumpleaños
2. _____ pierna	6. _____ agua	10. _____ camión
3. _____ problema	7. _____ mano	11. _____ costumbre
4. _____ día	8. _____ lección	12. _____ ciudad

C *Write the plural form of the following nouns.*

1. casa _____
2. libro _____
3. esquí _____
4. ladrón _____
5. ciudad _____
6. lápiz _____
7. orden _____
8. lunes _____
9. domingo _____
10. el Sr. y la Sra. Pérez _____

NUMBERS

Cardinal Numbers

0 cero	30 treinta	60 sesenta
1 uno	31 treinta y uno	61 sesenta y uno
2 dos	32 treinta y dos	62 sesenta y dos
3 tres	33 treinta y tres	63 sesenta y tres
4 cuatro	34 treinta y cuatro	64 sesenta y cuatro
5 cinco	35 treinta y cinco	65 sesenta y cinco
6 seis	36 treinta y seis	66 sesenta y seis
7 siete	37 treinta y siete	67 sesenta y siete
8 ocho	38 treinta y ocho	68 sesenta y ocho
9 nueve	39 treinta y nueve	69 sesenta y nueve
10 diez	40 cuarenta	70 setenta
11 once	41 cuarenta y uno	71 setenta y uno
12 doce	42 cuarenta y dos	72 setenta y dos
13 trece	43 cuarenta y tres	73 setenta y tres
14 catorce	44 cuarenta y cuatro	74 setenta y cuatro
15 quince	45 cuarenta y cinco	75 setenta y cinco
16 dieciséis	46 cuarenta y seis	76 setenta y seis
17 diecisiete	47 cuarenta y siete	77 setenta y siete
18 dieciocho	48 cuarenta y ocho	78 setenta y ocho
19 diecinueve	49 cuarenta y nueve	79 setenta y nueve
20 veinte	50 cincuenta	80 ochenta
21 veintiuno	51 cincuenta y uno	81 ochenta y uno
22 veintidós	52 cincuenta y dos	82 ochenta y dos
23 veintitrés	53 cincuenta y tres	83 ochenta y tres
24 veinticuatro	54 cincuenta y cuatro	84 ochenta y cuatro
25 veinticinco	55 cincuenta y cinco	85 ochenta y cinco
26 veintiséis	56 cincuenta y seis	86 ochenta y seis
27 veintisiete	57 cincuenta y siete	87 ochenta y siete
28 veintiocho	58 cincuenta y ocho	88 ochenta y ocho
29 veintinueve	59 cincuenta y nueve	89 ochenta y nueve

90 noventa
91 noventa y uno
92 noventa y dos
93 noventa y tres
94 noventa y cuatro
95 noventa y cinco
96 noventa y seis
97 noventa y siete
98 noventa y ocho
99 noventa y nueve

100	cien	200	doscientos(-as)
101	ciento uno	300	trescientos(-as)
102	ciento dos	400	cuatrocientos(-as)
113	ciento trece	500	quinientos(-as)
129	ciento veintinueve	600	seiscientos(-as)
133	ciento treinta y tres	700	setecientos(-as)
142	ciento cuarenta y dos	800	ochocientos(-as)
154	ciento cincuenta y cuatro	900	novecientos(-as)
165	ciento sesenta y cinco		
176	ciento setenta y seis		
188	ciento ochenta y ocho		
197	ciento noventa y siete		

1000 mil
1492 mil cuatrocientos noventa y dos
1776 mil setecientos setenta y seis
1999 mil novecientos noventa y nueve
2000 dos mil

1.000.000 un millón
2.472.683 dos millones, cuatrocientos setenta y dos mil, seiscientos ochenta
y tres

Ordinal Numbers

1º primero(-a)   primer (*before masculine noun*)
2º segundo(-a)
3º tercero(-a)   tercer (*before masculine noun*)
4º cuarto(-a)
5º quinto(-a)
6º sexto(-a)
7º séptimo(-a)
8º octavo(-a)
9º noveno(-a)
10º décimo(-a)

11°	undécimo(-a)	30°	trigésimo(-a)
12°	duodécimo(-a)	40°	cuadragésimo(-a)
13°	decimotercero(-a)	50°	quincuagésimo(-a)
14°	decimocuarto(-a)	60°	sexagésimo(-a)
15°	decimoquinto(-a)	70°	septuagésimo(-a)
16°	decimosexto(-a)	80°	octogésimo(-a)
17°	decimoséptimo(-a)	90°	nonagésimo(-a)
18°	decimoctavo(-a)	100°	centésimo(-a)
19°	decimonoveno(-a)	1000°	milésimo(-a)
20°	vigésimo(-a)	1.000.000°	millonésimo(-a)
21°	vigesimoprimero(-a)		
22°	vigesimosegundo(-a)		
23°	vigesimotercero(-a)		

Fractions

½	un medio
⅔	dos tercios
¾	tres cuartos
⅘	cuatro quintos
⅚	cinco sextos
6/7	seis séptimos
⅝	cinco octavos
7/9	siete novenos
4/10	cuatro décimos

Review the numbers in the charts on the previous pages.

The Spanish and English numbering systems are very similar. There are, however, several notable differences.

Writing Numbers

In some countries, the numbers *1* and *7* are handwritten in a slightly different manner in Spanish.

uno   *1*   a one with a long tail (can look like a seven)
siete   *7*   a seven with a line through the center

In many, but not all, Spanish-speaking countries, a period is used to mark the thousands, and a comma is used for the decimal point—exactly the opposite of the English system.

2.763   *two thousand, seven hundred sixty-three*
3.892.359   *three million, eight hundred ninety-two thousand,*
                three hundred fifty-nine
4,25   *four point two five*
3,75   *three point seven five*

The Spanish equivalent of the English nd and th, as in 2nd or 4th, is o when referring to a masculine noun and a when referring to a feminine noun. The equivalent of the English st, as in 1st, and rd, as in 3rd, is ero when referring to a masculine noun and era when referring to a feminine noun. The ero is shortened to er (*primer* and *tercer*) before a masculine singular noun.

1ero	primero	3ero	tercero
1era	primera	3era	tercera
1er	primer	3er	tercer
2o	segundo	4o	cuarto
2a	segunda	4a	cuarta

Ones

■ Note the spelling of *seis* and *siete*.

seis   "SEH ees" (rhymes with English "face")
siete   "SYE teh"

Watch the spelling of *cuatro*.

AVOID THE *Blunder*

✗ sies   ✗ seite   ✗ quatro

■ The numbers from *dos* to *cien* ("two" to "one hundred") are never pluralized.

cuatro manzanas	*four apples*
siete alumnos	*seven students*
noventa personas	*ninety people*
cien libros	*a hundred books*

AVOID THE *Blunder*

✗ cuatros manzanas   ✗ sietes alumnos
✗ noventas personas   ✗ cientos libros

■ In Spanish there are several ways to indicate "one."

☐ The word for "one" is the same as the indefinite article, which has three forms.

un, uno, una   *one*

—¿Qué tienes?   *"What do you have?"*
—Tengo un libro.   *"I have a book."*

—¿Cuántos libros tienes?   *"How many books do you have?"*
—Tengo un libro. / Tengo uno.   *"I have one book." / "I have one."*

—¿Quiere un libro?   *"Do you want a book?"*
—Hay uno en la mesa.   *"There is one on the table."*

—¿Quiere una pluma?   *"Do you want a pen?"*
—Aquí está una.   *"Here is one."*

Numbers above 20 that contain "one" follow the same pattern.

Tengo veintiún libros.	*I have 21 books.*
Mi hermano tiene treinta y un libros.	*My brother has 31 books.*
Hay veinte niños y veintiuna niñas.	*There are 20 boys and 21 girls.*
Necesitamos cuarenta y una camisetas.	*We need 41 T-shirts.*

AVOID THE *Blunder*

Drop the *-o* from *uno* before a masculine noun. Use *una* before a feminine noun. Don't forget the accent mark above the *ú* in *veintiún*.

✗ uno libro   ✗ un pluma   ✗ veintiuno libros
✗ treinta y uno libros   ✗ veintiun libros

☐ *Ningún, ninguno,* or *ninguna* is used to express "not one."

No veo ningún libro.	*I don't see a book.*
	(I don't see any books.)
No hay ninguno.	*There aren't any.*
	(There isn't a single one.)
No tengo ningún amigo aquí.	*I don't have any friends here.*
—¿Cuántas personas vinieron?	*"How many people came?"*
—No vino ninguna.	*"Not a single one came."*

AVOID THE *Blunder*

In English, "zero"—or "not any"—is followed by a plural noun. Do not use a plural with *ninguno* in Spanish.

✗ No tengo ningunos libros.
✗ No hay ningunas personas.

☐ "Another one," "one more," and "a different one" are expressed with *otro(-a)* in Spanish. Alternatively, *uno(-a) más* can be used for "one more" and *uno(-a) distinto(-a)* can be used for "a different one."

Tengo un libro. Quiero otro.	*I have a book. I want another one.*
Quiero otro. / Quiero uno más.	*I want one more.*
Quiero otro. / Quiero uno distinto.	*I want a different one.*
Tiene una pluma. Quiere otra.	*He has a pen. He wants another one.*
Quiere otra. / Quiere una más.	*He wants one more.*
Quiere otra. / Quiere una distinta.	*He wants a different one.*

AVOID THE *Blunder*

Do not use *un, uno,* or *una* before *otro* or *otra.*

✗ un otro libro   ✗ una otra amiga

In English, numbers are placed before the word "other." In Spanish, they are placed after *otros(-as).* (See pages 71–72.)

Tenemos otros dos primos.	*We have two other cousins.*
Necesitan otras cuatro sillas.	*They need four more chairs.*

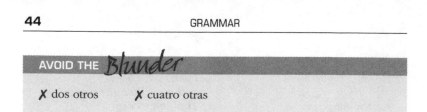

AVOID THE Blunder

✗ dos otros   ✗ cuatro otras

Tens

Watch the numbers *once, doce, trece, catorce,* and *quince.*

AVOID THE Blunder

✗ diez y tres   ✗ diez y cuatro   ✗ diez y cinco

Note that the numbers from 16 through 29 are expressed as one word. It is no longer common to separate these into three-word expressions.

AVOID THE Blunder

✗ diez y seis   ✗ veinte y nueve

Note that the numbers 16, 22, 23, and 26 require an accent mark on the final syllable.

dieciséis   veintidós   veintitrés   veintiséis

Watch the spelling and pronunciation of *veinte.* The first syllable is spelled and pronounced like the English word "vein." Similarly, the vowels in the first syllable of *treinta* are pronounced (but not spelled) like the vowels in the English word "train."

AVOID THE Blunder

✗ viente   ✗ trienta

Hundreds

Ciento is shortened to *cien* when it immediately precedes a noun and when it stands alone.

Hay cien alumnos.   *There are a hundred students.*
Tenemos cien cajas de libros.   *We have a hundred boxes*
                                     of books.
Hay cien.   *There are a hundred.*

In English, the number "one" or "a" can precede "hundred." In Spanish, *ciento* and *cien* are never preceded by a form of *uno*.

Hay cien chicos.	*There are a/one hundred boys.*
Hay ciento veinte chicas.	*There are a/one hundred and twenty girls.*

AVOID THE *Blunder*

✗ un ciento ✗ una cien

In spoken English, there is a tendency to insert "and" after the hundreds. In Spanish, there is no *y* after the hundreds. In Spanish, *y* ("and") is used in the tens.

ciento tres	*one hundred and three*
quinientos veinte	*five hundred and twenty*
doscientos cuarenta y cuatro	*two hundred and forty-four*

AVOID THE *Blunder*

✗ ciento y tres ✗ quinientos y veinte
✗ cuarenta cuatro ✗ treinta dos

Multiple hundreds are always plural and are masculine or feminine to agree with the nouns they modify.

doscientos dólares	*two hundred dollars*
trescientos pesos	*three hundred pesos*
cuatrocientas libras	*four hundred pounds*

Thousands

In English, the number "one" or "a" can precede "thousand." In Spanish, *mil* is preceded by *un* only in cases of ambiguity.

$1.000	mil dólares	*one thousand dollars*
$400.000	cuatrocientos mil dólares	*four hundred thousand dollars*
$401.000	cuatrocientos un mil dólares	*four hundred and one thousand dollars*

AVOID THE *Blunder*

✗ un mil dólares

In English, years above 1000 are often expressed as multiples of hundreds. In Spanish, *mil* is used.

1867	mil ochocientos sesenta y siete
1959	mil novecientos cincuenta y nueve

AVOID THE *Blunder*

Do not use this format to express 1959.

✗ diecinueve cincuenta y nueve

Millions, Billions, and Trillions

Millón, billón, and *trillón* are preceded by *un* to express "one." To express more than one, they are pluralized.

un millón	*one million*
dos millones	*two million*
tres billones	*three billion*
un trillón	*one trillion*

When the item being counted is stated, it is preceded by *de.*

un millón de dólares	*one million dollars*
tres billones de pesos	*three billion pesos*

AVOID THE *Blunder*

✗ un millón dólares　　✗ tres millones pesos

Using Cardinal Numbers
Comparisons

When a comparison includes a number, "more than" is expressed by *más de*; "less than" is expressed by *menos de.*

Tengo que esperar más de dos horas.	*I have to wait more than two hours.*
Tiene menos de cien pesos.	*He has less than a hundred pesos.*

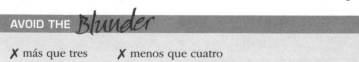

AVOID THE *Blunder*

✗ más que tres　　✗ menos que cuatro

Dates

In Spanish, when numbers are used to designate a calendar date, the first number indicates the day, the second number indicates the month, and the third number indicates the year.

3/6/05	*June 3, 2005*
4/7/76	*July 4, 1976*
6/10/64	*October 6, 1964*

AVOID THE *Blunder*

Do not use this format to express November 23, 1974.

✗ 11/23/74

Do not use this format to express March 6, 2006.

✗ 3/6/06

Telephone Numbers

Telephone numbers are expressed as a sequence of two-digit numbers in Spanish. When there are three digits in a group, the first number is stated in isolation, and the second two as a two-digit number.

64.98.31	sesenta y cuatro, noventa y ocho, treinta y uno
453-8679	cuatro, cincuenta y tres, ochenta y seis, setenta y nueve
301-220-0290	tres cero uno, dos veinte, cero dos, noventa

Street Addresses

Street addresses typically begin with the name of the street followed by the street number, then the floor and apartment or room number, if applicable.

Calle Villamil, 27 3^{ero}B	*27 Villamil Street, Third Floor, Apt. B*

AVOID THE *Blunder*

✗ 27 Villamil Calle

Telling Time

¿Qué hora es? asks for the current time. Following are some common responses. (See page 58.)

Es la una de la madrugada.	*It's one o'clock in the morning./ It's 1 A.M.*
Son las diez y cuarto de la mañana.	*It's a quarter after ten in the morning./It's 10:15 A.M.*
Son las cinco y media de la tarde.	*It's 5:30 in the afternoon./ It's 5:30 P.M.*
Es mediodía.	*It's 12 noon.*
Es medianoche.	*It's 12 midnight.*

AVOID THE *Blunder*

Use *es la* with "one o'clock" and *son las* with other times.

✗ son la una   ✗ es las tres   ✗ es cinco

En la mañana, en la tarde, and *en la noche* are correct when used to refer to parts of the day, when the actual time is not expressed. The abbreviation "A.M." is expressed with *de la mañana* and "P.M." is expressed with *de la tarde* or *de la noche.*

AVOID THE *Blunder*

✗ Son las diez en la mañana.
✗ Es la una en la tarde.
✗ Son las once en la noche.

¿A qué hora es? asks the time of an event. The answer is also expressed with *a* when a specific time is mentioned.

¿A qué hora es la reunión?	*What time is the meeting?*
Es en la mañana./Es por la mañana.	*It's in the morning.*
Es a las once de la mañana.	*It's at 11 o'clock in the morning./ It's at 11 A.M.*
Es en la tarde./Es por la tarde.	*It's in the afternoon.* OR *It's in the evening.*
Es a las siete y media de la tarde.	*It's at 7:30 in the evening./ It's at 7:30 P.M.*
Es en la noche./Es por la noche.	*It's in the evening.* OR *It's at night.*
Es a las diez de la noche.	*It's at 10 o'clock at night./ It's at 10 P.M.*

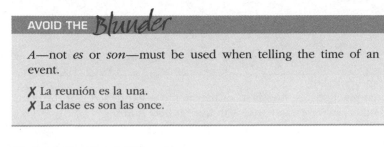

A—not *es* or *son*—must be used when telling the time of an event.

✗ La reunión es la una.
✗ La clase es son las once.

Using Ordinal Numbers

Review the ordinal numbers in the chart on pages 39–40.

Two ordinal numbers, *primero* and *tercero,* are shortened to *primer* and *tercer* when used before masculine singular nouns.

el primer presidente   *the first president*
el tercer piso   *the third floor*

AVOID THE Blunder

✗ el primero año   ✗ el tercero hombre

All ordinal numbers change the final *-o* to *-a* before a feminine noun.

la primera presidente   *the first president*
la tercera calle   *the third street*
la quinta milla   *the fifth mile*

Primero and *primera* can be used in the plural.

los primeros días de enero   *the first days in January*
las primeras llamadas del día   *the first calls of the day*

Although there are ordinals in Spanish for "eleventh" and above, cardinal numbers are usually used for ordinals higher than *décimo*.

Está en el piso once.   *It's on the eleventh floor.*
Vamos a la Calle Cincuenta   *Let's go to Fifty-fourth Street.*
  y cuatro.

In spoken language, the names of kings and popes are expressed without the article *el.*

Carlos V   Carlos quinto   *Carlos the Fifth*
Alfonso XII   Alfonso doce   *Alfonso the Twelfth*
Juan XXIII   Juan veintitrés   *John the Twenty-third*

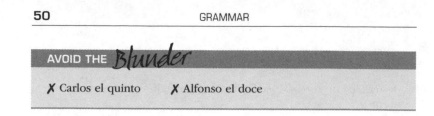

AVOID THE Blunder

✗ Carlos el quinto   ✗ Alfonso el doce

When giving dates, the "first" of the month is expressed with *primero*. All other days are expressed with the cardinal number.

el primero de enero	*January 1*
el dos de febrero	*February 2*
el dieciséis de septiembre	*September 16*
el veintiocho de diciembre	*December 28*

AVOID THE Blunder

✗ el tercero de marzo   ✗ el cuarto de julio

Using Fractions

"One-half" is expressed by using *medio(-a)* followed by a noun of quantity.

Déme medio kilo de mantequilla.	*Give me a half-kilo of butter. /* *Give me half a kilo of butter.*
He traído media docena de huevos.	*I brought a half-dozen eggs. /* *I brought half a dozen eggs.*

AVOID THE Blunder

Do not use *un, uno, una* before *medio* + noun.

✗ un medio kilo   ✗ una media docena

"One and a half" is expressed by naming the noun of quantity followed by *y medio(-a)*.

Esperamos hora y media.	*We waited an hour and a half.*
Ella compró kilo y medio de harina.	*She bought a kilo and a half of flour.*
Tomé taza y media de café.	*I drank a cup and a half of coffee.*

> ### AVOID THE *Blunder*
>
> Do not use *un, uno, una* before a quantity noun if a fraction follows.
>
> ✗ una taza y media   ✗ una hora y media

"Half of" a commodity can be expressed by *la media parte de* or *la mitad de.*

Pablo vendió la media parte de sus tierras.	*Pablo sold half of his land.*
Ella le robó la mitad de sus bienes.	*She robbed him of half of his assets.*

> ### AVOID THE *Blunder*
>
> Be sure to use *la* and *de* with these expressions.
>
> ✗ media parte sus tierras   ✗ una mitad sus bienes

A whole number plus a half is always separated by a noun of quantity.

Esperamos dos horas y media.	*We waited two and a half hours.*
He perdido tres kilos y medio.	*I've lost three and a half kilos.*

> ### AVOID THE *Blunder*
>
> Do not put *y medio* or *y media* before the noun.
>
> ✗ dos y media horas   ✗ tres y medio kilos

When the top number of a fraction is "one," use *la* + the ordinal number + *parte de.*

la tercera parte de	*one-third of*
la cuarta parte de	*one-fourth of / a quarter of*
la séptima parte de	*one-seventh of*
la décima parte de	*one-tenth of*

> ### AVOID THE *Blunder*
>
> ✗ una tercera de   ✗ una cuarta de

Exercises

A *Write the words for the following numbers.*

1. 2   _____
2. 10   _____
3. 14   _____
4. 22   _____
5. 39   _____
6. 146   _____
7. 473   _____
8. 511   _____
9. 1984   _____
10. 2007   _____

B *Write the words for the ordinal numbers in the chart.*

	MASCULINE		FEMININE	
1. *first*	*el primer*	libro	_____	novela
2. *second*	_____	piso	_____	vez
3. *third*	_____	edificio	_____	casa
4. *fourth*	_____	año	_____	calle
5. *fifth*	_____	día	_____	persona

C *Express in words.*

1. 21 chicos   _____
2. 21 chicas   _____
3. 100 libros   _____
4. 203 niños   _____
5. $2.000.000   _____
6. 2/10/77   _____
7. 202-490-3361   _____
8. 10:30 A.M.   _____
9. ½ kilo   _____
10. 2½ kilos   _____

NOUN DETERMINERS

Definite Articles

el, la, los, las   *the*

Indefinite Articles

un, una   *a, an*
unos, unas   *some*

Demonstratives

este, esta, esto   *this*
estos, estas   *these*

ese, esa, eso   *that*
esos, esas   *those*

aquel, aquella   *that (over there)*
aquellos, aquellas   *those (over there)*

Possessives

BEFORE A NOUN		ALONE OR AFTER AN ARTICLE OR NOUN	
mi/mis	*my*	mío(-a/-os/-as)	*mine/my*
tu/tus/su/sus	*your*	tuyo(-a/-os/-as)/ suyo(-a/-os/-as)	*yours/your*
su/sus	*his*	suyo(-a/-os/-as)	*his/his*
su/sus	*her*	suyo(-a/-os/-as)	*hers/her*
su/sus	*its*		
nuestro(-a/-os/-as)	*our*	nuestro(-a/-os/-as)	*ours/our*
vuestro(-a/-os/-as)/su/sus	*your*	vuestro(-a/-os/-as)/ suyo(-a/-os/-as)	*yours/your*
su/sus	*their*	suyo(-a/-os/-as)	*theirs/their*
cuyo(-a/-os/-as)	*whose*		

Other Determiners

algún/alguna(-os/-as)	*some*
otro(-a/-os/-as)	*other, another*
cierto(-a/-os/-as)	*(a) certain*
propio(-a/-os/-as)	*one's own*
mucho(-a/-os/-as)	*a lot of*
poco(-a/-os/-as)	*little*
tanto(-a/-os/-as)	*so much, so many*
todo(-a/-os/-as)	*all, every*
el/la mismo(-a)	*the same*
los/las mismos(-as)	*the same*
el/la único(-a)	*the only*
los/las únicos(-as)	*the only*
ambos(-as)	*both*
los/las demás	*the rest*
varios(-as)	*several*
unos(-as) cuantos(-as)	*several*
unos(-as) pocos(as)	*a few*
cada	*each*
tal	*the aforementioned*
semejante(s)	*such (a)*
medio(-a)	*half a*
cualquier/cualquiera	*any*

Review the forms in the charts on the previous pages.

Noun determiners help identify nouns and are usually placed before the noun, with a few exceptions.

Definite Articles

The definite article—masculine singular *el*, feminine singular *la*, masculine plural *los*, feminine plural *las*—like English "the," refers to a particular noun.

The definite article may refer to the only noun possible or simply to one that both the speaker and hearer have mutual knowledge of.

el hijo de Juan	*Juan's son*
la cocina	*the (only) kitchen (in this house or restaurant)*
los hijos de Juan	*Juan's children*
las llaves de mi casa	*the keys to my house*

■ Purely for pronunciation purposes, feminine singular nouns that begin with a stressed *a*- or *ha*- are preceded by *el* instead of *la* (see page 29).

el agua	*the water*
el águila	*the eagle*
el área	*the area*
el alma	*the soul*
el hambre	*the hunger*

El does not replace *la* in the following situations, however:

- If another determiner or an adjective separates the definite article from the noun.

Es la primera águila que vemos.	*It's the first eagle we've seen.* ✓
La otra área es más bonita.	*The other area is prettier.*

- If the *el* or *la* distinguishes whether the person referred to is male or female.

el árabe	*the Arab (male)*
la árabe	*the Arab (female)*

- If the noun and definite article are plural.

las aguas	*the waters*
las águilas	*the eagles*
las áreas	*the areas*
las almas	*the souls*

All other determiners and adjectives that relate to these nouns are feminine.

el agua pura	*the clean water*
el águila bella	*the beautiful eagle*
el área seca	*the dry area*
poca agua	*very little water*
mucha hambre	*a lot of hunger*

AVOID THE *Blunder*

✗ la área ✗ todo el área ✗ este área

✗ los almas ✗ mucho hambre

■ When *el* is preceded by the preposition *a*, it must be contracted to *al*. When preceded by *de*, it must be contracted to *del*. This does not apply to *El* when it is part of a proper name.

Vamos al mercado.	*We're going to the market.*
Vamos a El Salvador.	*We're going to El Salvador.*
Soy del sur del país.	*I'm from the south of the country.*
Soy del sur de El Salvador.	*I'm from the south of El Salvador.*

AVOID THE *Blunder*

✗ a el país ✗ de el hermano

■ In Spanish, as in English, no article is used before a title when addressing someone.

Buenos días, Sr. Ochoa.	*Good morning, Mr. Ochoa.*
Hola, Sra. Rodríguez.	*Hello, Mrs. Rodríguez.*
Hasta luego, Srta. Díaz.	*See you later, Miss Díaz.*

In Spanish, a definite article is required before a title such as *señor, señora, señorita, doctor, doctora,* or *ingeniero* when speaking about someone, even though no article would be used in English.

El señor Ochoa me llamó anoche.	*Mr. Ochoa called me last night.*
Quiero presentarte a la señora Rodríguez.	*I want to introduce you to Mrs. Rodríguez.*
Voy a visitar a la señorita Díaz cuando vaya a Chile.	*I'm going to visit Miss Díaz when I go to Chile.*
Conocimos al doctor Páez el viernes pasado.	*We met Dr. Páez last Friday.*

AVOID THE *Blunder*

✗ Hola, la señorita López.
✗ Sr. Ochoa me llamó.

Do not forget the "personal *a*" before a direct object that is a person. When it immediately precedes the article *el*, the two words are contracted to *al*.

✗ Conocimos doctor Páez.
✗ Conocimos el doctor Páez.

No article is used when referring to people with the titles *don, doña, fray, sor, monseñor, San, Santa,* or *Santo.*

Anoche hablé con don Pablo.	*Last night I talked to don Pablo.*
Quiero presentarte a fray Luis.	*I want to introduce you to Brother Luis.*

■ The article *el* is used before the name of a day to indicate action occurring on that day.

Te veo el lunes.	*I'll see you on Monday.*
El martes vamos a la playa.	*On Tuesday we're going to the beach.*
Se fue el miércoles.	*She left on Wednesday.*
No tenemos clase el jueves.	*We don't have class on Thursday.*

AVOID THE *Blunder*

✗ en lunes   ✗ en el martes

The article *los* is used before the name of a day to indicate action that occurs regularly on that day of the week.

Tenemos clase los lunes.	*We have class on Mondays.*
Hay partidos de fútbol los domingos.	*There are soccer games on Sundays.*
Se divierten los fines de semana.	*They have fun on weekends.*

AVOID THE *Blunder*

✗ en lunes   ✗ en los lunes   ✗ en los fines de semanas

In telling time, the article *la* is used to express one o'clock and *las* is used to express the other hours. No article is used to express noon and midnight. (See page 48.)

Es la una.	*It's one o'clock.*
Son las diez.	*It's 10 o'clock.*
Nos vamos a las ocho.	*We're leaving at eight.*
La fiesta terminó a medianoche.	*The party ended at midnight.*
Ellos comen a mediodía.	*They eat at noon.*

In Spanish the definite article is required before the names of seasons.

No hay clases en el verano.	*There are no classes in (the) summer.*
Esquían en el invierno.	*They go skiing in (the) winter.*
La primavera es una temporada hermosa.	*Spring is a beautiful season.*

AVOID THE *Blunder*

✗ en verano   ✗ en otoño   ✗ Me encanta primavera.

■ Definite article usage varies to express movement to, movement from, and presence at certain familiar places.

As in English, no article is used to express movement to, movement from, or presence at one's own home.

Voy a casa.	*I'm going home.*
Salgo de casa a las ocho.	*I leave home at eight.*
Estamos en casa.	*We're at home.*

As in English, no article is used to express movement to or from a church service or class session.

Voy a misa.	*I'm going to mass.*
Salimos de misa a las once.	*We get out of mass at eleven.*
¿Van Uds. a clase?	*Are you all going to class?*
Salgo de clase a las cuatro.	*I get out of class at four.*

In Spanish, an article is used to express movement to certain common destinations, as well as presence at certain locations. English typically does not use an article in these cases.

Voy a la ciudad/a la iglesia/ a la escuela.	*I'm going to town/to church/ to school.*
Está en la ciudad/en la iglesia/ en la escuela/en el trabajo.	*He's in town/at church/ at school/at work.*

AVOID THE *Blunder*

✗ Voy a ciudad.
✗ Va a iglesia.
✗ Está en escuela.

■ In Spanish, an article is used to indicate "in care of": *al cuidado de.*

Te mandé un paquete al cuidado   *I sent you a package in care*
   del Sr. Alberto Sánchez.   *of Mr. Alberto Sánchez.*

■ In Spanish, a definite article is used to refer to parts of the body and articles of clothing.

Me lavo las manos.   *I wash my hands.*
Se lava los dientes.   *She brushes her tooth.*
Se quitó el sombrero.   *He took off his hat.*

AVOID THE *Blunder*

✗ Lavo mis manos.
✗ Lava sus dientes.
✗ Se quitó su sombrero.

In Spanish, when referring to one item that pertains to more than one person, the singular noun is used and means "one each." As in English, when more than one item is referred to, the plural noun is used.

Los chicos se quitaron el sombrero.   *The boys took off their hats.*
                                          (one each)
Los chicos se quitaron los zapatos.   *The boys took off their shoes.*

AVOID THE *Blunder*

Use the singular noun, unless you mean each one took off more than one hat.

✗ Los chicos se quitaron los sombreros.

Use the plural noun, unless you mean each one took off only one shoe.

✗ Los chicos se quitaron el zapato.

■ In Spanish, a definite article is used to indicate price per quantity. English uses "a" or "per."

50 centavos la docena	*50 cents a dozen*
30 pesos el kilo	*30 pesos a kilo*
20 euros el metro	*20 euros a meter*

AVOID THE *Blunder*

✗ 50 centavos una docena   ✗ 30 pesos un kilo

■ In Spanish, the names of languages are generally preceded by a definite article. English does not use a definite article before names of languages.

El español es el idioma más hablado en la América del Sur.	*Spanish is the most commonly spoken language in South America.*
El español y el francés son los idiomas que se enseñan en este colegio.	*Spanish and French are the languages taught at this school.*
Van a traducirlo del español al inglés.	*They're going to translate it from Spanish to English.*
Están estudiando la gramática del inglés.	*They're studying English grammar.*

AVOID THE *Blunder*

✗ Español es difícil.
✗ Español y francés son los idiomas que se enseñan.
✗ Van a traducirlo de español a inglés.
✗ la gramática de inglés

The Spanish article is generally not used when *en* or a form of *hablar* precedes the name of the language.

El artículo está escrito en chino.	*The article is written in Chinese.*
Mi hijo habla español.	*My son speaks Spanish.*

AVOID THE *Blunder*

✗ Hablamos el español.
✗ Está escrito en el chino.

■ As in English, nouns that represent some but not all of the members of a class are not preceded by an article in Spanish.

Comemos enchiladas.	*We eat enchiladas.*
Tiene flores en el balcón.	*She has flowers on the balcony.*
Hay enchiladas hoy.	*There are enchiladas today.*
Había flores de toda clase.	*There were all kinds of flowers.*

■ Spanish nouns used in a general sense to represent all members of a class are preceded by a definite article. English does not use an article.

El pollo es rico.	*Chicken (all chicken) is delicious.*
El pollo me gusta.	*I like chicken. (Chicken appeals to me.)*
Las enchiladas son ricas.	*Enchiladas (all enchiladas) are delicious.*
El ruido es un estorbo.	*Noise (in general) is a disturbance.*
Las flores son caras.	*Flowers (in general) are expensive.*
Las novelas me fascinan.	*Novels (all novels) fascinate me.*

AVOID THE *Blunder*

Do not eliminate the article before the subject.

✗ Pollo es rico.   ✗ Mc gusta pollo.
✗ Flores son caras.   ✗ Me fascinan novelas.

■ Spanish nouns that name abstract notions are generally preceded by a definite article. English usually does not use an article.

La contaminación del agua es un problema muy grande.	*Water pollution is a big problem.*
La salud es más importante que la riqueza.	*Health is more important than wealth.*

AVOID THE *Blunder*

✗ Contaminación es un problema.
✗ Salud es importante.

■ Definite articles are sometimes used with proper nouns.

El or *la* before a first name can have a derogatory connotation unless there is a descriptive adjective between the article and the noun.

Viene con la Anita.	*He's coming with that Anita.*
Viene con la adorable Anita.	*He's coming with adorable Anita.*

El can be part of a proper name, as in *El Salvador*, where it is always capitalized. The names of certain other countries, cities, and places are traditionally preceded by a lowercase definite article. This usage varies, so these must be learned individually. Following are some common examples.

la Argentina	la Habana
el Ecuador	el Perú
los Estados Unidos	El Morro

When the name of a place is modified by an adjective or phrase, it is preceded by a definite article.

la España del siglo XVI	*16th-century Spain*
la bella Madrid	*splendid Madrid*

In an appositive phrase that is placed next to a noun and defines it, no article is used in Spanish.

Washington, ciudad capital de los EE.UU.	*Washington, the capital of the United States*
Miguel Alonso, director del colegio	*Miguel Alonso, the school principal*

AVOID THE Blunder

✗ Washington, la ciudad capital de los EE.UU.
✗ Miguel Alonso, el director del colegio

As in English, in an appositive phrase that expresses a superlative or simply gives information about the noun, an article is used in Spanish.

Washington, la ciudad más grande del área	*Washington, the largest city in the area*
Miguel Alonso, el director que asistió a la conferencia	*Miguel Alonso, the director who attended the meeting*

Names of bodies of water and mountains are preceded by a definite article.

el Río Grande*	*the Rio Grande*	los Andes	*the Andes*
el Guadalquivir	*the Guadalquivir*	los Pirineos	*the Pyrenees*
el Misisipi	*the Mississippi*	los Alpes	*the Alps*

* The river at the border of the United States and Mexico is called "the Rio Grande" north of the border and *el Río Bravo* south of the border.

■ Names of the points of the compass are preceded by a definite article.

el norte	*north*	al norte de	*north of*
el sur	*south*	al sur de	*south of*
el este	*east*	en el norte de	*in the north of*
el oeste	*west*	hacia el este	*toward the east*

AVOID THE *Blunder*

✗ Oregón es norte de California.
✗ Florida es sur de Georgia.

■ The article is omitted in certain expressions with prepositions.

con objeto de	*for the purpose of*
con motivo de	*for the purpose of*
a orillas de	*on the banks of*
en nombre de	*in the name of*

Indefinite Articles

The indefinite article—masculine singular *un*, feminine singular *una*, masculine plural *unos*, and feminine plural *unas*—like English "a," "an," and "some," refers to an unspecified example of a noun.

Tengo un libro.	*I have a book.*
Buscamos unas revistas.	*We're looking for some magazines.*

■ The indefinite article is not used when expressing nationality or professional, religious, or other affiliation in Spanish. English often uses the indefinite article in such cases.

Miguel es ecuatoriano.	*Miguel is an Ecuadorean./ Miguel is Ecuadorean.*
Sara es médico.	*Sara is a doctor.*
Humberto es católico.	*Humberto is a Catholic./ Humberto is Catholic.*

However, as in English, when an adjective is added to further describe the person as a member of that category, an indefinite article is used in Spanish.

Miguel es un ecuatoriano famoso.	*Miguel is a famous Ecuadorean.*
Sara es una médico comprensiva.	*Sara is an understanding doctor.*

✗ Soy un profesor.
✗ Es una mexicana.
✗ Es médico bueno.

■ The indefinite article may be omitted before *gran, buen, buena, mal,* or *mala* when showing a certain "affiliation" with a type.

Es muy buena amiga.	*She's a good friend.*
Es buen católico.	*He's a good Catholic.*
Es mala persona.	*He's a bad person.*

■ The indefinite article is not used before *otro, cierto, medio(-a), cien,* and *mil,* or after *¡Qué!.*

Quiero otro libro.	*I want another book.*
Noto cierto aire de indiferencia.	*I note a certain air of indifference.*
Quiero medio kilo de azúcar.	*I want a half kilo of sugar.*
No tenemos mil dólares, sino cien.	*We don't have a thousand dollars; we have a hundred.*
¡Qué bella vista!	*What a beautiful view!*
¡Qué chica más inteligente!	*What a smart girl!*

✗ un otro libro
✗ un medio kilo
✗ un mil dólares
✗ ¡Qué una bella vista!
✗ ¡Qué una chica inteligente!

■ When the indefinite article is omitted after the verb *tener,* a general, rather than specific, meaning is implied.

Mi amigo tiene un coche.	*My friend has a car.*
Mi amigo tiene coche.	*My friend has his own transportation.*
Ella tiene un novio guapo.	*She has a cute boyfriend.*
Ella tiene novio.	*She is unavailable.*
Tengo un trabajo interesante.	*I have an interesting job.*
Tengo trabajo.	*I am employed.*

No article is used after *tener* in the following expressions of a condition. English generally uses the indefinite article in such cases.

Tiene fiebre.   *She has a fever.*
Tiene resfriado.   *He has a cold.*
Tengo tos.   *I have a cough.*

Nevertheless, when an adjective describes the noun, the indefinite article is used.

Tiene una tos terrible.   *She has a terrible cough.*

AVOID THE *Blunder*

✗ Tiene una fiebre.
✗ Tengo una tos.
✗ Tiene resfriado terrible.

■ The indefinite article is not used when expressing what one doesn't have.

No tengo coche.   *I don't have a car.*
No tenemos visita.   *We don't have a visitor/ any visitors.*

AVOID THE *Blunder*

✗ No tengo un coche.
✗ No tenemos una visita.
✗ No tenemos visitas.

■ The indefinite article is generally not used after *sin*.

Lo hace sin problema.   *She does it without a problem/ without any problems.*
Viaja sin maleta.   *He travels without a suitcase.*
Asistió al concierto sin boleto.   *He attended the concert without a ticket.*

AVOID THE *Blunder*

✗ sin un problema
✗ sin una maleta
✗ sin un boleto

■ The indefinite article is generally not used when indicating purpose after *por* or *como*.

Tiene por mesa una caja de cartón.	*He has a cardboard box for a table.*
Usa su abrigo como manta.	*She uses her coat as a blanket.*

AVOID THE *Blunder*

✗ por una mesa   ✗ como una manta

■ The indefinite article is generally not used as the first word in the title of a book or article in Spanish.

Comparación de estilos	*A Comparison of Styles*
Nuevo método para leer rápido	*A New Method for Speed Reading*
Acercamiento al aprendizaje de lenguas	*An Approach to Language Learning*

AVOID THE *Blunder*

✗ Una comparación de estilos
✗ Un nuevo método para leer rápido
✗ Un acercamiento al aprendizaje de lenguas

■ The omission of an article can indicate a slight change in meaning.

Es la verdad.	*It's the truth.*
Es verdad.	*It's true.*
Es una mentira.	*It's a lie.*
Es mentira.	*It's not true.*

■ A plural indefinite article—*unos* or *unas*—can indicate an approximation.

Están esperando unas veinte personas.	*About 20 people are waiting.*
Tengo que leer unas cincuenta páginas.	*I have to read about 50 pages.*

Demonstratives

Demonstratives indicate specific nouns in relationship to their distance from the speaker. Demonstratives also serve as pronouns when it is unnecessary to state the noun. Use of an accent mark above the first vowel of a demonstrative pronoun is now optional.

■ *Este(-a/-os/-as)* is used to indicate something that is so close that the speaker can touch it.

Este libro es interesante.	*This book is interesting.*
Éste/Este es interesante.	*This one is interesting.*
Esta novela es larga.	*This novel is long.*
Ésta/Esta es larga.	*This one is long.*
Estos exámenes están corregidos.	*These exams are corrected.*
Éstos/Estos están corregidos.	*These are corrected.*
Estas respuestas no son correctas.	*These answers are not correct.*
Éstas/Estas no son correctas.	*These are not correct.*

When the demonstrative is placed after the noun, it has a negative connotation.

La niña esta me está fastidiando.	*This pesky little girl is annoying me.*

The demonstrative can also refer to time.

esta mañana	*this morning*
esta noche	*tonight*
esta semana	*this week*
este año	*this year*
estos días	*these days*

■ *Ese(-a/-os/-as)* indicates something that is farther away from the speaker, perhaps close to the person being spoken to.

Ese libro es aburrido.	*That book is boring.*
Ése/Ese es aburrido.	*That one is boring.*
Esa novela es corta.	*That novel is short.*
Ésa/Esa es corta.	*That one is short.*
Esos exámenes no están corregidos.	*Those exams aren't corrected.*
Ésos/Esos no están corregidos.	*Those aren't corrected.*
Esas respuestas son correctas.	*Those answers are correct.*
Ésas/Esas son correctas.	*Those are correct.*

AVOID THE *Blunder*

Do not use the pronouns *esto* and *eso* before nouns.

✗ esto año   ✗ eso beso

When the demonstrative is placed after the noun, it has a negative connotation.

El chico ese vive cerca de mi casa.	*That annoying kid lives near my house.*

The demonstrative can also refer to time.

esa mañana	*that morning*
esa tarde	*that afternoon*
esa noche	*that night*
ese día	*that day*

■ *Aquel/aquella/aquellos/aquellas* refers to something farther away, not close to either the speaker or the person being spoken to.

Aquel libro es carísimo.	*That book over there is really expensive.*
Aquella novela no es cara.	*That novel over there isn't expensive.*
Aquellos exámenes no son míos.	*Those exams over there aren't mine.*
Aquellas respuestas son interesantes.	*Those answers over there are interesting.*

The demonstrative can also refer to a distant time.

aquel día	*that day*
aquella semana	*that week*
aquella primavera	*that spring*
aquellos años	*those years*

AVOID THE *Blunder*

Always put the demonstrative before the noun unless you want to indicate a negative connotation.

✗ la mujer esa   ✗ el profesor aquel   ✗ los hombres aquellos

Possessives

The possessives, *mi(s), tu(s), su(s), nuestro(-a/-os/-as)*, and *vuestro(-a/-os/-as)* identify the possessor or owner of something. In Spanish, they are not used with parts of the body. (See page 59.)

mi libro	*my book*
mis libros	*my books*
mi casa	*my house*
mis casas	*my houses*

tu libro	*your book*
tus libros	*your books*
tu casa	*your house*
tus casas	*your houses*
su libro	*your book, his book, her book, their book,* *your* (pl.) *book*
sus libros	*your books, his books, her books, their books,* *your* (pl.) *books*
su casa	*your house, his house, her house, their house,* *your* (pl.) *house*
sus casas	*your houses, his houses, her houses, their houses,* *your* (pl.) *houses*
nuestro libro	*our book*
nuestros libros	*our books*
nuestra casa	*our house*
nuestras casas	*our houses*
vuestro libro	*your* (pl.) *book*
vuestros libros	*your* (pl.) *books*
vuestra casa	*your* (pl.) *house*
vuestras casas	*your* (pl.) *houses*

AVOID THE *Blunder*

✗ nuestros libro   ✗ sus casa
✗ mi libros   ✗ nuestras casa

■ Remember that *su(s)* can mean "your," "his," "her," and "their." An -*s* at the end means that the things possessed are plural.

To distinguish between "your," "his," "her," and "their," a phrase with *de* may be used.

su coche el coche de usted }	*your car*
sus coches los coches de usted }	*your cars*
el coche de él los coches de él	*his car* *his cars*
el coche de ella los coches de ella	*her car* *her cars*

el coche de ustedes	*your* (pl.) *car*
los coches de ustedes	*your* (pl.) *cars*
el coche de ellos/ellas	*their car*
los coches de ellos/ellas	*their cars*

■ The possessive adjectives *mío, tuyo,* and *suyo* follow the verb *ser*, an article, or a noun, and agree with the noun (or pronoun) in number and gender.

Este coche es mío. El suyo está allí.	*This car is mine. Yours is over there.*
¿Es tuya esta chaqueta? No puedo encontrar la mía.	*Is this jacket yours? I can't find mine.*
Esos paquetes son suyos. Los nuestros están aquí.	*Those packages are theirs. Ours are here.*
Las flores son nuestras. No sé dónde están las suyas.	*The flowers are ours. I don't know where hers are.*

AVOID THE *Blunder*

Suyo(-a/-os/-as) can mean "yours," "his," "hers," and "theirs." Be sure the ending agrees in number and gender with the item that is possessed.

✗ Los coches son mío.
✗ La chaqueta es suyos.
✗ Esos paquetes son suyo.

"Yours" (with *usted* and *ustedes*), "his," "hers," and "theirs" can also be expressed with a phrase using *de*.

El coche es de usted.	*The car is yours.*
El coche es de él.	*The car is his.*
El coche es de ella.	*The car is hers.*
Los coches son de ustedes.	*The cars are yours* (pl.).
Los coches son de ellos.	*The cars are theirs.*
Los coches son de ellas.	*The cars are theirs.*

"Mine" and "yours" (for *tú*) are not expressed with a phrase.

| El coche es mío. | *The car is mine.* |
| El coche es tuyo. | *The car is yours.* |

AVOID THE *Blunder*

✗ El coche es de mí.   ✗ El coche es de ti.

Other Determiners

algún

Algún/alguna(-os/-as) refers to particular, but unidentified, nouns.

Algún día será feliz.	*One day/Some day he'll be happy.*
Quiere invitar a alguna chica.	*He wants to invite a girl. (I don't know which one.)*
Algunos chicos vienen con nosotras.	*Some boys are coming with us.*
¿Conoce alguna novela buena?	*Do you know of a good novel?*

cualquier

Cualquier and *cualquiera* indicate any one of a class or group. *Cualquier* is used before a masculine or feminine noun. *Cualquiera* is used after a noun.

Me llamó como cualquier otro día. ⎫	*He called me just like any*
Me llamó como un día cualquiera. ⎬	*other day.*

Tráeme cualquier chaqueta. ⎫	
Tráeme una chaqueta cualquiera. ⎬	*Bring me any old jacket.*

AVOID THE *Blunder*

Do not change *cualquier* according to gender, but rather according to its position before or after the noun.

✗ cualquiera día   ✗ cualquiera persona
✗ cualquiera manera   ✗ un día cualquier

unos cuantos and unos pocos

Unos(-as) cuantos(-as) and *unos(-as) pocos(-as)* indicate "several" or "a few."

Tengo unos cuantos amigos en esta ciudad.	*I have several friends in this city.*
Quiero comprar unas pocas cosas.	*I want to buy a few things.*

otro

Otro(-a/-os/-as) indicates one or several more of a noun, or one or several different ones. (See pages 43–44.)

Quiero otro profesor.	*I want another (a different) teacher.*
¿Tienen otros juguetes?	*Do you have any other toys?*
Tengo otras ideas.	*I have some other ideas.*

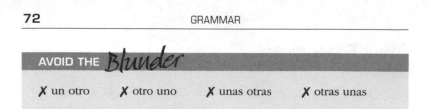

| ✗ un otro | ✗ otro uno | ✗ unas otras | ✗ otras unas |

Muchos(-as) and *pocos(-as)* can be placed before or after *otros(-as)*.

Conoce a muchas otras personas.   *He knows a lot of other people.*
Tiene otras pocas ideas.   *He has a few other ideas.*

Numbers are placed after *otros(-as)*—never before.

Quiero ver otras dos películas.   *I want to see two other movies.*
Mi vecino tiene otros tres coches.   *My neighbor has three other cars.*

| ✗ dos otros libros | ✗ tres otros amigos |

poco

Poco(-a/-os/-as) indicates a small number or amount of something.

Gana poco dinero.   *He earns very little money.*
Tenemos poca agua en el campo.   *We have very little water in the
                                      country.*

Hay pocos alumnos en esa   *There are few students at that
escuela.   school.*
Hay pocas cosas que hacer allí.   *There are very few things to do
                                      there.*

Do not confuse *poco* with *un poco*. *Poco* emphasizes a lack; *un poco*
means "some."

Gana poco dinero.   *He earns very little money.*
Gana un poco de dinero.   *He earns a little money.*

Hay poca contaminación.   *There is very little pollution.*
Hay un poco de contaminación.   *There is some pollution.*

Do not use *de* with *poco*. Do not leave it out after *un poco*.

✗ Gana poco de dinero.
✗ Hay un poco contaminación.

mucho

Mucho(-a/-os/-as) indicates a large number or amount of something.

Hay mucho ruido en la calle.	*There is a lot of noise in the street.*
Tengo mucha hambre.	*I'm very hungry. (I have a lot of hunger.)*
Lee muchos libros en el verano.	*He reads a lot of books in summer.*
Tengo muchas ganas de verte.	*I'm looking forward to seeing you. (I have a lot of wishes to see you.)*

Many expressions with *tener* and *hacer* indicate a state or condition that is expressed with "be" in English. In English, these are enhanced by "very." In Spanish they are enhanced by *mucho(-a)*. (See page 311.)

Tengo mucho miedo/frío/calor/ suerte.	*I am very afraid/cold/hot/lucky.*
Tengo mucha hambre/sed.	*I am very hungry/thirsty.*
Hace mucho frío/calor/viento.	*It's very cold/hot/windy.*

AVOID THE *Blunder*

✗ Tengo muy miedo.
✗ Tengo muy hambre.
✗ Hace muy frío.

tanto

Tanto(-a/ os/ as) refers to a number or amount that has consequences.

Hay tanto trabajo que no sé dónde empezar.	*There is so much work that I don't know where to start.*
Tenía tanta sed que casi se muere.	*She was so thirsty she almost died.*
Tiene tantos problemas que ya no puede más.	*He has so many problems that he can't go on.*
Ella tiene tantas deudas que no las puede pagar.	*She has so many debts that she can't pay them.*

AVOID THE *Blunder*

✗ tan mucho
✗ tan muchos

todo

The entirety of something is expressed by *todo el, toda la, todos los,* or *todas las* plus the noun.

Voy a trabajar todo el día.	*I'm going to work all day.*
Toda la clase está aquí.	*The whole class is here.*
Trabajo todos los días.	*I work every day.*
Todas las chicas están aquí.	*All the girls are here.*

Another way to emphasize the whole of a singular noun is by placing *entero(-a)* after it.

Voy a trabajar el día entero.	*I'm going to work the whole day.*
La clase entera está aquí.	*The entire class is here.*

"Everybody" can be expressed three ways, using *todo el mundo, todos,* or *el mundo entero.*

Todo el mundo va a la fiesta.	
Todos van a la fiesta.	*Everybody is going to the party.*
Lo van a saber todos.	*Everybody is going to find out*
Lo va a saber el mundo entero.	*about it.*

AVOID THE *Blunder*

Use a singular verb with *todo el mundo* and *el mundo entero.* Use a plural verb with *todos.*

✗ Todo el mundo van a la fiesta.
✗ Lo van a saber el mundo entero.
✗ Todos va a la fiesta.

Another way to emphasize the totality of the members of a category is *todo(-a)* plus a singular noun.

Todo trabajador merece un descanso.	*Every worker deserves a break.*
Toda niña necesita una muñeca.	*Every little girl needs a doll.*

Todo un or *toda una* plus a noun emphasizes the achievement of becoming the embodiment of the noun.

Su hijo es todo un hombre.	*Your son is all grown up (a complete man).*
Ella es toda una mujer.	*She's all grown up (a complete woman).*
Ya es toda una estrella de cine.	*Now he/she is a real movie star (in every sense of the word).*

cada

Cada is used to indicate all the items, emphasizing one at a time. It can be used before *uno* and *una*.

Cada alumno recibió su diploma.	*Each student received his diploma.*
Cada uno recibió su diploma.	*Each one received his diploma.*
BUT	
Todos los alumnos recibieron su diploma.	*All the students received their diplomas.*
Cada madre recogió a sus niños.	*Each mother picked up her children.*
Cada una recogió a sus niños.	*Each one picked up her children.*
BUT	
Todas las madres recogieron a sus niños.	*All the mothers picked up their children.*

AVOID THE *Blunder*

Do not use *cada* for "all" unless you want to emphasize the individuality of each member.

ambos

Ambos(-as) is used to indicate the same, but separate, state or action of two people, animals, or things. *Los dos* and *las dos* are used to indicate either joint or separate states or actions.

Ambos chicos fueron a casa.	*Each boy went home./Both boys went home (separately).*
Los dos chicos fueron a casa.	*Both boys went home (separately or together).*
Los dos chicos fueron a casa juntos.	*Both boys went home (together)./ The two boys went home together.*
Vine a visitar a los dos.	*I came to visit both of you (together).*

AVOID THE *Blunder*

Do not use *ambos(-as)* unless you want to indicate separate circumstances. To emphasize joint action, use *los dos* or *las dos* and add *juntos(-as)*.

✗ Vine a visitar a ambos de ustedes.

los demás

Los demás or *las demás* refers to "the rest" or "the others."

Miguel, Juan y los demás chicos ya se fueron.	*Miguel, Juan, and all the other boys left.*
Ana y las demás chicas se quedaron.	*Ana and the rest of the girls stayed.*

sólo, solamente, ni un solo

Sólo and *solamente* emphasize the small number or small amount of something.

Sólo tres coches estaban en el garaje.	*Only three cars were in the garage.*
Me compró solamente una camiseta.	*She only bought me a T-shirt.*

A negative statement with the determiner *un solo* or *una sola* indicates a total lack.

No me dio un solo centavo.	*He didn't give me a red cent.*
No tengo ni una sola amiga aquí.	*I don't have even one friend here.*

único

A definite article plus *único(-a/-os/-as)* indicates the only one of something.

Es el único lápiz que tengo.	*It's the only pencil I have.*
Es la única cosa que me queda.	*It's the only thing I have left.*
Son los únicos músicos en el pueblo.	*They're the only musicians in this town.*
Son las únicas flores que había.	*They're the only flowers there were.*

AVOID THE *Blunder*

✗ el sólo lápiz	✗ la sóla cosa
✗ los sólos músicos	✗ las sólas flores

tal

Tal can refer to something already mentioned, usually of a negative nature.

Mi hermana nunca hizo tal cosa.	*My sister never did anything like that.*

Un tal or *una tal* plus a noun indicates someone unknown to the speaker.

¿Conoces a un tal Miguel Márquez?	*Do you know a Miguel Márquez?*
Te llamó una tal Jennifer.	*Somebody named Jennifer called you.*

Determiners with Different Meanings

The determiners in the examples below have different meanings when they are placed after the noun.

Hay cierto riesgo.	*There's a certain risk.*
Hay un riesgo cierto.	*There's a definite risk.*
Necesitas media taza de azúcar.	*You need half a cup of sugar.*
Es de la clase media.	*He's middle class.*
Es la misma mujer.	*It's the same woman.*
La mujer misma apareció.	*The woman herself appeared.*
Tiene su propia casa.	*He has his own house.*
Tiene una casa propia.	*He has an appropriate house.*
No haría semejante cosa.	*I wouldn't do such a thing.*
Ella hizo una cosa semejante.	*She did a similar thing.*
Es el único chico de la clase.	*He's the only boy in the class.*
Es un chico único.	*He's a unique boy.*
Es su único hijo.	*It's his only son.*
Es hijo único.	*He's an only child.*
Tenemos varios amigos.	*We have several friends.*
Tenemos amigos varios.	*We have diverse friends.*

AVOID THE *Blunder*

Put the determiner before the noun. Put the descriptive adjective after it.

✗ No haría una semejante cosa.
✗ Es de la media clase.
✗ Es su hijo único.

Exercises

A Complete the chart with the corresponding singular or plural noun and its determiner.

SINGULAR	PLURAL
1. _____	las águilas
2. este libro	_____
3. _____	las lecciones
4. el agua	_____
5. _____	aquellos días
6. aquella persona	_____
7. _____	algunos chicos
8. un libro	_____

B Fill in the blank with the word or words necessary to complete each expression. If no word is necessary, write an "X" in the blank.

1. _____ martes (*on Tuesday*)

2. _____ martes (*on Tuesdays*)

3. _____ verano (*in summer*)

4. _____ norte (*in the north*)

5. _____ norte de (*north of*)

6. Me gusta _____ pollo. (*I like chicken.*)

7. Samuel Bueno, _____ presidente de la clase (*Samuel Bueno, the president of the class*)

8. Elena es _____ maestra. (*Elena is a teacher.*)

9. _____ persona (*another person*)

10. _____ personas (*two other people*)

11. _____ persona (*nobody*)

12. Tiene _____ fiebre. (*He has a fever.*)

13. Tiene _____ coche nuevo. (*He has a new car.*)

14. No tiene _____ bicicleta. (*He doesn't have a bicycle.*)

15. Se lava _____ manos. (*She washes her hands.*)

16. 30 centavos _____ docena (*30 cents a dozen*)

17. Ella cocina sin _____ libro de cocina. (*She cooks without a cookbook.*)

C *Match the words in the left column with the words in the right column that complete a sentence.*

_____ 1. Alberto es   a. a la Srta. Ruiz.

_____ 2. Buenas tardes,   b. Srta. Ruiz.

_____ 3. El libro está   c. las cuatro.

_____ 4. Éste es el libro   d. a las cuatro.

_____ 5. La película empieza   e. a casa.

_____ 6. No conozco   f. en la casa de mi amigo.

_____ 7. Son   g. español.

_____ 8. Van a traducirlo   h. de español.

_____ 9. Voy   i. al español.

D *Indicate the correct order of the nouns in relation to their determiners.*

1. ese / hombre

   _____ es el padre de Carlos.
   (*That man is Carlos's father.*)

2. cualquiera / libro

   Traiga un _____ a la reunión.
   (*Bring any book to the meeting.*)

3. cualquier / libro

   Traiga _____ a la reunión.
   (*Bring any book to the meeting.*)

4. propio / negocio

   Este es mi _____ .
   (*This is my own business.*)

5. propio / negocio

   Este es un _____ para esta comunidad.
   (*This is an appropriate business for this community.*)

6. única / mujer

   Ella es la _____ en la oficina.
   (*She's the only woman in the office.*)

7. única / mujer

   Ella es una _____ .
   (*She's a unique woman.*)

8. cierto / problema

   Hay _____ que tenemos que hablar.
   (*There's a certain problem we have to talk about.*)

DESCRIPTIVE ADJECTIVES

	MASCULINE		FEMININE	
	SINGULAR	PLURAL	SINGULAR	PLURAL
-e	-e	-es	-e	-es
-ista	-ista	-istas	-ista	-istas
-or	-or	-ores	-ora	-oras
-ón	-ón	-ones	-ona	-onas
-ín	-ín	-ines	-ina	-inas
-z	-z	-ces	-z	-ces
any other consonant	*consonant*	-es	*consonant*	-es
-o	-o	-os	-a	-as

Review the forms in the chart above.

Forms

In Spanish, descriptive adjectives generally are placed after the nouns they describe, and their endings change to agree with them in gender and number.

■ Many adjectives end in *-o* to describe masculine nouns and *-a* to describe feminine nouns. Their plurals end in *-os* and *-as*, respectively.

el hombre alto	*the tall man*
la mujer alta	*the tall woman*
el edificio alto	*the tall building*
la casa pequeña	*the small house*
los hombres altos	*the tall men*
las mujeres altas	*the tall women*
los edificios altos	*the tall buildings*
las casas pequeñas	*the small houses*

A number of adjectives end in -*e* to describe both masculine and feminine nouns. Their plurals end in -*es*.

el muchacho inteligente	*the smart boy*
la muchacha inteligente	*the smart girl*
los muchachos inteligentes	*the smart boys*
las muchachas inteligentes	*the smart girls*

A number of adjectives end in -*ista* to describe both masculine and feminine nouns. Their plurals end in -*istas*.

el hombre optimista	*the optimistic man*
la mujer optimista	*the optimistic woman*
los hombres optimistas	*the optimistic men*
las mujeres optimistas	*the optimistic women*

A number of adjectives end in -*or* to describe masculine nouns. Their feminine counterparts end in -*ora*. Their plurals end in -*ores* and -*oras*, respectively.

el chico encantador	*the charming boy*
la chica encantadora	*the charming girl*
los chicos encantadores	*the charming boys*
las chicas encantadoras	*the charming girls*

Adjectives that end in -*in* and -*ón* describe masculine nouns. Their feminine counterparts end in -*ina* and -*ona* (without accent marks), respectively.

Adjectives that end in other consonants have the same form to describe masculine and feminine nouns. Their plurals end in -*es*. (Note that a final -*z* changes to -*c*- in the plural. See pages 11 and 33.)

el lápiz azul	*the blue pencil*
la mujer joven	*the young woman*
la niña feliz	*the happy girl*
los lápices azules	*the blue pencils*
las mujeres jóvenes	*the young women*
las niñas felices	*the happy girls*

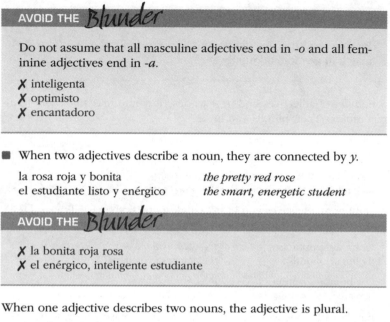

Do not assume that all masculine adjectives end in -*o* and all feminine adjectives end in -*a*.

✗ inteligenta
✗ optimisto
✗ encantadoro

■ When two adjectives describe a noun, they are connected by *y*.

la rosa roja y bonita	*the pretty red rose*
el estudiante listo y enérgico	*the smart, energetic student*

✗ la bonita roja rosa
✗ el enérgico, inteligente estudiante

When one adjective describes two nouns, the adjective is plural.

el coche y el camión nuevos	*the new car and truck*
la falda y la blusa caras	*the expensive skirt and blouse*
la casa y el jardín hermosos	*the beautiful house and garden*

Do not use a singular adjective to describe more than one noun.

✗ la casa y el jardín hermoso
✗ la falda y el vestido caro

When two adjectives describe all components of a plural noun, both adjectives are plural.

las flores rojas y bonitas	*(both/all) the beautiful red flowers*
los estudiantes listos y enérgicos	*(both/all) the smart, energetic students*

When two separate items are described by two different adjectives, both adjectives are singular.

las rosas roja y amarilla	*both the red rose and the yellow one*
los coches blanco y azul	*both the white car and the blue one*

> **AVOID THE** *Blunder*
>
> Do not use a plural adjective to describe one component of a plural noun.
>
> Use singular adjectives to express one red rose and one yellow one.
>
> ✗ las rosas rojas y amarillas
>
> Use singular adjectives to express one white car and one blue one.
>
> ✗ los coches blancos y azules

■ While English nouns can function like adjectives when placed before other nouns, Spanish nouns must be preceded by a preposition in order to modify another noun.

un libro de español	*a Spanish book**
una mesa de vidrio	*a glass table*
una bolsa de papel	*a paper bag*
una casa de adobe	*an adobe house*

**Un libro de español* is a book for learning Spanish. *Un libro español* is a book written, manufactured, or published in Spain.

> **AVOID THE** *Blunder*
>
> ✗ una mesa vidrio
> ✗ una bolsa papel
> ✗ una casa adobe

Adjective Position

The placement of descriptive adjectives varies in Spanish.

■ An adjective generally follows the noun it describes.

Adjectives of nationality and religion, as well as adjectives that classify a noun as part of a specific group, always follow the noun.

una mujer norteamericana	*a North American woman*
un hombre judío	*a Jewish man*
la cocina mexicana	*Mexican cuisine*
una casa de estilo colonial	*a colonial-style house*

AVOID THE *Blunder*

✗ un judío hombre
✗ la mexicana cocina

Adjectives that describe a physical quality and distinguish the noun from others of its kind generally follow the noun.

el lápiz amarillo	*the yellow pencil*
la casa grande	*the big house*
el coche viejo	*the old car*
el pelo rizado	*the curly hair*
el muchacho guapo	*the cute boy*
la chica lista	*the smart girl*

AVOID THE *Blunder*

✗ el amarillo lápiz
✗ el rizado pelo

■ When a descriptive adjective precedes a noun, it indicates that the quality is already known or inseparable from the noun. Compare the following examples.

las bonitas flores	*the beautiful flowers (all of which are beautiful)*
las flores bonitas	*the beautiful flowers (only the beautiful ones)*
las caras tiendas del barrio	*the expensive neighborhood stores (all of which are expensive)*
las tiendas caras del barrio	*the expensive neighborhood stores (only the expensive ones)*
mi nuevo novio	*my new boyfriend (whom you know about)*
mi novio nuevo	*my new boyfriend (not my old one)*

The adjectives *bueno* and *malo* are shortened when they immediately precede masculine singular nouns.

la buena muchacha	*the good girl (who is known to be good)*
el buen muchacho	*the good boy (who is known to be good)*
la mala mujer	*the bad woman (who is known to be bad)*
el mal hombre	*the bad man (who is known to be bad)*

The adjective *grande* is shortened before both masculine and feminine nouns, and it has a different meaning when placed before the noun. Compare the following examples.

la mujer grande	*the big woman*
la gran mujer	*the great woman*
el hombre grande	*the big man*
el gran hombre	*the great man*
la ciudad grande	*the big city*
la gran ciudad	*the great city*

The adjectives listed below also have slightly different meanings depending on whether they are placed before or after the noun. Compare the following examples.

la antigua capital	*the former capital city*
la capital antigua	*the very old capital city*
la tela de baja calidad	*the cloth of low quality*
la chica baja	*the short girl*
las dichosas llamadas	*the annoying calls*
las chicas dichosas	*the lucky girls*
diferentes maneras	*various ways*
maneras diferentes	*different ways*
distintos hombres	*various men*
hombres distintos	*different men*
el pobre muchacho	*the unfortunate boy*
el muchacho pobre	*the poor boy*
el raro pájaro	*the rare bird*
el pájaro raro	*the strange bird*
un simple error	*a mere error*
una casa simple	*a modest house*
mi viejo amigo	*my long-time friend*
mi amigo viejo	*my friend who's old*

AVOID THE *Blunder*

Make sure you don't call your best friend old!

Usage

Descriptive adjectives can be used in different ways in a sentence.

■ In English, "the" plus an adjective plus "one(s)" distinguishes one or more persons or things from the others in a group. In Spanish, "one(s)" is not expressed.

la roja	*the red one*	los pequeños	*the small ones*
el grande	*the big one*	las últimas	*the last ones*

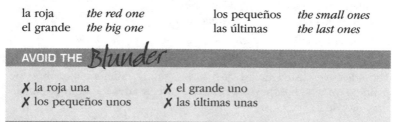

AVOID THE *Blunder*

✗ la roja una   ✗ el grande uno
✗ los pequeños unos   ✗ las últimas unas

Plural adjectives preceded by a definite article can be used as nouns that refer to an entire class.

los ricos	*the rich (ones)*
los orgullosos	*the proud (ones)*
los famosos	*the famous (ones)*
los ridículos	*the ridiculous (ones)*

■ An adjective can be used as the subject of a sentence by placing *lo* before it. (See pages 226–227.)

Lo bueno es que ella está contenta.	*The good thing (about it) is that she is happy.*
Lo malo es que vive muy lejos.	*The bad thing is that she lives so far away.*

AVOID THE *Blunder*

✗ la buena cosa   ✗ la cosa mala

Lo before an adjective can also indicate the intensity of the adjective. (See pages 226–227.)

No te imaginas lo difícil que es.	*You can't imagine how hard it is.*
Me habla de lo aburrido que está.	*He tells me how bored he is.*

AVOID THE *Blunder*

✗ como difícil que es   ✗ como aburrido es

■ The past participle of a verb (see page 122) can be used as an adjective. Its ending reflects the gender and number of the noun it modifies. Participles express different meanings, depending on whether they are used with *ser* or *estar*.

A sentence with *ser* plus a past participle gives information about how an action is done. A sentence with *estar* plus a past participle tells the result of an action.

La puerta es abierta por el guardia.	*The door is opened by the guard.*
La puerta está abierta.	*The door is open.*
La pareja va a ser casada por el cura.	*The couple is going to be married by the priest.*
La pareja está casada.	*The couple is married.*
Estas mesas son hechas en México.	*These tables are made in Mexico.*
Estas mesas están hechas.	*These tables are finished (already made).*
Los libros son publicados en este país.	*The books are published in this country.*
Los libros ya están publicados.	*The books are already published.*

AVOID THE *Blunder*

Remember that a participle used after *ser* or *estar* is an adjective, and its ending changes to agree with the noun it describes.

✗ La puerta está abierto.
✗ Estas mesas son hecho en México.

Adjectives generally express different meanings, depending on whether they are used with *ser* or *estar*. (See page 309.)

abierto

La muchacha es abierta.	*The girl is frank.*
La puerta está abierta.	*The door is open.*

aburrido

El maestro es aburrido.	*The teacher is boring.*
El maestro está aburrido.	*The teacher is bored.*

alegre

El niño es alegre.	*The child has a happy nature.*
El niño está alegre.	*The child is enjoying himself.*

bajo

Mi hermana es baja.	*My sister is short.*
Mi hermana está baja en la lista.	*My sister is way down on the list.*

bonito

Eres muy bonita.	*You are a very pretty girl.*
¡Estás muy bonita!	*You look pretty today!*

callado

La jefa es muy callada.	*The boss is not a big talker.*
La jefa está muy callada.	*The boss is very quiet today.*

débil

El joven es débil.	*The boy is a weakling.*
El joven está débil.	*The boy is in a weak condition.*

despierto

La mujer es despierta.	*The woman is bright.*
La mujer está despierta.	*The woman is awake.*

divertido

La chica es divertida.	*The girl is a lot of fun.*
La chica está divertida.	*The girl is having fun.*

frío

Esa mujer es fría.	*That woman is unfeeling.*
Esta comida está fría.	*This food is cold.*

fuerte

El actor es fuerte.	*The actor is a strong man.*
El actor está fuerte.	*The actor is in shape.*

gordo

Soy muy gorda.	*I'm very fat.*
Estoy muy gorda.	*I've gained a lot of weight.*

listo

El estudiante es listo.	*The student is smart.*
El estudiante está listo.	*The student is ready.*

loco

El pobre es loco.	*The poor guy is crazy.*
¡Estás loco!	*You must be crazy!*

nervioso

Soy nerviosa.	*I'm a nervous person.*
Tengo un examen y estoy nerviosa.	*I have an exam, and I'm nervous.*

seguro

Esta zona es segura.	*This area is safe.*
Ella está segura de lo que hace.	*She's sure about what she's doing.*

verde

Estas uvas son verdes.	*These grapes are green.*
Estas uvas están verdes.	*These grapes aren't ripe.*

viejo

Tú no eres viejo.	*You're not old.*
Tú estás viejo.	*You look old.*

vivo

Esa mujer es viva.	*That woman is "smart like a fox."*
Esa mujer está viva.	*That woman is alive.*

AVOID THE *Blunder*

Use *ser* with an adjective to describe natural qualities. Use *estar* to indicate a present condition.

✗ Soy nervioso por el examen.
✗ La mujer no murió. Es viva.
✗ La puerta es abierta.

■ Certain adverbs used before an adjective make the adjective more or less intense.

un poco	medio	bastante	muy	demasiado	tan ____ que
				bien	
				sumamente	
				extremadamente	
				re-/reque-/requete-	

El coche es un poco caro.	*The car is a little expensive.*
La blusa es medio cara.	*The blouse is somewhat expensive.*
Los boletos son bastante caros.	*The tickets are quite expensive.*
Las clases son muy caras.	*The classes are very expensive.*
La universidad es demasiado cara.	*The university is extremely expensive.*
Ese restaurante es bien caro.	*That restaurant is very expensive.*
Los libros son recaros/requecaros/ requetecaros.	*The books are really expensive.*
Ese coche es tan caro que no lo puedo comprar.	*That car is so expensive that I can't buy it./That car is too expensive.*
Estoy tan cansada que no puedo caminar más.	*I'm so tired that I can't walk any farther./I'm too tired to walk.*

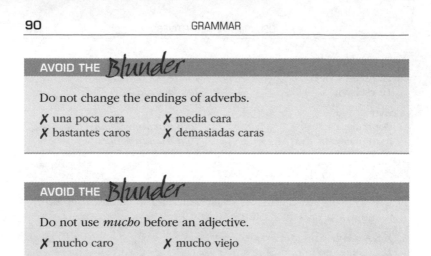

AVOID THE *Blunder*

Do not change the endings of adverbs.

✗ una poca cara   ✗ media cara
✗ bastantes caros   ✗ demasiadas caras

AVOID THE *Blunder*

Do not use *mucho* before an adjective.

✗ mucho caro   ✗ mucho viejo

Demasiado is often translated as "too"; however, it is better translated as "extremely" because it does not imply a negative result.

Ese coche es demasiado caro.   *That car is extremely expensive (no particular implication).*

Ese coche es muy caro y no lo puedo comprar / no lo quiero comprar.   *That car is too expensive and I can't buy it / I won't buy it.*

AVOID THE *Blunder*

Do not use *demasiado* to imply that you are not going to buy it.

✗ El vestido es demasiado caro.

Do not confuse *re-* before an adjective with *re-* before a verb. Before a verb *re-* means, as it does in English, "to do again." Before an adjective it means "very."

Tienes que reescribir la carta.   *You have to rewrite the letter.*
Es una clase reaburrida.   *It's a very boring class.*

AVOID THE *Blunder*

Frijoles refritos are well known in English as "refried beans." However, rather than being "refried," they are actually "well fried."

■ To indicate the opinion of the speaker or writer, adjectives that end in a vowel can be intensified by dropping the final vowel and adding *-ísimo, -ísima, -ísimos, -ísimas.*

la carta importantísima	*the extremely important letter*
el actor guapísimo	*the gorgeous actor*

After the final vowel has been dropped, some consonants change before adding *-ísimo*:

- If the final consonant is *c*, it changes to *qu* before *-ísimo* (see page 10).

el maestro simpatiquísimo	*the really nice teacher*
la comida riquísima	*the delicious meal*

- If the final consonant is *g*, it changes to *gu* before *-ísimo* (see page 10).

la película larguísima	*the very long movie*

Adjectives that end in *-ble* add an *i* between the *b* and the *l*.

la mujer amabilísima	*the really, really nice woman*
el hombre notabilísimo	*the very distinguished man*

For adjectives that end in *-l*, add *-ísimo, -ísima, -ísimos, -ísimas.*

la lección facilísima	*the really easy lesson*
el curso dificilísimo	*the very difficult course/academic year*

For adjectives that end in *-n*, add *-císimo, -císima, -císimos, -císimas.*

el jefe jovencísimo	*the very young boss*

If the final consonant is *z*, it changes to *c* before *-ísimo* (see page 11).

el animal ferocísimo	*the very fierce animal*
la niña felicísima	*the extremely happy child*

AVOID THE *Blunder*

✗ jovenísimo	✗ ricímo	✗ simpaticísimo
✗ felizísimo	✗ ferozísimo	✗ terriblísimo

■ Descriptive adjectives can be used with *más* ____ *que* and *menos* ____ *que* to compare people or things.

Este coche es más caro que ese.	*This car is more expensive than that one.*
Ese coche es menos caro que este.	*That car is less expensive than this one.*

María es más alta que yo.	*María is taller than I am.*
Yo soy menos alta que María.	*I'm not as tall as María.*
Los zapatos blancos son más bonitos que los negros.	*The white shoes are prettier than the black ones.*

AVOID THE *Blunder*

Always compare subjects with subjects, and possessives with possessives.

✗ María es más alta que mi.

There are four irregular comparative forms: *mejor, peor, mayor,* and *menor.*

Esteban es mejor que Pablo.	*Esteban is better than Pablo.*
Pablo es peor que Esteban.	*Pablo is worse than Esteban.*
Esteban y Pablo son mejores que los otros.	*Esteban and Pablo are better than the others.*
Los otros son peores que Esteban y Pablo.	*The others are worse than Esteban and Pablo.*
Esteban es mayor que Pablo.	*Esteban is older than Pablo.*
Pablo es menor que Esteban.	*Pablo is younger than Esteban.*
Esteban y Ricardo son mayores que Pablo.	*Esteban and Ricardo are older than Pablo.*
Pablo y Juan son menores que Esteban.	*Pablo and Juan are younger than Esteban.*

AVOID THE *Blunder*

Do not use *más bueno* unless you mean that Esteban is more saintly.

✗ Esteban es más bueno que Pablo.

Do not use *más malo* unless you mean that Pablo is more diabolical.

✗ Pablo es más malo que Esteban.

Mayor can mean *más grande* and, when it refers to people, *más viejo.*
Menor can mean *más pequeño* and, when it refers to people, *más joven.*

Ella va con su hermana mayor.	*She's going with her older sister.*
Ella es menor que su hermana.	*She is younger than her sister.*

■ Descriptive adjectives can be used with *tan* ___ *como* to show equality between people or things.

Tu libro es tan caro como el mío.	*Your book is as expensive as mine.*
Tus libros son tan caros como los míos.	*Your books are as expensive as mine.*
Esta computadora es tan ligera como la otra.	*This computer is as light as the other one.*
Estas son tan buenas como esas.	*These are as good as those.*

AVOID THE *Blunder*

Do not use *que* in place of *como*.

✗ tan caro que el otro

Do not forget the article before a possessive.

✗ tan caro como mío
✗ tan buenas como tuyas

■ Descriptive adjectives can be used to single out people or things as superlative.

Ese es mi mayor problema.	*That's my biggest problem.*
Ese es su mejor vestido.	*That is her best dress.*
Es la ciudad más bella del mundo.	*It's the most beautiful city in the world.*
Este coche es el más caro de todos.	*This car is the most expensive of all.*
Julia es la más alta de todas las chicas.	*Julia is the tallest of the girls.*
Esteban es el mejor de la clase.	*Esteban is the best (one) in the class.*
Julia es la más alta del grupo.	*Julia is the tallest (one) in the group.*
Mario y Juanita son los mejores de la escuela.	*Mario and Juanita are the best in the school.*

AVOID THE *Blunder*

Do not use *en* in place of *de*.

✗ más grande en el mundo
✗ la más bonita en el mundo
✗ los mejores en la clase

Exercises

A *Complete the chart below with the feminine equivalent of the masculine noun phrase, and the masculine equivalent of the feminine noun phrase.*

MASCULINE	FEMININE
1. el chico interesante	_____
2. _____	la mujer optimista
3. los jóvenes encantadores	_____
4. _____	las niñas felices
5. _____	la muchacha alta

B *Write the correct form and order of the Spanish nouns and adjectives for each English phrase.*

1. hermoso / pequeño / casa

   _____

   (*the pretty little house*)

2. nuevo / blusa / falda

   _____

   (*the new blouse and skirt*)

3. azul / bonito / zapatos

   _____

   (*the pretty blue shoes*)

4. rojo / blanco / blusas

   _____

   (*the red blouse and the white blouse*)

C *Circle the noun-adjective combination that reflects the English meaning.*

1. *This is the new car I told you about.*

   Éste es mi **coche nuevo | nuevo coche**.

2. *The professor is a great man.*

   El profesor es un **hombre grande | gran hombre**.

3. *These are the ruins of the former city.*

   Éstas son las ruinas de la **ciudad antigua | antigua ciudad**.

4. *The girl comes from a poor family.*

   La chica es de una **familia pobre | pobre familia**.

5. *Yesterday I saw my old friend, Mateo.*

   Ayer vi a mi **amigo viejo | viejo amigo**, Mateo.

D *Write the Spanish equivalent of the following English expressions.*

1. *the green one* _____

2. *the big ones* _____

3. *the good thing* _____

4. *the interesting thing* _____

5. *the interesting ones* _____

E *Write es or está in the blank before each adjective to reflect the English meaning.*

1. El niño _____ listo.
   The child is smart.

2. La estudiante _____ aburrida.
   The student is bored.

3. La muchacha _____ alegre.
   The girl has a happy nature.

4. El chico _____ divertido.
   The boy is a lot of fun.

5. El dormitorio _____ grande.
   The bedroom is big.

6. La mujer _____ gorda.
   The woman has gained weight.

7. El jefe _____ seguro de eso.
   The boss is sure about that.

8. La niña _____ nerviosa.
   She's a nervous child.

F *Write the Spanish equivalent of the English expressions in parentheses.*

1. Samuel es _____ enérgico. (*very*)

2. Martín es _____ perezoso. (*a little*)

3. Diego es _____ listo. (*extremely*)

4. Enrique es list_____. (*extremely*)

5. Jorge es _____.
   (*the tallest boy in the class*)

6. Ana es _____.
   (*more energetic than Esteban*)

7. Marta es nervios_____. (*extremely nervous*)

8. Susana es _____.
   (*the most serious girl in the school*)

VERBS
the infinitive

Verbs are listed in the dictionary in their basic form, the infinitive. The Spanish infinitive is not equivalent to the English infinitive, "to" plus the basic verb. It is simply the basic verb.

The infinitive ending, *-ar*, *-er*, or *-ir*, indicates how the verb is conjugated. Each infinitive ending has a different conjugation pattern in each tense.

Additional Information in the Dictionary

Most dictionaries provide additional information about a verb.

- One or two vowels in parentheses after the infinitive indicate the verb's stem changes in the present tense and present subjunctive (see page 161). *-Ir* verbs of this type also have a second vowel in parentheses, which indicates the verb's stem changes in the preterite, the gerund, the imperfect subjunctive, and the *nosotros* and *vosotros* forms of the present subjunctive (see page 161).

- An infinitive with *-se* attached after the *-ar*, *-er*, or *-ir* ending indicates that the verb must always be accompanied by a reflexive pronoun (see pages 103 and 208–214).

Constructions with the Infinitive
Conjugated Verb + Infinitive

Certain verbs may be immediately followed by the infinitive form of another verb. Following are some examples.

deber	*be obligated to*	preferir (ie, i)	*prefer to*
esperar	*hope to*	querer (ie)	*want to*
necesitar	*need to*	saber	*know how to*
pensar (ie)	*plan to*	encantar	*love to* (see page 106)
poder (ue)	*be able to*	gustar	*like to* (see page 106)

Debes pagar la multa.	*You have to pay the fine.*
Esperamos visitar los museos.	*We hope to visit the museums.*
Piensan salir temprano.	*They're planning to leave early.*
No puedo ir contigo.	*I am not able to/can't go with you.*
Prefiere vivir solo.	*He prefers to live alone.*
Quiero dormir.	*I want to sleep.*
Mi hermano no sabe manejar.	*My brother doesn't know how to drive.*
No le gusta bailar.	*She doesn't like to dance.*

AVOID THE *Blunder*

Do not add *a* before the infinitive after these verbs.

✗ Quiero a dormir.   ✗ Prefiere a vivir.
✗ Necesitan a descansar.   ✗ No le gusta a bailar.

Preposition + Infinitive

In English, certain prepositions are followed by the infinitive form of a verb ("to" + verb), and others are followed by a verb in the "-ing" form. In Spanish, a verb that follows a preposition is always in the infinitive form.

Mis padres vienen **a comer** con nosotros.	*My parents are coming **to eat** with us.*
Fue a la biblioteca **para estudiar**.	*He went to the library **to study**.*
Diego lleva dos meses **sin trabajar**.	*Diego has gone two months **without working**.*
Están cansados **de esperar**.	*They're tired **of waiting**.*

AVOID THE *Blunder*

✗ sin trabajando   ✗ cansados de esperando

Conjugated Verb + Preposition + Infinitive

Many common verb + preposition combinations are followed by an infinitive in Spanish.

+ a			
aprender a	*learn to*	empezar (ie) a	*begin to, start to*
ayudar a	*help to*	ir a	*be going to*
comenzar (ie) a	*begin to, start to*	volver (ue) a	*_____ again*

+ de

acabar de	*have just _____ed*
deber de	*must be _____ing*
dejar de	*stop _____ing*
haber de	*have to*
tratar de	*try to*

+ en

insistir en	*keep on _____ing*
pensar (ie) en	*concentrate on _____ing*
empeñarse en	*be determined to*

+ para

ofrecerse para	*offer to*

+ que*

haber que	*be necessary to*
tener que	*have to*

*Que acts like a preposition after *haber* and *tener*.

Está aprendiendo a cocinar.	*She's learning to cook.*
Empiezo/Comienzo a trabajar el lunes.	*I start working on Monday.*
Vamos a hacer una fiesta el viernes.	*We're going to have a party on Friday.*
Mintió y volvió a mentir.	*She lied and she lied again.*
Acaba de terminar el trabajo.	*She has just finished the paper.*
Debe de estar en la oficina.	*He must be at the office.*
Dejó de fumar el año pasado.	*He stopped smoking last year.*
He de hacerlo por mi madre.	*I have to do it for my mother's sake.*
Insiste en llamarme cada noche.	*He keeps on calling me every night.*
Sólo piensa en estudiar medicina.	*All she thinks about is studying medicine.*
Ella se ofreció a recogernos.	*She offered to pick us up.*
Hay que leer mucho en ese curso.	*You have to read a lot in that course.*
Tenemos que ir a casa.	*We have to go home.*

Two or more expressions of this type can be used in sequence, following an initial conjugated verb.

Voy a tener que empezar a trabajar.	*I'm going to have to start working.*
Acaba de aprender a nadar.	*She just learned to swim.*

AVOID THE *Blunder*

Do not leave out the preposition.

✗ Aprende cocinar.
✗ Empiezo trabajar.
✗ Tenemos ir.

Ver and oír + Infinitive

The infinitive follows the verbs *ver* and *oír* to refer to the object's action.

Vi entrar al profesor.	*I saw the teacher walk in.*
Anoche oímos a Sara tocar el piano.	*Last night we heard Sara play the piano.*

AVOID THE *Blunder*

Do not forget the *a* to indicate that the direct object is a person.

✗ Vi entrar el profesor.
✗ Oímos Sara tocar el piano.

Other Uses of the Infinitive

Expressing Orders

As an alternative to the subjunctive, the infinitive can be used after verbs that allow, order, demand, force, prevent, or prohibit another's action. (See page 168 for the use of the subjunctive.) Following are some typical verbs of this type.

aconsejar	*advise*	dejar	*allow*
recomendar (ie)	*recommend*	permitir	*allow*
sugerir (ie, i)	*suggest*		
		impedir (i, i)	*prevent*
decir (i)	*tell*	prohibir	*prohibit*
exigir	*demand*		
hacer	*make, cause*		

El profesor le exigió disculparse.	*The teacher demanded that she apologize.*
Mi mamá nos hizo limpiar la casa.	*My mom made us clean the house.*

El maestro nos dejó salir.	*The teacher let us leave.*
El guardia le permitió hacer una llamada.	*The guard let him make a call.*
Sus padres les impidieron verse.	*Their parents prevented them from seeing one another.*
Mi tío me prohibió hablar con mi amiga.	*My uncle prohibited me from talking to my friend.*

AVOID THE *Blunder*

Do not use English word order. Use indirect object-pronouns with these verbs.

✗ El maestro no dejó nos salir.
✗ El guardia permitió lo hacer una llamada.
✗ Mi mamá hizo nos limpiar la casa.

Do not add prepositions.

✗ El maestro nos dejó a salir.
✗ El guardia le permitió a hacer una llamada.

Expressing Subjects

The infinitive can be used as a noun.

It can be the subject of a sentence; the masculine article *el* is optional.

(El) vivir en la ciudad puede ser peligroso.	*Living in the city can be dangerous.*
Querer es poder.	*Wanting to is being able to.*
Caminar sola por la noche no es buena idea.	*Walking alone at night isn't a good idea.*

AVOID THE *Blunder*

✗ Viviendo en la ciudad es peligroso.
✗ Caminando sola no es buena idea.
✗ Queriendo es pudiendo.

The infinitive is used after *al* to indicate two simultaneous actions.

Al ver el océano, me sentí contenta.	*When I saw the ocean, I felt happy.*
Recordó el nombre al llegar a casa.	*He remembered the name as soon as he got home.*

Describing Activities

As in English, Spanish uses an infinitive directly after an adjective to describe an activity.

ENGLISH PATTERN   "be" + adjective + infinitive
SPANISH PATTERN   *ser* + adjective + infinitive

Es fácil leer este libro.   *It's easy to read this book.*
Será difícil encontrarlo.   *It will be difficult to find him.*

Describing Nouns

To describe a noun, an infinitive follows an adjective + *de*.

ENGLISH PATTERN   noun + "be" + adjective + infinitive
SPANISH PATTERN   noun + *ser* + adjective + *de* + infinitive

Este libro es fácil de leer.   *This book is easy to read.*
Él será difícil de encontrar.   *He will be difficult to find.*

Expressing Commands

The infinitive is often used to give commands to the general public.

No fumar.   *No smoking.*
No pisar el césped.   *Do not walk on the grass.*
No entrar.   *Do not enter.*

Exercise

A   Use an infinitive construction to write the Spanish equivalent of each of the following English sentences.

1. We have to study more. _____

2. She wrote the exercise again. _____

3. They want to stop smoking. _____

4. We love to go shopping. _____

5. I saw the boss leave. _____

6. She made me work. _____

7. Knowing how to ride a bike is important in this city.

   _____

8. He has just arrived. _____

9. It's hard to study here. _____

10. These books are easy to understand.

   _____

VERBS
types of verbs

Spanish verbs can be subdivided into several categories according to their usage with or without object nouns and pronouns.

Intransitive Verbs

Intransitive verbs in Spanish, like intransitive verbs in English, have no object.

PATTERN subject + verb (+ adverb or prepositional phrase)

Typical intransitive verbs follow.

caminar	*walk*	llorar	*cry*
correr	*run*	nadar	*swim*
ir	*go*	salir	*leave (go out)*

Eva corre.	*Eva runs.*
Eva corre rápido.	*Eva runs fast.*
Eva corre en el parque.	*Eva runs in the park.*
El niño lloró.	*The child cried.*
El niño lloró mucho.	*The child cried a lot.*
El niño lloró en los brazos de su mamá.	*The child cried in his mother's arms.*

AVOID THE *Blunder*

Do not use object pronouns when there is no object.

✗ El niño lo lloró.
✗ Eva lo corre en el parque.

Do not use reflexive pronouns with verbs that do not have *-se* attached to the infinitive.

✗ Eva se corre.

-Se Verbs

Verbs that are listed in the dictionary with *-se* attached to the infinitive are always used with a reflexive pronoun (*me, te, se, nos, os*). These verbs are commonly referred to as reflexive verbs, although some of them do not have a reflexive meaning. (See pages 211–214.)

PATTERN   subject + reflexive pronoun + verb
(+ adverb or prepositional phrase)

Lastimarse "to hurt oneself" is a typical verb with reflexive meaning.

Verónica se lastimó en el partido   *Verónica hurt herself in the*
de fútbol.   *soccer match.*

Levantarse "to get up" ("to raise oneself up") is a typical verb with reflexive meaning, although the meaning is not expressed as a reflexive in English.

Octavio se levanta a las seis.   *Octavio gets up at six.*

Quejarse "to complain" is a typical verb with no reflexive meaning, even though it requires a reflexive pronoun.

David y sus amigos se quejan   *David and his friends complain*
de todo.   *about everything.*

AVOID THE *Blunder*

If a verb is listed with *-se* at the end, always use the reflexive pronoun that refers to the same person as the subject of the sentence.

✗ Verónica lastimó en el partido.
✗ Octavio levanta a las seis.
✗ David y sus amigos quejan de todo.

Transitive Verbs

Transitive verbs that have only direct objects depict action by the subject on or toward a target—the direct object (see pages 104–106). Typical verbs that take direct objects follow.

amar	*love*	mirar	*look at*
anunciar	*announce*	preferir (ie, i)	*prefer*
dejar	*leave (something)*	querer (ie)	*want, love*
escuchar	*listen to*	recoger	*pick up*
llamar	*call*	ver	*see*
manejar	*drive*	visitar	*visit*

PATTERN 1   subject + verb + direct object noun
                (+ adverb or prepositional phrase)

Germán llamaba a su papá todas las noches.	*Germán called his dad every night.*
Germán llamó el número equivocado.	*Germán called the wrong number.*
Vamos a ver la película.	*We're going to watch the movie.*
Vamos a ver a la profesora.	*We're going to see the teacher.*

AVOID THE *Blunder*

When the direct object is a person or people, do not forget to precede it with the "personal *a*."

✗ Germán llama su papá.
✗ Vamos a ver la profesora.

Several common transitive verbs are translated into English using a verb followed by a preposition (see page 215). These verbs are normally not followed by a preposition in Spanish. However, when the direct object is a person or people, the "personal *a*" is required.

buscar	*look for*	esperar	*wait for*
escuchar	*listen to*	mirar	*look at*

Estoy buscando un libro interesante.	*I'm looking for an interesting book.*
Estoy buscando a mi hijo.	*I'm looking for my son.*
Roberto escucha la música.	*Roberto listens to the music.*
Roberto escucha a la profesora.	*Roberto listens to the teacher.*
Esperamos el autobús.	*We're waiting for the bus.*
Esperamos a los niños.	*We're waiting for the children.*
Las chicas miran los zapatos.	*The girls are looking at the shoes.*
Las chicas miran a los chicos.	*The girls are looking at the boys.*

AVOID THE *Blunder*

✗ Estoy buscando por un libro.   ✗ Roberto escucha a la música.
✗ Estoy buscando para mi hijo.   ✗ Las chicas miran a los zapatos.
✗ Esperamos por el autobús.

PATTERN 2   (subject) + direct object pronoun + verb
(+ adverb or prepositional phrase)

Germán lo llamó dos veces.	*Germán called it (the number)* *two times.*
Germán lo llamó anoche.	*Germán called him (his father)* *last night.*
Vamos a verla.	*We're going to see it (the movie).*
Vamos a verla.	*We're going to see her (the teacher).*

AVOID THE *Blunder*

Do not use *a* + object pronoun (*a él, a ella, a mí, a nosotros*) for direct objects that refer to people. Use the direct object pronoun instead, and place it before the verb.

✗ Germán llama a él.
✗ Vamos a ver a ella.

"Exchange" Verbs

Certain transitive verbs have both a direct and an indirect object. These verbs indicate an exchange of something (the direct object) from the subject to another person (the indirect object). Contrary to English usage, the indirect object pronoun must always appear before the conjugated verb in Spanish, even if it is also otherwise named. Typical "exchange" verbs follow.

dar	*give*	decir (i)	*tell*
entregar	*hand to, deliver*	contar (ue)	*tell, relate*
mostrar (ue)	*show*	enviar	*send*
demostrar (ue)	*demonstrate*	mandar	*send*
enseñar	*teach, show*		
		pedir (i, i)	*ask for*

PATTERN 1   (subject) + indirect object pronoun + verb
+ direct object noun (+ *a* + indirect object)

Miguel me da el dinero (a mí).	*Miguel gives me the money.*
Norman te muestra las fotos (a ti).	*Norman shows you the pictures.*

PATTERN 2   (subject) + indirect object pronoun
+ direct object pronoun + verb (+ *a* + indirect object)

Miguel me lo da (a mí).	*Miguel gives it to me.*
Norman te las muestra (a ti).	*Norman shows them to you.*

> AVOID THE *Blunder*
>
> Do not leave out the indirect object pronoun before the verb.
>
> ✗ Miguel da el dinero a mí.
> ✗ Miguel lo da a mí.
> ✗ Norman muestra las fotos a ti.
> ✗ Norman las muestra a ti.

Verbs of Feeling

Certain verbs require an indirect object pronoun but do not have a direct object (see pages 220–223). Typical verbs of this type follow.

encantar	*enchant*	gustar	*please, appeal to*
faltar	*lack*	molestar	*bother*
fascinar	*fascinate*		

PATTERN (*A* + noun/pronoun) + indirect object pronoun
+ verb + subject

A mí me falta el tiempo.	*I don't have time. (Time is lacking to me.)*
A Alejandro le fascina la película.	*The movie fascinates Alejandro.*
¿Te gustan mis zapatos nuevos?	*Do you like my new shoes? (Do my new shoes appeal to you?)*
A él le molestan los mosquitos.	*Mosquitoes annoy him.*

In English, when the subject is not stated, it is replaced by a pronoun. In Spanish, the subject pronoun (*él, ella, ellos*) may be used if the subject is a person or people. If the subject is a thing, no pronoun is used.

A Alejandro le fascina Ana.	*Ana fascinates Alejandro.*
A Alejandro le fascina (ella).	*She fascinates Alejandro.*
A Alejandro le fascina la película.	*The movie fascinates Alejandro.*
A Alejandro le fascina.	*It fascinates Alejandro.*
¿Te gustan mis zapatos?	*Do you like my shoes?*
¿Te gustan?	*Do you like them? (Do they appeal to you?)*
A él le molestan los mosquitos.	*Mosquitoes bother him.*
A él le molestan.	*They bother him.*

AVOID THE *Blunder*

Do not use direct object pronouns with these verbs to translate "it" or "them." Keep in mind that it is the subject ("it" or "they") that "sends the feeling" to the indirect object.

✗ A él le molestan los.
✗ ¿Te los gustan?

The subjects of sentences of this type often occur after the verb, whereas in English the usual position of the subject is before the verb.

Me gustan los zapatos rojos.   *The red shoes appeal to me.*
Le molesta el tráfico.   *Traffic bothers him.*

In English, an article is not used with plural and noncount nouns when they are used in a general sense. In Spanish, an article must be used before a noun subject, whether it is singular, plural, or noncount.

Me gusta el chocolate.   *I like chocolate. (Chocolate appeals to me.)*

Me gustan los chocolates.   *I like chocolates. (Chocolates appeal to me.)*

AVOID THE *Blunder*

Do not leave out the article before the subject.

✗ Me gusta chocolate.
✗ Me gustan chocolates.

Verbs Indicating Advice or Control

Certain verbs that indicate advice or control over the actions of others are preceded by an indirect object pronoun and followed by a clause in the subjunctive (see pages 167–168 and 188–189).

PATTERN   subject clause + indirect object pronoun + verb
    (+ *a* + noun/pronoun) + *que* + subjunctive clause

La maestra les aconseja a los estudiantes que estudien.   *The teacher advises the students to study.*
Los padres le prohíben al chico que vea la televisión.   *The parents don't allow the child to watch television.*

Verbs Indicating Unplanned Occurrences

Certain verbs indicate unplanned occurrences (see pages 224–225). Typical verbs of this type follow.

acabársele	*end, run out of*	perdérsele (ie)	*lose*
caérsele	*fall*	quedársele	*remain*
olvidársele	*forget*	rompérsele	*break*

(A mí) se me olvidó el libro.	*I forgot my book. (The book forgot itself, and it is affecting me.)*
A Pedro se le perdió la llave.	*Pedro lost his key. (The key lost itself, and it is affecting Pedro.)*
A Jorge se le quedaron los cuadernos en el coche.	*Jorge left the notebooks in the car. (The notebooks stayed in the car, and it is affecting Jorge.)*

AVOID THE *Blunder*

Do not use a possessive adjective before the noun with these verbs.

✗ Se me olvidó mi libro.
✗ Se le perdió su llave.
✗ Se le quedaron sus cuadernos.

Exercise

A *Underline the main verb in each of the following sentences, then indicate which of the following is the appropriate category for the verb. (Hint: There are three verbs in each category.)*

    a. Intransitive verbs (with no object)

    b. Verbs with a reflexive pronoun only

    c. Verbs with a direct object (noun or pronoun) only

    d. Verbs that indicate an exchange, with both an indirect object pronoun and a direct object

    e. Verbs that indicate a person's feelings, with an indirect object pronoun

    f. Verbs that indicate advice or control over another person's actions, with an indirect object pronoun and a subjunctive clause

    g. Verbs that indicate unplanned occurrences, with reflexive and indirect object pronouns

1. ¿A qué hora sales? _____

2. Me levanto temprano. _____

3. Los chicos caminan en el parque. _____

4. Sara llama a su mamá. _____

5. Ella me cuenta sus ideas. _____

6. Marcos se queja mucho. _____

7. La profesora nos las envía. _____

8. Se le pierden las llaves. _____

9. Le encantan las chicas. _____

10. Se lo da a su jefe. _____

11. Se me olvida el nombre. _____

12. Mi amigo me visita los sábados. _____

13. Les dice que trabajen. _____

14. Se nos acaba la gasolina. _____

15. Les fascina el teatro. _____

16. Los jugadores se lastiman mucho. _____

17. Me gusta mucho el cuento. _____

18. Te aconsejo que estudies. _____

19. Me sugiere que escriba más. _____

20. Te quiero mucho. _____

21. Todos vamos en el coche. _____

VERBS
the indicative mood

The indicative mood is used to indicate that the action or condition stated by the verb is an objective fact.

VERBS
the present tense

Tense Formation

Stem (infinitive minus *-ar/-er/-ir*) + endings

Tense Endings

-ar VERBS

yo	-o	nosotros(-as)	-amos
tú	-as	vosotros(-as)	-áis
usted/él/ella	-a		
ustedes/ellos/ellas	-an		

-er VERBS

yo	-o	nosotros(-as)	-emos
tú	-es	vosotros(-as)	-éis
usted/él/ella	-e		
ustedes/ellos/ellas	-en		

-ir VERBS

yo	-o	nosotros(-as)	-imos
tú	-es	vosotros(-as)	-ís
usted/él/ella	-e		
ustedes/ellos/ellas	-en		

VERBS THAT END IN *-uir*

huir		**construir**	
huyo	huimos	construyo	construimos
huyes	huís	construyes	construís
huye		construye	
huyen		construyen	

Verbs with Irregular *yo* Forms

dar	doy	**decir**	digo	**poner**	pongo
estar	estoy	**hacer**	hago	**tener**	tengo
ir	voy	**oír**	oigo	**venir**	vengo
		traer	traigo	**salir**	salgo

Also, verbs that end in -*cer*, for example:

conocer conozco
parecer parezco

Also, verbs that end in -*ger/-gir*, for example:

dirigir dirijo
recoger recojo

Stem-changing Verb Patterns

With these verbs, the last vowel in the stem is replaced by another vowel or vowels in the forms for *yo, tú, usted/él/ella,* and *ustedes/ellos/ellas.* The change is normally indicated in a dictionary by an annotation after the infinitive. The stem does not change in the forms for *nosotros(-as)* and *vosotros(-as).* An example is given below for each stem-changing pattern.

-*ar* VERBS

e > ie		o > ue		u > ue	
pensar (ie)		**almorzar** (ue)		**jugar** (ue)	
pienso	pensamos	almuerzo	almorzamos	juego	jugamos
piensas	pensáis	almuerzas	almorzáis	juegas	jugáis
piensa		almuerza		juega	
piensan		almuerzan		juegan	

-*er* VERBS

e > ie		e > ie		o > ue	
perder (ic)		**tener** (ie)		**poder** (ue)	
pierdo	perdemos	tengo	tenemos	puedo	podemos
pierdes	perdéis	tienes	tenéis	puedes	podéis
pierde		tiene		puede	
pierden		tienen		pueden	

-*ir* VERBS

e > ie		e > ie		o > ue	
sentir (ie, i)		**venir** (ie, i)		**dormir** (ue, u)	
siento	sentimos	vengo	venimos	duermo	dormimos
sientes	sentís	vienes	venís	duermes	dormís
siente		viene		duerme	
sienten		vienen		duermen	

e > i		e > i	
pedir (i, i)		**decir** (i, i)	
pido	pedimos	**digo**	decimos
pides	pedís	dices	decís
pide		dice	
piden		dicen	

Gerunds

-*ar* VERBS

No stem change

	hablar	**pensar**	**almorzar**	**jugar**
Stem + -*ando*	hablando	pensando	almorzando	jugando

-*er* VERBS

No stem change

	comer	**perder**	**volver**
Stem + -*iendo*	comiendo	perdiendo	volviendo

	leer	**creer**	**caer**
Stem ending in vowel + -*yendo*	leyendo	creyendo	cayendo

-*ir* VERBS

Stem change as indicated below

	abrir	**partir**	**vivir**
Stem + -*iendo*	abriendo	partiendo	viviendo

	construir	**oír**
Stem ending in vowel + -*yendo*	construyendo	oyendo

All -*ir* verbs that have stem changes in the present tense have stem changes in the gerund. These changes are indicated by the second annotation after the infinitive.

e > i	**sentir** (ie, i)	**venir** (ie, i)
	sintiendo	viniendo
o > u	**dormir** (ue, u)	**morir** (ue, u)
	durmiendo	muriendo
e > i	**servir** (i, i)	**decir** (i, i)
	sirviendo	diciendo

Review the forms on the preceding pages.

Spanish tenses express a different range of meanings than similarly named English tenses.

Uses of the Present Tense

The present tense is used with certain time expressions.

ahora	*now*	esta semana	*this week*
en este momento	*at the moment*	este mes	*this month*
actualmente	*currently*	este semestre	*this semester*
hoy	*today*	este año	*this year*
esta mañana	*this morning*	estos días	*these days*
esta tarde	*this afternoon*		
esta noche	*tonight*		

Stating Facts

The Spanish present tense, like the present tense in English, is used to state facts about the present.

Soy responsable.	*I'm responsible.*
Tenemos los boletos.	*We have the tickets.*
Perú está en Sudamérica.	*Peru is in South America.*
Viven en Nueva York.	*They live in New York.*

Describing Usual Action

The Spanish present tense, like the present tense in English, is used to describe usual action.

Trabajo a las nueve los lunes.	*I work at nine o'clock on Mondays.*
Come después de las clases.	*She eats after school.*
Vamos a la playa en el verano.	*We go to the beach in the summer.*
Llevan sus paraguas cuando llueve.	*They take their umbrellas when it rains.*

AVOID THE *Blunder*

Be sure to use the correct verb ending to correspond with the subject of the sentence. When the subject is not stated, the conjugated ending of the verb acts as the subject of the sentence.

Describing Action in Progress

The Spanish present tense, unlike the present tense in English, can be used to describe action in progress, that is, action that has begun but has not finished.

A progressive construction, formed by conjugating *estar* in the present tense and adding a verb in the gerund form (ending in *-ndo*), can be used as an alternative; this is comparable to the English present progressive. (Review the gerund forms on page 113.)

ENGLISH PATTERN   "be" + "_____ing"

SPANISH PATTERN   present tense of *estar*
+ _____ *ando* OR _____ *iendo/yendo*

¿Qué haces?
¿Qué estás haciendo? } *What are you doing?*

Trabajo ahora.
Estoy trabajando. } *I'm working.*

¿Adónde van?* *Where are you all going?*

Come en este momento.
Está comiendo } *She's eating.*

Llevan sus paraguas.
Están llevando sus paraguas. } *They're carrying their umbrellas.*

*The progressive form of *ir* (*yendo*) is not used in this construction.

AVOID THE *Blunder*

✗ ¿Adónde estás yendo?

The gerund is also used after a conjugated form of the verbs *andar*, *ir*, and *seguir*.

Mi prima anda diciendo mentiras. *My cousin goes around telling lies.*

El chico va cantando por la calle. *The boy goes down the street singing.*

Las chicas siguen bailando. *The girls keep on dancing.*

The Spanish present tense, unlike the present tense in English, is used to tell how long a current action has been taking place.

ENGLISH PATTERNS   "have/has" + past participle + "for"
+ period of time
"have/has" + "been _____ing" + "for"
+ period of time

SPANISH PATTERN 1   present tense of *llevar* + period of time + gerund

Llevo dos años trabajando aquí.
$\left\{\begin{array}{l}\textit{I have worked here for two years.}\\ \textit{I have been working here for two years.}\end{array}\right.$

SPANISH PATTERN 2   *hace* + period of time + *que*
+ present tense / present progressive tense

Hace dos años que trabajo aquí.
Hace dos años que estoy
   trabajando aquí.
$\left.\begin{array}{l}\\ \\ \\ \end{array}\right\}\left\{\begin{array}{l}\textit{I have worked here for two years.}\\ \textit{I have been working here for two years.}\end{array}\right.$

SPANISH PATTERN 3   present tense / present progressive tense
+ *desde hace* + period of time

Trabajo aquí desde hace dos años.
Estoy trabajando aquí desde hace
   dos años.
$\left.\begin{array}{l}\\ \\ \\ \end{array}\right\}\left\{\begin{array}{l}\textit{I have worked here for two years.}\\ \textit{I have been working here for two years (since two years ago).}\end{array}\right.$

AVOID THE *Blunder*

Do not use the word-for-word equivalent of the English present perfect tense to tell how long an action has been taking place.

✗ He trabajado aquí por dos años.
✗ He estado trabajando aquí por dos años.

The present tense is used to indicate how long it has been since the last time an action occurred.

ENGLISH PATTERN   "haven't/hasn't" + past participle + "for"
+ period of time

SPANISH PATTERN   present tense of *llevar* + period of time
+ *sin* + infinitive

Llevo tres años sin ver a mi mejor amigo.	*I haven't seen my best friend for three years.*
Lleva dos meses sin fumar.	*He hasn't smoked in two months.*

AVOID THE *Blunder*

✗ No he visto a mi amigo por tres años.
✗ No ha fumado en dos meses.

The Spanish present tense, unlike the present tense in English, is used to state when an action began.

ENGLISH PATTERN   "have/has" + past participle + "since"
                 + time activity began

SPANISH PATTERN   present tense + *desde* + time activity began

Trabajo aquí desde enero de 2003. Estoy trabajando aquí desde enero de 2003.	*I have worked here since January of 2003.* *I have been working here since January of 2003.*

AVOID THE *Blunder*

Do not use the word-for-word equivalent of the English present perfect tense when stating when an action began.

✗ He trabajado aquí desde enero de 2003.
✗ He estado trabajando aquí desde enero de 2003.

The Spanish present tense, unlike the present tense in English, is used to state that an action is taking place for the first, second, third, etc. time.

ENGLISH PATTERN   "the first/second/tenth time" + "have/has"
                 + past participle

SPANISH PATTERN   *la primera/segunda/décima vez* + *que*
                 + present tense

Esta es la primera vez que estoy en México.	*This is the first time I have (ever) been in Mexico.*
Es la segunda vez que come en nuestra casa.	*It's the second time he has eaten at our house.*

AVOID THE *Blunder*

Do not use the word-for-word equivalent of the English present perfect tense when stating the number of times an action has taken place.

✗ Esta es la primera vez que he estado en México.
✗ Es la segunda vez que ha comido en nuestra casa.

Describing Future Action

The Spanish present tense, like the present tense in English, is used to state the time of a scheduled event.

El avión sale a las cinco y media.	*The plane leaves at 5:30.*
La película empieza a las ocho.	*The movie starts at eight.*

The Spanish present tense, unlike the present tense in English, is used to make a request.

ENGLISH PATTERN   future tense + question mark

SPANISH PATTERN   question mark + present tense + question mark

¿Me ayudas?	*Will you help me?*
¿Le traes un vaso de agua?	*Will you bring him a glass of water?*

The Spanish present tense is used to make an offer.

ENGLISH PATTERN   "can" + basic verb + question mark

SPANISH PATTERN   question mark + present tense + question mark

¿Te ayudo?	*Can I help you?*
¿Le traigo un vaso de agua?	*Can I bring him a glass of water?*

The Spanish present tense, unlike the present tense in English, is used to make a commitment or promise.

ENGLISH PATTERN   "will" + basic verb

SPANISH PATTERN   present tense

Te llamo esta noche.	*I'll call you tonight.*
Sí, me caso contigo en diciembre.	*Yes, I'll marry you in December.*

The present tense of *ir* + *a* + infinitive, like the English "be going to" + basic verb, is used to state a future plan. In English, the progressive—"be" + verb in "-ing" form—can be used as an alternative.

| ENGLISH PATTERNS | "be going to" + basic verb |
| | "be + ___ing" |

| SPANISH PATTERN | *ir* + *a* + infinitive form of verb |

Voy a cenar con él mañana.
$\left\{\begin{array}{l}\textit{I'm going to have dinner with}\\\textit{him tomorrow.}\\\textit{I'm having dinner with him}\\\textit{tomorrow.}\end{array}\right.$

Sí, nos vamos a casar el año próximo.
$\left\{\begin{array}{l}\textit{Yes, we're going to get married}\\\textit{next year.}\\\textit{Yes, we're getting married}\\\textit{next year.}\end{array}\right.$

AVOID THE *Blunder*

Do not use the progressive form as you would in English to state a future plan.

✗ Estoy cenando con él mañana.
✗ Sí, nos estamos casando el año próximo.

Describing Conditional Action

As in English clauses introduced by "if," the present tense is used in Spanish after the word *si* to express conditional future action.

| ENGLISH PATTERN | "if" + present tense + future clause |

| SPANISH PATTERN | *si* + present tense + future clause |

Si no llueve, voy a la playa.   *If it doesn't rain, I'm going to the beach.*

Si llegas tarde, no podrás ir.   *If you are late, you won't be able to go.*

Describing Past Action

The present tense of the verb *acabar* + *de* + infinitive is used to express recently completed action. This is expressed in English by the present perfect tense or the past tense with "just." (See pages 123–124 for an alternative way to express this meaning in Spanish.)

| ENGLISH PATTERNS | "have/has just" + past participle |
| | "just" + past tense |

| SPANISH PATTERN | present tense of *acabar* + *de* + infinitive |

Acabo de comer.	$\left\{\begin{array}{l} \text{\textit{I have just eaten.}} \\ \text{\textit{I just ate.}} \end{array}\right.$
Acaban de llegar.	$\left\{\begin{array}{l} \text{\textit{They have just arrived.}} \\ \text{\textit{They just arrived.}} \end{array}\right.$

In English, the present tense is often used to tell jokes or relate the events of a movie or play but not to write formal history. In Spanish the present tense can be used, both formally and informally, to narrate the past.

(En la película) la mujer y su esposo tienen una discusión y luego la mujer sale de la casa y empieza a llorar.	*(In the movie) the woman and her husband have an argument, and then she leaves the house and starts to cry.*
Cristóbal Colón descubre el Nuevo Mundo en 1492 y lo reclama para España.	*Christopher Columbus discovered the new world in 1492 and claimed it for Spain.*

The present tense is used in Spanish to express action that almost happened, but in fact didn't. English uses the past tense in this situation.

ENGLISH PATTERN   "almost" + past tense

SPANISH PATTERN   *por poco/casi* + present tense

Por poco me caigo.	*I almost fell.*
Casi se muere.	*He almost died.*

AVOID THE *Blunder*

Do not use a past tense in Spanish with *por poco* or *casi*.

✗ Por poco me caí.
✗ Casi se murió.

■ For additional Spanish equivalents of the English present tense, see the sections on the present subjunctive (pages 161–176) and reported speech (pages 200–203).

Exercises

A *Circle the correct verb form to complete the following sentences.*

1. ¿Qué **hace** | **compra** | **hacen** | **compras** los chicos ahora?

2. Mi amigo está **leyendo** | **lees** | **compras** | **lee** el libro.

3. Ana, Beatriz y yo **tener** | **tengo** | **tienen** | **tenemos** clase los lunes a las dos.

4. Si tú **estudies** | **estudian** | **estudias** | **estudien**, vas a aprobar el curso.

5. No hablo bien porque hace un año que no **hablo** | **he estudiado** | **han estudiado** | **hemos hablado** español.

6. Mi primo **ha estado** | **está** | **estás** | **hemos estado** aquí desde el viernes pasado.

7. En el verano voy a **estar** | **estoy** | **ir** | **vamos** a Costa Rica.

8. Mañana **estamos estudiando** | **voy a estudiar** | me están visitando | **estoy saliendo**.

9. Ayer, al caminar por la calle, mi amigo casi **me caigo** | **se cayó** | **se cae** | **caigo**.

10. Esta es la primera vez que mi amiga **cantamos** | **bailan** | **canta en público** | **ha cantado en público**.

B *Express the following in Spanish.*

1. They're building a new house.

   _____

2. We have lived in this city for ten years.

   _____

3. This is the first time I've ever eaten mole.

   _____

4. She has just read that novel. _____

5. Can we take you home? _____

6. They almost had an accident. _____

7. If you call me, I'll help you. _____

8. We're leaving at six, and the movie starts at seven.

   _____

9. Are you going out with your friends tomorrow night?

   _____

10. Will you help me? _____

VERBS
the preterite perfect tense

Tense Formation

Present tense of *haber* + past participle

The Present Tense of *haber*

yo	he	nosotros(-as)	hemos
tú	has	vosotros(-as)	habéis
usted/él/ella	ha		
ustedes/ellos/ellas	han		

Past Participle Formation

	-ar verbs	*-er* verbs	*-ir* verbs
Verb stem (infinitive minus *-ar/-er/-ir*) +	-ado	-ido	-ido
	hablar	**comer**	**vivir**
	hablado	comido	vivido

IRREGULAR PARTICIPLES

abrir	abierto	**poner**	puesto
cubrir	cubierto	**oponer**	opuesto
descubrir	descubierto	**proponer**	propuesto
decir	dicho	**ver**	visto
predecir	predicho	**prever**	previsto
escribir	escrito	**volver**	vuelto
describir	descrito	**devolver**	devuelto
prescribir	prescrito	**revolver**	revuelto
hacer	hecho	**resolver**	resuelto
morir	muerto	**romper**	roto

Review the forms on the preceding page.

AVOID THE *Blunder*

Be sure to learn the irregular past participle forms.

✗ abrido   ✗ escribido   ✗ hacido
✗ ponido   ✗ rompido

It is easy to make the mistake of thinking that this tense is equivalent to the English present perfect ("have" + past participle), because the formations are similar. In some cases, in fact, the uses are equivalent. In many cases, however, the uses are quite different.

Uses of the Past Tenses

The past tenses are used with certain time expressions.

ayer	*yesterday*
anoche	*last night*
anteayer	*the day before yesterday*
la semana pasada	*last week*
el mes pasado	*last month*
el año pasado	*last year*
hace dos semanas	*two weeks ago*
hace tres meses	*three months ago*
hace cinco años	*five years ago*

AVOID THE *Blunder*

Do not confuse "last" with "ago."

✗ dos semanas pasadas   ✗ tres meses pasados

Uses of the Preterite Perfect Tense

Describing Recent Action

The Spanish preterite perfect tense, like the present perfect tense in English, is used to express action that has been recently completed.

ENGLISH PATTERNS   subject + "have/has just" + past participle
                      subject + "just" + past tense

SPANISH PATTERN   (subject) + present tense of *haber* + participle

He hablado con Juan. $\begin{cases} \textit{I have just talked to Juan.} \\ \textit{I just talked to Juan.} \end{cases}$

Hemos comido. $\begin{cases} \textit{We have just eaten.} \\ \textit{We just ate.} \end{cases}$

Mi perro ha muerto. $\begin{cases} \textit{My dog has just died.} \\ \textit{My dog just died.} \end{cases}$

Sus amigos han llegado. $\begin{cases} \textit{Your friends have just arrived.} \\ \textit{Your friends just arrived.} \end{cases}$

This usage is more common in Spain than in Latin America, where the present tense of *acabar* + *de* + infinitive is more often used for this purpose (see pages 119–120).

In English, the word "just" is important in conveying the sense of recent action. In Spanish, an equivalent word is not necessary. Also note that in American English, it is common to use the past tense for this purpose.

Expressing Time of Action

In Spanish, the time of a recent action is often stated with the preterite perfect tense. In English, time is stated with the past tense—never with the present perfect tense.

He hablado con Juan a las tres.	*I talked to Juan at three o'clock.*
Hemos comido en la tarde.	*We ate in the afternoon.*
Mi perro ha muerto anoche.	*My dog died last night.*
Sus amigos han llegado hace poco.	*Your friends arrived a short time ago.*

AVOID THE *Blunder*

When translating from Spanish to English, do not use the present perfect if the time of action is stated. Use the past tense instead.

✗ My dog has died last night.
✗ Your friends have arrived a few minutes ago.

Expressing "Already" and "Not Yet"

The Spanish preterite perfect tense, like the English present perfect tense, is used to express action that has already occurred or that has not yet occurred. Note that the markers *ya* and *todavía* are necessary to convey this meaning in Spanish, but "already" and "yet" are optional in conveying this meaning in English.

Ya he hablado con Juan.	*I've (already) talked to Juan.*
Ya hemos comido.	*We have (already) eaten.*
No he escrito el trabajo todavía.	*I haven't written the paper (yet).*
Mis amigos no han llegado todavía.	*My friends haven't arrived (yet).*

AVOID THE *Blunder*

If you expect or hope that the action will occur, you must include the marker *todavía*.

Don't omit *todavía* if you plan to write the paper.

✗ No he escrito el trabajo.

Don't omit *todavía* if you expect your friends to arrive.

✗ No han llegado mis amigos.

Expressing the Frequency of an Action

The Spanish preterite perfect tense, like the English present perfect tense, is used to express the number of times an action has been performed.

He hablado dos veces con Juan.	*I have talked to Juan twice.*
Hemos comido muchas veces en este lugar.	*We have eaten at this place many times.*

Unlike the English present perfect tense, the Spanish preterite perfect tense is not used to express activity that is occurring now for the first, second, third, etc. time (see page 117).

ENGLISH PATTERN   "the first time (that)" + subject + "have/has" + past participle

SPANISH PATTERN   *la primera vez que* + (subject) + present tense

Esta es la primera vez que comemos en este lugar.	*This is the first time we have eaten at this place.*

AVOID THE *Blunder*

✗ Esta es la primera vez que hemos comido en este lugar.
✗ Es la segunda vez que he estado en este país.

The Spanish preterite perfect tense, unlike the English present perfect tense, is not used to express how long an activity has been taking place.

ENGLISH PATTERN   subject + "have/has" + "been _____ing"

SPANISH PATTERNS   (subject) + present tense
                       (subject) + present progressive tense

Hace diez minutos que hablo con Juan.⎫
Hace diez minutos que estoy hablando ⎬ *I've been talking to Juan*
  con Juan.   ⎭ *for 10 minutes.*

Hace seis meses que estoy en este país.   *I've been in this country*
                                           for six months.

AVOID THE *Blunder*

Don't use the preterite perfect tense unless you mean that the action is completed: "I talked to John for 10 minutes."

✗ He estado hablando con Juan por diez minutos.

Exercises

A *Change the verbs in the following sentences to the preterite perfect tense as an alternative to* acabar de.

EXAMPLE   Acabamos de ver esa película. → Hemos visto esa película.

1. Mis padres acaban de comer. _____

2. ¿Qué acabas de hacer? _____

3. Acabo de terminar con mis exámenes. _____

4. Ana acaba de recibir un mensaje. _____

B *Express the following in Spanish.*

1. *They just arrived.* _____

2. *We have already written the letters.* _____

3. *He hasn't sent his application yet.* _____

4. *She opened the window a few minutes ago.*

_____

5. *How many times have you all seen that movie?*

_____

VERBS
the preterite tense

Tense Formation

Stem (infinitive minus -ar/-er/-ir) + endings

Pattern 1 Verbs
Tense Endings

-*ar* VERBS

yo	ó	nosotros(-as)	-amos
tú	-aste	vosotros(-as)	-asteis
usted/él/ella	-ó		
ustedes/ellos/ellas	-aron		

-*er* AND -*ir* VERBS

yo	-í	nosotros(-as)	-imos
tú	-iste	vosotros(-as)	-isteis
usted/él/ella	-ió		
ustedes/ellos/ellas	-ieron		

Spelling Changes in *yo* Forms

Verbs that end in -*car*	-qué
Verbs that end in -*gar*	-gué
Verbs that end in -*guar*	-güé
Verbs that end in -*zar*	-cé

The Preterite Tense of *dar*

Dar is an -*ar* verb with -*er*/-*ir* endings in the preterite.

di	dimos
diste	disteis
dio	
dieron	

Stem-changing Verb Patterns

-*ar* VERBS

No stem change

-*er* VERBS

No stem change

-*ir* VERBS

Second stem change in third-person singular and plural

o > u
dormir (ue, u)

dormí	dormimos
dormiste	dormisteis
durmió	
durmieron	

Pattern 2 Verbs

The following verbs have irregular stems in the preterite and a different set
of conjugated endings.

Irregular Preterite Stems

INFINITIVE	STEM	1SG. FORM	INFINITIVE	STEM	1SG. FORM
andar	anduv-	anduve	**hacer**	hic-	hice
tener	tuv-	tuve	**querer**	quis-	quise
estar	estuv-	estuve	**venir**	vin-	vine
poder	pud-	pude	**decir**	dij-	dije*
poner	pus-	puse	**traer**	traj-	traje*
saber	sup-	supe			
haber	hub-	hube			

Tense Endings

yo	-e	nosotros(-as)	-imos
tú	-iste	vosotros(-as)	-isteis
usted/él/ella	-o		
ustedes/ellos/ellas	-ieron/-eron*		

*The third-person plural ends in -*eron* after *j*.

The Preterite Tense of *ir* and *ser*

fui	fuimos
fuiste	fuisteis
fue	
fueron	

Review the forms in the chart on the preceding pages.

Review the time expressions used with past tenses on page 123.

AVOID THE *Blunder*

Note that pattern 2 verbs do not have an accent mark in their endings.

✗ tuvé   ✗ hizó   ✗ pudé

Note automatic spelling changes in the *yo* forms of certain verbs ending in *-car, -gar, -zar*.

✗ sacé   ✗ jugé   ✗ almorzé

Note that there is no stem change in the preterite of *-ar* and *-er* verbs.

✗ piensé   ✗ juegó   ✗ almuercé   ✗ pierdió

Note the third-person stem change in *-ir* stem-changing verbs.

✗ sentió   ✗ dormió   ✗ servieron

Note that pattern 2 verbs whose stems end in *j* drop the *i* after the *j*.

✗ trajieron   ✗ dijieron

Uses of the Preterite Tense

Describing Terminated Actions

The preterite tense in Spanish is used to describe actions that began and terminated in the past, without giving details about other simultaneous or interrupting actions.

Estuve en clase (ayer).	*I was in class (yesterday).*
Fuimos a la fiesta (el viernes).	*We went to the party (on Friday).*
No comió nada (anoche).	*He didn't eat anything (last night).*
Aprendieron mucho (el año pasado).	*They learned a lot (last year).*

AVOID THE *Blunder*

Do not use the imperfect tense unless you intend to tell what happened while you were in class.

✗ Estaba en clase ayer.

Describing Actions Simultaneously Begun and Terminated

The Spanish preterite tense is used to describe actions that began and terminated at the same time.

Abrí la puerta.	*I opened the door.*
Salimos a las ocho.	*We left at eight o'clock.*
Estornudó.	*She sneezed.*
Empezaron a escribir.	*They started to write.*

This kind of action is often accompanied by the following types of expressions.

de repente	*suddenly*
de pronto	*suddenly*
a las tres y media	*at 3:30*

Describing Constant Past Action

The preterite tense is often used with *siempre* to emphasize that an action or feeling was constant during an entire period of time; it is used with *nunca* to emphasize that an action did not occur during an entire period of time.

Siempre lo supo.	*He always knew it.*
Flora nunca estuvo de acuerdo conmigo.	*Flora never agreed with me.*

Narrating

The preterite tense is used in combination with the imperfect tense to narrate a story or an event. For details and examples, see pages 135–137.

Exercises

A Write accent marks where necessary in the following preterite forms.

1. jugue	7. estuvo	13. pudo	19. escribi
2. almorzo	8. estudie	14. oiste	20. visito
3. fuimos	9. volvio	15. leyo	21. lei
4. tuve	10. dormi	16. dio	22. fui
5. corrio	11. hizo	17. vi	23. sintio
6. hicieron	12. comi	18. busco	24. supe

B Rewrite each of the following sentences, changing the verb from the present tense to the preterite tense.

1. Yo siempre pago las cuentas.

2. Jorge baila bien.

3. Vamos al cine el sábado.

4. No hacemos nada el jueves.

5. ¿Adónde vas?

6. Nuestro equipo juega bien.

7. Los niños duermen toda la noche.

8. A Beatriz no le gusta la película.

9. Me da mucho gusto conocerlo.

10. Está muy cansado.

VERBS
the imperfect tense

Tense Formation

Stem (infinitive minus *-ar/-er/-ir*) + endings

Tense Endings

-ar VERBS

yo	-aba	nosotros(-as)	-ábamos
tú	-abas	vosotros(-as)	-abais
usted/él/ella	-aba		
ustedes/ellos/ellas	-aban		

-er AND *-ir* VERBS

yo	-ía	nosotros(-as)	-íamos
tú	-ías	vosotros(-as)	-íais
usted/él/ella	-ía		
ustedes/ellos/ellas	-ían		

The Imperfect Tense of Irregular Verbs

ser		ir		ver	
era	éramos	iba	íbamos	veía	veíamos
eras	erais	ibas	ibais	veías	veíais
era		iba		veía	
eran		iban		veían	

Formation of the Imperfect Progressive Tense

Imperfect tense of *estar* + gerund

estaba	estábamos	
estabas	estabais	
estaba		} + hablando/comiendo/escribiendo
estaban		

Review the forms in the chart on the preceding page.

Review the time expressions used with past tenses on page 123.

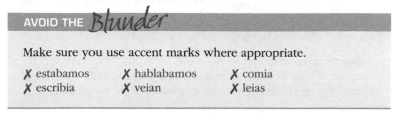

AVOID THE *Blunder*

Make sure you use accent marks where appropriate.

✗ estabamos ✗ hablabamos ✗ comia
✗ escribia ✗ veian ✗ leias

Uses of the Imperfect Tense

Describing the Past

The Spanish imperfect tense is used to describe a past period of time—the way things were in the past.

Cuando yo tenía 10 años, era pequeña y muy tímida.	*When I was 10 years old, I was little and very shy.*
Tenía una amiga que vivía cerca de mi casa.	*I had a friend who lived near my house.*
Había tres escuelas en la ciudad.	*There were three schools in the city.*
Teníamos mucho tiempo libre.	*We had a lot of free time.*
Nuestra casa era muy bonita.	*Our house was really pretty.*
Mis abuelos vivían en el campo.	*My grandparents lived in the country.*

AVOID THE *Blunder*

Do not use the preterite tense to describe a past period of time.

✗ Nuestra casa fue muy bonita.
✗ Mis abuelos vivieron en el campo.

When describing a past period of time, activities that occurred on a regular basis are expressed with the imperfect tense. In English, this can be expressed in three different ways.

Hacía mis tareas en la tarde. {
I (always) did my assignments in the afternoon.
I (always) used to do my assignments in the afternoon.
I would (always) do my assignments in the afternoon.
}

Jugábamos en la calle. $\left\{\begin{array}{l} \textit{We (always) played in the street.} \\ \textit{We (always) used to play in the street.} \\ \textit{We would (always) play in the street.} \end{array}\right.$

AVOID THE Blunder

Rather than translate word for word from English, consider the purpose of your remarks. If you are describing activities that took place on a regular basis, use the imperfect tense in Spanish.

AVOID THE Blunder

Do not use the imperfect progressive tense if you are describing activities that took place on a regular basis.

✗ Estaba haciendo mis tareas todos los días.
✗ Estábamos jugando en la calle cada tarde.
✗ Se estaba preocupando todas las noches.

Describing Simultaneous Past Actions

The imperfect or the imperfect progressive tense is used to express an action that was in progress at the same time that another action was in progress. In English, this type of action can be expressed in the past tense or the past progressive.

Mientras José leía el periódico, Juana veía la televisión.	*While José read the newspaper, Juana watched TV.*
Cuando estábamos jugando, nuestros padres estaban hablando.	*When we were playing, our parents were talking.*

AVOID THE Blunder

Do not use the preterite tense to express two simultaneous past actions.

✗ Mientras José leyó el periódico, Juana vio la televisión.
✗ Cuando jugamos, nuestros padres hablaron.

Narrating

■ In a narrative, the imperfect or imperfect progressive tense is used to describe an action that had started, but not ended, when another action (expressed in the preterite) began (see pages 129–130). In English, the past progressive tense is used for this purpose.

Pepe leía el periódico cuando llamó Marta.	*Pepe was reading the newspaper when Marta called.*
Pepe estaba leyendo el periódico cuando llamó Marta.	

Jugábamos en el jardín cuando Ana se cayó.	*We were playing in the yard when Ana fell down.*
Estábamos jugando en el jardín cuando Ana se cayó.	

■ The Spanish imperfect tense is used to describe a condition or state that had started, but not ended, when the preterite action occurred. In English, verbs that describe states or conditions are usually expressed in the past tense, not the past progressive, even though they represent "being in the middle of" a state or condition.

COMMON VERBS DESCRIBING AN ONGOING STATE OR CONDITION IN THE PAST

INFINITIVE	3SG. IMPERFECT	ENGLISH PAST TENSE
comprender	comprendía	*understood*
contener	contenía	*contained*
creer	creía	*believed*
encantar	encantaba	*loved*
existir	existía	*existed*
gustar	gustaba	*liked*
necesitar	necesitaba	*needed*
odiar	odiaba	*hated*
oír	oía	*heard*
oler	olía	*smelled* (intransitive)*
olvidar	olvidaba	*forgot*

continued on next page

*As an intransitive verb, *oler* refers to the state of something, not to the conscious act of smelling (*oler,* transitive).

INTRANSITIVE

El cuarto olía mal.	*The room smelled bad.*

TRANSITIVE

Quería oler tu perfume.	*I wanted to smell your perfume.*

**COMMON VERBS DESCRIBING AN ONGOING STATE
OR CONDITION IN THE PAST** (continued)

INFINITIVE	3SG. IMPERFECT	ENGLISH PAST TENSE
parecer	parecía	*appeared, seemed*
pensar	pensaba	*thought*
poseer	poseía	*owned*
preferir	prefería	*preferred*
querer	quería	*wanted*
recordar	recordaba	*remembered*
saber	sabía	*knew*
saber	sabía	*tasted* (intransitive)*
ser/estar	era/estaba	*was*
tener	tenía	*had*
ver	veía	*saw*

*As an intransitive verb, *saber* refers to the state of something, not to the conscious act of tasting (*probar*, transitive).

INTRANSITIVE

La carne sabía rica.   *The meat tasted delicious.*

TRANSITIVE

Probamos la carne.   *We tasted the meat.*

While the Spanish imperfect tense is used to describe ongoing states or feelings in the past, the English past tense (rather than the past progressive) is usually used for this purpose.

Quería seguir durmiendo.   *I wanted to keep on sleeping.*
                                                   (NOT *was wanting*)

Tenía tres coches cuando   *He had three cars when I met him.*
   lo conocí.   (NOT *was having*)

Yo no recordaba su nombre   *I didn't remember his name at the time.*
   en ese momento.   (NOT *wasn't remembering*)

AVOID THE *Blunder*

Do not use the preterite to express ongoing feelings or conditions.

✗ Quise seguir durmiento.
✗ Tuvo tres coches cuando lo conocí.
✗ No recordé su nombre en ese momento.

The Imperfect vs. the Preterite

Certain Spanish verbs have different English translations, depending on whether they express an already-started (imperfect) action or condition or a newly initiated or terminated (preterite) action or condition.

Cuando llegué a esta ciudad, conocía a dos personas.	*When I arrived in this city, I (already) knew two people.*
Cuando llegué a esta ciudad, conocí a dos personas.	*When I arrived in this city, I met two people.*
La mujer tenía dos niños.	*The woman (already) had two children.*
La mujer tuvo un niño.	*The woman gave birth to a child.*
Sabía que él estaba casado.	*She knew he was married.*
Supo que él estaba casado.	*She found out he was married.*
Ella estaba aquí a las ocho	*She was (already) here at eight.*
Ella estuvo aquí a las ocho.	*She got here at eight o'clock.*
Cuando Carlos salió de la fiesta, quería ir a su casa.	*When Carlos left the party, he wanted to go home.*
Cuando Carlos salió de la fiesta, quiso ir a su casa.	*When Carlos left the party, he tried to go home (but was unable to).*
Cuando salió de la fiesta, no quería ir a su casa.	*When he left the party, he didn't want to go home.*
Cuando salió de la fiesta, no quiso ir a su casa.	*When he left the party, he refused to go home.*

Expressing "Could" and "Had to"

Both the imperfect and the preterite of *poder* may be translated as "could," and both the imperfect and the preterite of *tener que* may be translated as "had to." The imperfect is used to describe a situation before its resolution. The preterite refers to a situation after its resolution.

Pedro llamó a su hijo porque no podía arreglar su computadora.	*Pedro called his son because he couldn't fix his computer.*
Pedro compró una computadora nueva porque su hijo no pudo arreglar la otra.	*Pedro bought a new computer because his son couldn't fix the other one.*
Eran las diez de la noche. Ana quería ir a una fiesta pero no podía porque tenía que estudiar.	*It was 10 P.M. Ana wanted to go to a party, but she couldn't because she had to study.*
Ana no fue a la fiesta anoche. No pudo ir porque tuvo que estudiar.	*Ana didn't go to the party last night. She couldn't go because she had to study.*

Expressing Past Detail

When telling what happened in the past, use the imperfect if you intend to describe the situation in further detail. Use the preterite if you don't intend to say any more about it.

Ayer estaba en la casa de mi amigo cuando empezó a nevar.	*Yesterday I was at my friend's house when it started to snow.*
Ayer estuve en la casa de mi amigo por dos horas. Luego fui a mi clase.	*Yesterday I was at my friend's house for two hours. After that I went to my class.*
Mi papá leía el periódico y vio una noticia que le sorprendió.	*My dad was reading the newspaper and saw an item that surprised him.*
Anoche mi papá llegó a casa a las ocho, leyó el periódico y salió de nuevo.	*Last night my dad got home at 8 o'clock, read the newspaper, and then went out again.*

AVOID THE *Blunder*

✗ Ayer estaba en la casa de mi amigo y luego fui a mi clase.
✗ Mi papá leía el periódico y luego salió de la sala.
✗ Anoche mi papá llegaba a casa a las ocho, leía el periódico y salía de nuevo.

Exercises

A *Rewrite the sentences below, changing the verbs from the present tense to the imperfect tense to describe activities that regularly occurred during a period of time in the past.*

1. Soy pequeña y un poco seria.

   _____

2. Tengo un perro y me gusta jugar con él.

   _____

3. Voy al cine con mis amigas todos los miércoles.

   _____

4. Mi familia y yo comemos en la casa de mi abuela los domingos por la tarde.

   _____

5. Escribo mis tareas en la tarde después de las clases.

_____

6. Mis hermanas y yo ayudamos en la casa.

_____

7. Mis amigos van a la playa en el verano y a veces yo los acompaño.

_____

8. La actividad que me gusta más es leer.

_____

B *Fill in the blanks by writing the correct form of the verb in parentheses, using the imperfect tense or the preterite tense, as appropriate.*

1. Mientras mi mamá _____ (cocinar), mi papá

_____ (ver) las noticias en la televisión.

2. Anoche, cuando yo _____ (entrar) en la casa, mis hermanos

_____ (jugar) en la sala.

3. Nosotros _____ (estar) estudiando cuando de repente se

_____ (apagar) la luz.

4. Cuando tú me _____ (llamar) ayer, yo

_____ (estar) en la biblioteca.

5. El viernes pasado Juan y yo estábamos en un club. No me sentía bien. Por eso

le dije que _____ (querer, yo) ir a casa.

6. Juan me respondió que no _____ (poder, él) llevarme a casa

todavía porque _____ (tener que, él) esperar a unos amigos.

Por eso, _____ (ir, yo) a casa en un taxi.

VERBS
the pluperfect tense

Tense Formation

Imperfect tense of *haber* + past participle

The Imperfect Tense of *haber*

yo	había	nosotros(-as)	habíamos
tú	habías	vosotros(-as)	habíais
usted/él/ella	había		
ustedes/ellos/ellas	habían		

Past Participle Formation

	-*ar* verbs	-*er* verbs	-*ir* verbs
Verb stem (infinitive minus -*ar*/-*er*/-*ir*) +	-ado	-ido	-ido
	hablar	**comer**	**vivir**
	hablado	comido	vivido

IRREGULAR PARTICIPLES

abrir	abierto	**poner**	puesto
cubrir	cubierto	**oponer**	opuesto
descubrir	descubierto	**proponer**	propuesto
decir	dicho	**ver**	visto
predecir	predicho	**prever**	previsto
escribir	escrito	**volver**	vuelto
describir	descrito	**devolver**	devuelto
prescribir	prescrito	**revolver**	revuelto
hacer	hecho	**resolver**	resuelto
morir	muerto	**romper**	roto

Review the forms in the chart on the preceding page.

AVOID THE *Blunder*

Remember to use accent marks in all forms of the imperfect of *haber*.

Be sure to learn the irregular past participle forms.

✗ habia volvido
✗ habiamos resolvido
✗ habian descubrido

Uses of the Pluperfect Tense

Describing Pre-past Action

The pluperfect tense in Spanish, like the past perfect tense in English, is used to describe actions that terminated before other past actions began.

María llegó a casa muy cansada. Había trabajado nueve horas seguidas.	*María got home exhausted. She had worked nine hours straight.*
Juan no aprobó el examen porque no había estudiado.	*Juan didn't pass the test because he hadn't studied.*

Expressing "Already" and "Not Yet"

The Spanish pluperfect, like the past perfect in English, is used to tell what had already happened or had not yet happened. (See *ya, todavía* on pages 124–125.)

Le ofrecí el periódico, pero ya lo había leído.	*I offered him the newspaper, but he had already read it.*
Eran las dos de la madrugada y mi hermana todavía no había aparecido.	*It was 2 A.M. and my sister still hadn't shown up.*

Reporting What Was Said

The Spanish pluperfect, like the past perfect in English, is used to report what someone said about a past action (see pages 200–203).

Sara dijo que su hermana no había vuelto a la casa.	*Sara said that her sister hadn't returned home.*
Mis amigos me dijeron que me habían llamado.	*My friends told me that they had called me.*

Describing the Frequency of an Action

The Spanish pluperfect, like the English past perfect, is used to express the number of times an action had been performed.

Había hablado dos veces con Juan.	I had talked to Juan twice.
Habíamos comido muchas veces en este lugar.	We had eaten at this place many times.

Unlike the English past perfect, the Spanish pluperfect is not used to express activity that was occurring for the first, second, third, etc. time.

ENGLISH PATTERN "the first time (that)" + subject + "had" + past participle

SPANISH PATTERN *la primera vez que* + (subject) + imperfect tense

Fue la primera vez que comíamos en ese lugar.	That was the first time we had eaten at that place.
Era la segunda vez que estaba en ese país.	It was the second time I had been in that country.

AVOID THE *Blunder*

✗ Fue la primera vez que habíamos comido en ese lugar.
✗ Era la segunda vez que había estado en ese país.

Exercise

A Use the pluperfect tense to complete the sentences below.

1. Javier leyó el periódico antes de ir a la oficina.

   Cuando Javier llegó a la oficina, ya sabía las noticias porque

   _____.

2. Comí a las doce. A la una, Mario me invitó a comer.

   Cuando Mario me invitó a comer, le dije que no, porque

   _____.

3. Margarita no estudió para el examen. Margarita suspendió el examen ayer.

   Margarita suspendió el examen ayer porque _____.

VERBS
the future tense

Tense Formation

Infinitive + endings

Tense Endings

yo	-é	nosotros(-as)	-emos
tú	-ás	vosotros(-as)	-éis
usted/él/ella	-á		
ustedes/ellos/ellas	-án		

Irregular Future-tense Stems

STEMS THAT DROP *e* FROM THE INFINITIVE

INFINITIVE	FUTURE STEM	1SG. FUTURE
haber	habr-	habré
poder	podr-	podré
querer	querr-	querré
saber	sabr-	sabré
caber	cabr-	cabré

STEMS THAT REPLACE *e* OR *i* WITH *d*

INFINITIVE	FUTURE STEM	1SG. FUTURE
poner	pondr-	pondré
salir	saldr-	saldré
tener	tendr-	tendré
valer	valdr-	valdré
venir	vendr-	vendré

OTHER IRREGULAR STEMS

INFINITIVE	FUTURE STEM	1SG. FUTURE
decir	dir-	diré
hacer	har-	haré

Review the forms on the preceding page.

AVOID THE Blunder

Do not use an accent mark in the *nosotros* form of the future tense.

✗ hablarémos   ✗ harémos   ✗ vendrémos

Be sure to learn the future stems of irregular verbs.

✗ teneré   ✗ quererán
✗ ponerá   ✗ veniremos

Uses of the Future Tense

The future tense is used with certain time expressions.

mañana	*tomorrow*
pasado mañana	*the day after tomorrow*
la próxima semana	*next week*
el próximo mes	*next month*
el próximo año	*next year*
pronto	*soon*
dentro de dos días	*in two days*
algún día	*some day*
nunca	*never*

Making a Prediction

The Spanish future tense is used to predict the future.

Mi hijo será médico.	*My son will be a doctor.*
Usted tendrá buena suerte.	*You will have good luck.*
Todos viajaremos a la luna.	*We will all travel to the moon.*
Algún día me graduaré.	*Some day I'll graduate.*

Stating a Probable Action

The Spanish future tense is used to indicate probability.

Lloverá en la tarde.	*It will probably rain this afternoon.*
Los muchachos llegarán tarde.	*The boys will probably be late.*
Te llamará esta noche.	*He'll probably call you tonight.*
Iré al centro la próxima semana.	*I'll probably go downtown next week.*

Stating Conjecture

The Spanish future tense is used to indicate conjecture about a present state or situation.

Estarás cansada.	*You must be tired.*
Serán las seis.	*It must be about 6 o'clock.*
Estarán enojados.	*They're probably mad.*
Estarán llegando ahora.	*They must be arriving about now.*

Expressing "I wonder . . ."

The future tense is used in a question to indicate speculation about a present action.

¿Dónde estará mi hermano?	*I wonder where my brother is.*
¿Qué hora será?	*I wonder what time it is.*

ALTERNATIVE CONSTRUCTION FOR EXPRESSING FUTURE ACTIONS

In Spanish, as in English, plans for the near future are usually expressed with a "going to" expression. The present tense of *ir* + *a* + infinitive is used.

Vamos a comprar una casa nueva.   *We're going to buy a new house.*

The future tense in Spanish is *not* used to ask or offer favors. These and other uses of the English "will" should be expressed in the present tense in Spanish (see page 118).

AVOID THE *Blunder*

Do not assume that the future tense is the exact equivalent of the English future tense with "will." Many uses of the English "will" are better expressed in Spanish in the present tense.

Clauses After the Future Tense

Expressing Intended or Expected Action

Certain expressions follow a present or future tense verb to indicate action intended or expected in the future. These expressions are followed by a clause with the verb in the present subjunctive (see pages 170–171).

cuando	*when (as soon as)*	hasta que	*until*
en cuanto	*as soon as*	antes que	*before*
tan pronto como	*as soon as*	después que	*after*
mientras	*when/while (at the same time as)*		

ENGLISH PATTERN   subject + future verb + time expression
                      + present indicative verb

SPANISH PATTERN   (subject) + future verb + time expression
                      + present subjunctive verb

Te sentirás mejor cuando salgas del hospital.	*You'll feel better when you leave the hospital.*
Lo llamaré en cuanto llegue a casa.	*I'll call him as soon as I get home.*
Ella estará bien tan pronto como reciba una carta.	*She'll be okay as soon as she gets a letter.*
Comeremos antes que regresen los otros.	*We'll eat before the others get back.*
Estudiaré después que termine este programa.	*I'll study after this program is over.*
Viviremos en esta casa hasta que se vayan nuestros hijos.	*We'll live in this house until our children leave.*
Nos divertiremos mientras estén ustedes en la ciudad.	*We'll have a good time when you all are in town.*

AVOID THE *Blunder*

When these Spanish expressions appear in clauses after a verb in the future tense, they are followed by a subjunctive verb, not a verb in the indicative.

✗ cuando sales   ✗ después que termina
✗ en cuanto llego   ✗ hasta que se van
✗ tan pronto como recibe ✗ mientras están
✗ antes que regresan

Expressing Conditional Future Action

Certain expressions indicate conditions on which future action depends. These expressions introduce a clause with the verb in the present subjunctive (see pages 172–173).

con tal (de) que	*provided that, as long as*
siempre y cuando	*provided that, as long as*
sin que	*without (something happening/ someone knowing)*
a menos que	*unless*
en caso (de) que	*if it should happen that, in case*

ENGLISH PATTERN subject + future verb + conditional marker
+ present indicative verb

SPANISH PATTERN (subject) + future verb + conditional marker
+ present subjunctive verb

Le prestaré el dinero con tal (de) que me lo devuelva.	*I'll lend him the money as long as he returns it.*
Haremos una fiesta siempre y cuando los niños se porten bien.	*We'll have a party provided the children behave.*
Trabajaré sin que mi familia lo sepa.	*I'll work without my family knowing about it.*
Viajará este verano a menos que tenga que trabajar.	*He will travel this summer unless he has to work.*
Llevará su licencia en caso (de) que quiera manejar.	*He'll take his license in case he wants to drive.*

AVOID THE *Blunder*

Do not use the present indicative tense after these expressions when they appear in clauses after a verb in the future tense.

✗ con tal de que me lo devuelve
✗ siempre y cuando se portan bien
✗ sin que mi familia lo sabe
✗ a menos que tengo que trabajar
✗ en caso que quiere manejar

Both the conditional markers *si* "if" and *por si acaso* "just in case" are followed by a verb in the present indicative, not the subjunctive.

Haremos una fiesta si los niños se portan bien.	*We'll have a party if the children behave.*
Viajará este verano si no tiene que trabajar.	*He'll travel this summer if he doesn't have to work.*
Llevará su licencia por si acaso quiere manejar.	*He'll take his license just in case he wants to drive.*

AVOID THE *Blunder*

✗ si los niños se porten bien
✗ si no tenga que trabajar

Expressing the Purpose of Future Action

Certain conjunctions indicate the purpose of future action. These expressions are followed by a clause with the verb in the present subjunctive.

para que	so that (expected result)
a fin de que	so that (hoped-for result)

Mi papá me manda dinero para que pueda ir a visitarlo.

My father sends me money so I can go visit him.

Nos vamos a acostar temprano esta noche a fin de que nos podamos despertar temprano mañana.

We're going to bed early tonight so we can wake up early tomorrow.

AVOID THE *Blunder*

Do not use the present indicative tense after the expressions *para que* and *a fin de que*.

✗ para que puede ir   ✗ a fin de que puedo comprarlo

Exercises

A *Fill in the blanks with the future tense of the verb in parentheses.*

1. Muy pronto _____ (tener, yo) un coche nuevo.

2. Tú _____ (encontrar) un tesoro.

3. Su espíritu _____ (vivir).

4. Ella no _____ (venir) a tiempo.

B *Complete the following sentences by writing the appropriate form of the verb in parentheses.*

1. Voy a llamarlo cuando _____ (regresar) de las vacaciones.

2. Ella se graduará siempre y cuando _____ (estudiar) mucho.

3. Haremos una fiesta mientras _____ (estar, ustedes) aquí en diciembre.

4. Te vas a enfermar si no _____ (comer) más.

5. No descansaré hasta que _____ (tener) el dinero para el viaje.

VERBS
the future perfect tense

Tense Formation

Future tense of *haber* + past participle

The Future Tense of *haber*

yo	habré	nosotros(-as)	habremos
tú	habrás	vosotros(-as)	habréis
usted/él/ella	habrá		
ustedes/ellos/ellas	habrán		

Past Participle Formation

	-*ar* verbs	-*er* verbs	-*ir* verbs
Verb stem (infinitive minus -*ar*/-*er*/-*ir*) +	-ado	ido	ido
	hablar	comer	vivir
	hablado	comido	vivido

IRREGULAR PARTICIPLES

abrir	abierto	**poner**	puesto
cubrir	cubierto	**oponer**	opuesto
descubrir	descubierto	**proponer**	propuesto
decir	dicho	**ver**	visto
predecir	predicho	**prever**	previsto
escribir	escrito	**volver**	vuelto
describir	descrito	**devolver**	devuelto
prescribir	prescrito	**revolver**	revuelto
hacer	hecho	**resolver**	resuelto
morir	muerto	**romper**	roto

Review the forms on the preceding page.

Review the time expressions used with future tenses on page 144.

AVOID THE *Blunder*

Note that all forms of *haber* in the future tense have an accent mark except the *nosotros* form.

Be sure to learn the irregular past participle forms.

✗ habre vido   ✗ habrémos hacido   ✗ habran escribido

Uses of the Future Perfect Tense

Predicting Termination of Future Action

The future perfect is used to predict action that will have terminated by a certain future time.

En una semana ya se habrá casado.	*In a week he will have already gotten married.*
En julio ya me habré graduado.	*In July I will have already graduated.*

Stating Conjecture About Past Action

The future perfect is used to indicate conjecture about past action.

Habrás trabajado mucho.	*You must have worked hard.*
Nos habrán visto.	*They must have seen us.*

Exercise

A *Predict what will have happened by the year 2030 by filling in the blanks.*

En el año 2030:

1. Los científicos _____ descubierto la cura del cáncer.

2. Alguien _____ viajado a Marte.

3. Nosotros _____ aprendido mucho sobre el medio ambiente.

4. Yo _____

_____.

VERBS
the conditional

The simple conditional expresses what someone would do if the facts or circumstances were different. It can also be used to express probability or conjecture about the past.

The conditional perfect expresses what someone would have done if the facts or circumstances had been different. It can also be used to express probability or conjecture about what had occurred before another past event.

VERBS
the simple conditional

Formation

Infinitive + endings

Endings

yo	-ía	nosotros(-as)	-íamos
tú	-ías	vosotros(-as)	-íais
usted/él/ella	-ía		
ustedes/ellos/ellas	-ían		

Irregular Conditional Stems

STEMS THAT DROP *e* FROM THE INFINITIVE

INFINITIVE	CONDITIONAL STEM	1SG. CONDITIONAL
haber	habr-	habría
poder	podr-	podría
querer	querr-	querría
saber	sabr-	sabría

STEMS THAT REPLACE *e* OR *i* WITH *d*

INFINITIVE	CONDITIONAL STEM	1SG. CONDITIONAL
poner	pondr-	pondría
salir	saldr-	saldría
tener	tendr-	tendría
venir	vendr-	vendría

OTHER IRREGULAR STEMS

INFINITIVE	CONDITIONAL STEM	1SG. CONDITIONAL
decir	dir-	diría
hacer	har-	haría

Review the forms in the chart on the preceding page.

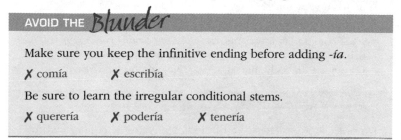

AVOID THE *Blunder*

Make sure you keep the infinitive ending before adding *-ía*.

✗ comía ✗ escribía

Be sure to learn the irregular conditional stems.

✗ querería ✗ podería ✗ tenería

Uses of the Conditional

Speculating About the Past

The conditional in Spanish is used in a question to indicate speculation about a past situation.

¿Qué hora sería?	*I wonder what time it was.*
	(What time would it have been?)
¿Dónde estarían mis amigos?	*I wonder where my friends were.*
	(Where would my friends have been?)

AVOID THE *Blunder*

Do not try to translate "I wonder." Use the conditional in a question instead.

Indicating Probability About Past Action

The conditional is used to indicate the probability of a past situation.

Serían las dos y media.	*It must have been about 2:30.*
Estarían en el centro.	*They were probably downtown.*
Tendría hambre.	*He must have been hungry.*
Mario sabría la verdad.	*Mario probably knew the truth.*

Expressing Conditional Action

The conditional is used in connection with *si* and the imperfect subjunctive (see page 195) to express conjecture.

—¿Qué haría usted si fuera el jefe?	*"What would you do if you were the boss?"*
—Yo sería más organizado.	*"I would be more organized."*

—¿Adónde irían ustedes si
tuvieran vacaciones?

—Iríamos a Chile.

—¿Qué comprarías si tuvieras
más dinero?

—Compraría un coche nuevo.

*"Where would you all go if you
had time off?"*

"We would go to Chile."

*"What would you buy if you had
more money?"*

"I would buy a new car."

AVOID THE *Blunder*

Do not use a past tense in the indicative after a conditional followed by *si*, as you would in English. Use the imperfect subjunctive instead.

✗ ¿Adónde irían ustedes si tenían vacaciones?

✗ ¿Qué comprarías si tenías más dinero?

Do not use an accent mark on *si* in these constructions.

✗ ¿Qué haría sí fuera el jefe?

Exercise

A *Use the simple conditional to express the following in Spanish.*

1. *You must have been cold.*

_____

2. *She was probably sick.*

_____

3. *If I were you, I wouldn't go out.*

_____

4. *If I had more money, I would buy a house.*

_____

5. *What would you do?*

_____

VERBS
the conditional perfect

Formation

Conditional of *haber* + past participle

The Conditional of *haber*

yo	habría	nosotros(-as)	habríamos
tú	habrías	vosotros(-as)	habríais
usted/él/ella	habría		
ustedes/ellos/ellas	habrían		

Past Participle Formation

	-ar verbs	*-er* verbs	*-ir* verbs
Verb stem (infinitive minus -*ar*/'-*er*/'-*ir*) +	-ado	-ido	-ido
	hablar	**comer**	**vivir**
	hablado	comido	vivido

IRREGULAR PARTICIPLES

abrir	abierto	**poner**	puesto
cubrir	cubierto	**oponer**	opuesto
descubrir	descubierto	**proponer**	propuesto
decir	dicho	**ver**	visto
predecir	predicho	**prever**	previsto
escribir	escrito	**volver**	vuelto
describir	descrito	**devolver**	devuelto
prescribir	prescrito	**revolver**	revuelto
hacer	hecho	**resolver**	resuelto
morir	muerto	**romper**	roto

Review the forms in the chart on the preceding page.

AVOID THE *Blunder*

Note that the conditional stem of *haber* drops the *e* from the infinitive.

✗ habería   ✗ haberían   ✗ haberíamos

Be sure to learn the irregular past participle forms.

✗ habría decido   ✗ habría hacido   ✗ habría morido

Uses of the Conditional Perfect

Expressing "I wonder..."

The conditional perfect in Spanish is used in a question to indicate speculation about an action completed in the past.

¿Qué habrían hecho?	*I wonder what they would have done.*
¿Qué habría dicho tu papá?	*I wonder what your father would have said.*

Indicating Probability

The conditional perfect is used to indicate the probability of a past action.

Ellos habrían luchado.	*They would have struggled.*
Mi papá habría dicho la verdad.	*My dad would have told the truth.*

Expressing Conjecture

The conditional perfect is used in connection with *si* and the pluperfect subjunctive (see page 198) to express conjecture about the past.

—¿Qué habrías hecho si hubieras sido el jefe?	*"What would you have done if you had been the boss?"*
—Habría sido más organizado.	*"I would have been more organized."*
—¿Adónde habrían ido si hubieran tenido más tiempo?	*"Where would you all have gone if you had had more time?"*
—Habríamos ido a la Argentina también.	*"We would have gone to Argentina as well."*

The conditional perfect can also be used after the expression *de* + *haber* + past participle to express conjecture about the past.

De haberlo conocido antes, te lo habría presentado.	*If I had known him before, I would have introduced him to you.*
De haber oído ese rumor, se lo habría dicho.	*If I had heard that rumor, I would have told him.*

Exercise

A *Use the conditional perfect to express the following in Spanish.*

1. *I wonder what we would have done.*

_____

2. *If I had had time, I would have called you.*

_____

3. *If your brother had been there, you wouldn't have done that.*

_____

4. *If we had known the truth, we wouldn't have worked here.*

_____

VERBS
the subjunctive mood

Expressions That Signal Use of the Subjunctive

- **Lack of knowledge or existence**

no existir	*not exist*
no haber nada/nadie que	*not be anything/anybody that*
no saber nada que	*not know anything that*
no conocer a nadie que	*not know anybody who*

- **Desire, need, or search for the unknown**

buscar algo / a alguien que	*look for something/somebody that*
necesitar algo / a alguien que	*need something/somebody that*
querer algo / a alguien que	*want something/somebody that*

- **Desire for action by others**

querer que alguien	*want somebody to*
preferir que alguien	*prefer that somebody*
esperar que alguien	*hope that somebody*
desear que alguien	*desire that somebody*
ojalá que	*hope that*

- **Attempt to control the actions of others**

pedirle a alguien que	*ask somebody to*
rogarle a alguien que	*beg somebody to*
suplicarle a alguien que	*beg somebody to*
implorarle a alguien que	*implore somebody to*
recomendarle a alguien que	*recommend to somebody that*
aconsejarle a alguien que	*advise somebody to*
sugerirle a alguien que	*suggest to somebody that*
exigirle a alguien que	*demand that somebody*
mandarle a alguien que	*command somebody to*
ordenarle a alguien que	*order somebody to*
decirle a alguien que	*tell somebody to*
prohibirle a alguien que	*prohibit somebody from*
impedirle a alguien que	*stop somebody from*

■ **Declaration of feeling**

ser bueno que	*be good that*
ser maravilloso que	*be wonderful that*
ser fantástico que	*be fantastic that*
ser sorprendente que	*be surprising that*
ser malo que	*be bad that*
ser horrible que	*be horrible that*
ser una lástima que	*be a shame that*
alegrarse de que	*be glad that*
estar contento de que	*be happy that*
sentir que	*be sorry that*
lamentar que	*regret that*

■ **Doubt**

dudar que	*doubt that*
no creer que	*not believe that*
no estar seguro (de) que	*not be sure that*
no es seguro que	*it's not certain that*
no es cierto que	*it's not true that*
ser posible que	*be possible that*
ser imposible que	*be impossible that*
ser probable que	*be probable that*
ser improbable que	*be improbable that*
tal vez	*maybe*
quizá/quizás	*perhaps*
acaso	*perhaps*

■ **Later action**

cuando	*when*
mientras	*while*
en cuanto	*as soon as*
tan pronto como	*as soon as*
antes que	*before*
después que	*after*
hasta que	*until*

■ **Conditional action**

siempre y cuando	*as long as*
con tal (de) que	*providing*
a menos que	*unless*
en caso (de) que	*in case*

■ **Avoidance of interference**

sin que	*without*

- **Purpose of action**

para que	*so that*
a fin de que	*so that*
por que	*so that*

- **Wish**

ojalá (que)*	*wish (that)*

*This triggers use of the imperfect subjunctive.

In Spanish, verbs are expressed in the subjunctive mood according to set patterns when the subject feels some emotion, uncertainty, or desire about the action or situation. The subject's feelings are expressed with an indicative verb in a beginning clause that triggers use of the subjunctive in the clause that follows.

Review the expressions that trigger use of the subjunctive in the chart above.

VERBS
the present subjunctive

Formation

Stem (*yo* form of the present indicative tense minus *o/oy*) + endings

hablar **pensar** **comer** **volver** **decir** **escribir** **pedir** **tener**

hablar	pensar	comer	volver	decir	escribir	pedir	tener
hablo	pienso	como	vuelvo	digo	escribo	pido	tengo
habl-	piens-	com-	vuelv-	dig-	escrib-	pid-	teng-

Endings

-*ar* VERBS

yo	-e	nosotros(-as)	-emos
tú	-es	vosotros(-as)	-éis
usted/él/ella	-e		
ustedes/ellos/ellas	-en		

-*er* AND -*ir* VERBS

yo	-a	nosotros(-as)	-amos
tú	-as	vosotros(-as)	-áis
usted/él/ella	-a		
ustedes/ellos/ellas	-an		

Stem Changes

-*Ar* and -*er* stem-changing verbs do not change stems in the *nosotros* and *vosotros* forms. -*Ir* stem-changing verbs have a stem change (the second one indicated in parentheses) in the *nosotros* and *vosotros* forms.

INFINITIVE	*nosotros* FORM	*vosotros* FORM
arrepentir (ie, i)	arrepintamos	arrepintáis
divertir (ie, i)	divirtamos	divirtáis
sentir (ie, i)	sintamos	sintáis
pedir (i, i)	pidamos	pidáis
servir (i, i)	sirvamos	sirváis
dormir (ue, u)	durmamos	durmáis
morir (ue, u)	muramos	muráis

Automatic Spelling Changes in Conjugations

VERBS THAT END IN -*car*

yo	-que	nosotros(-as)	-quemos
tú	-ques	vosotros(-as)	-quéis
usted/él/ella	-que		
ustedes/ellos/ellas	-quen		

VERBS THAT END IN -*gar*

yo	-gue	nosotros(-as)	-guemos
tú	-gues	vosotros(-as)	-guéis
usted/él/ella	-gue		
ustedes/ellos/ellas	-guen		

VERBS THAT END IN -*guar*

yo	-güe	nosotros(-as)	-güemos
tú	-gües	vosotros(-as)	-güéis
usted/él/ella	-güe		
ustedes/ellos/ellas	-güen		

VERBS THAT END IN -*zar*

yo	-ce	nosotros(-as)	-cemos
tú	-ces	vosotros(-as)	-ceis
usted/él/ella	-ce		
ustedes/ellos/ellas	-cen		

VERBS THAT END IN -*ger* OR -*gir*

yo	-ja	nosotros(-as)	-jamos
tú	-jas	vosotros(-as)	-jáis
usted/él/ella	-ja		
ustedes/ellos/ellas	-jan		

Verbs That Are Irregular in the Present Subjunctive

ser		**ver**		**saber**	
sea	seamos	vea	veamos	sepa	sepamos
seas	seáis	veas	veáis	sepas	sepáis
sea		vea		sepa	
sean		vean		sepan	

ir		**haber**	
vaya	vayamos	haya	hayamos
vayas	vayáis	hayas	hayáis
vaya		haya	
vayan		hayan	

Commands

Affirmative Commands

	usted	ustedes	nosotros	tú	vosotros
			SUBJUNCTIVE		INFINITIVE
	SUBJUNCTIVE	SUBJUNCTIVE	*nosotros*	INDICATIVE	MINUS *r*
INFINITIVE	*Ud.* FORM	*Uds.* FORM	FORM	*Ud.* FORM	PLUS *d*
hablar	hable	hablen	hablemos	habla	hablad
comer	coma	coman	comamos	come	comed
escribir	escriba	escriban	escribamos	escribe	escribid

Object pronouns are attached to the end of affirmative commands.

comer	cómalo	cómanlo	comámoslo	cómelo	comedlo
sentarse	siéntese	siéntense	sentémonos+	siéntate	sentados
dar	déselo	dénselo	démoselo*	dáselo	dádselo

*Drop the s from *-mos* when it is followed by *nos* or *se*.

IRREGULAR FORMS OF AFFIRMATIVE *tú* COMMANDS

hacer	haz
ir	ve
poner	pon
salir	sal
tener	tén
venir	ven

Negative Commands

	usted	ustedes	nosotros	tú	vosotros
			no +		*no* +
	no +	*no* +	SUBJUNCTIVE	*no* +	SUBJUNCTIVE
	SUBJUNCTIVE	SUBJUNCTIVE	*nosotros*	SUBJUNCTIVE	*vosotros*
INFINITIVE	*Ud.* FORM	*Uds.* FORM	FORM	*tu* FORM	FORM
hablar	no hable	no hablen	no hablemos	no hables	no habléis
comer	no coma	no coman	no comamos	no comas	no comáis
escribir	no escriba	no escriban	no escribamos	no escribas	no escribáis

Object pronouns are placed between *no* and the verb.

comer	no lo coma	no lo coman	no lo comamos	no lo comas	no lo comáis
sentarse	no se siente	no se sienten	no nos sentemos	no te sientes	no os sentéis
dar	no se lo dé	no se lo den	no se lo demos	no se lo des	no se lo deis

Review the forms in the charts on the preceding pages.

AVOID THE *Blunder*

Be sure to use the *yo* form of the present indicative tense to determine the correct subjunctive stem.

✗ tena   ✗ haca   ✗ pona

Be sure to make stem changes in *-ar* and *-er* verbs.

✗ pense   ✗ volva   ✗ perda

Do not make stem changes in the *nosotros* and *vosotros* forms of *-ar* and *-er* verbs.

✗ piensemos   ✗ vuelvamos   ✗ pierdais

Be sure to make stem changes in the *nosotros* and *vosotros* forms of *-ir* verbs.

✗ dormamos   ✗ divertamos   ✗ servamos

Be aware of automatic spelling changes.

✗ almuerze   ✗ busce   ✗ juege
✗ averigue   ✗ recoga   ✗ finga

Uses of the Present Subjunctive

When the verb that triggers subjunctive use is in the present or future tense, the verb in the clause that follows is in the present subjunctive.

Expressing What Seems Not to Exist

The present subjunctive in Spanish is used to express that somebody or something doesn't exist, at least in the opinion of the speaker.

No hay ningún trabajo que me interese.	*There is no job that interests me.*
No veo nada que me guste.	*I don't see anything I like.*
No hay nadie que me comprenda.	*There is nobody who understands me.*
No existe nadie que cocine mejor.	*There's nobody who cooks better.*

AVOID THE *Blunder*

✗ No hay nada que me gusta.
✗ No hay nadie que me comprende.
✗ No conozco a nadie que vive aquí.

Expressing Desired Characteristics

The present subjunctive is used to describe the characteristics desired in someone or something, but the actual person or object sought is as yet unknown.

INDICATIVE
Busco a mi amigo que habla
   español.

*I'm looking for my friend who
   speaks Spanish.*

SUBJUNCTIVE
Busco un amigo que hable
   español.

*I'm looking for a (possible) friend
   who speaks Spanish.*

INDICATIVE
Nuestros amigos tienen una casa
   que tiene piscina.

*Our friends have a house that has
   a swimming pool.*

SUBJUNCTIVE
Nosotros queremos una casa que
   tenga piscina.

*We want (to find) a house that
   has a swimming pool.*

INDICATIVE
Germán tiene un puesto que le
   paga bien.

*Germán has a job that pays him
   well.*

SUBJUNCTIVE
Germán necesita un puesto que
   le pague bien.

*Germán needs (to find) a job that
   pays him well.*

AVOID THE *Blunder*

Use the indicative if you can picture the actual person or item in question. Use the subjunctive if you only have an idea about what the wished-for person or item should be like.

✗ Busco un asistente que habla español.
✗ Germán quiere un puesto que le paga bien.

■ The "personal *a*," indicating that the direct object is a person, is not used when the person is as yet unknown.

INDICATIVE
Necesito a mi novio, quien me
   comprende.

*I need my boyfriend, who
   understands me.*

SUBJUNCTIVE
Necesito un novio que me
   comprenda.

*I need (to find) a boyfriend who
   understands me.*

Nevertheless, the "personal *a*" is used before *alguien* and *nadie* when they are direct objects, even if they are unknown.

Busco a alguien que me pueda
ayudar.

No he encontrado a nadie que
sepa hacer esto.

*I'm looking for somebody who
can help me.*

*I haven't found anybody who
knows how to do this.*

AVOID THE *Blunder*

✗ Busco mi amiga Susana.
✗ Busco alguien.
✗ No busco nadie.

Expressing Desire for Action

The subjunctive is used when the subject expresses a desire for action
by another person or other people.

Quiero que estudies.
María prefiere que te vayas.
Esperamos que no lleguen tarde.
Mis padres prefieren que trabaje
con ellos.
Ojalá que no llueva.

Ojalá que podamos vernos este
verano.

I want you to study.
María would like you to leave.
We hope they don't arrive late.
*My parents prefer that I work with
them.*
*I hope it doesn't rain. (May God
grant that it not rain.)*
*I hope we will be able to see each
other this summer. (May God
grant that we see each other
this summer.)*

AVOID THE *Blunder*

Do not translate the English construction word for word.

✗ Quiero tú estudiar.
✗ Esperamos que no llegan tarde.
✗ Ojalá que no llueve.

When the action of the second verb is to be performed by the subject
of the first verb, an infinitive construction is used instead of the
subjunctive.

INFINITIVE—SAME SUBJECT
Quiero estudiar. *I want to study.*
SUBJUNCTIVE—DIFFERENT SUBJECTS
Quiero que estudies. *I want you to study.*

INFINITIVE—SAME SUBJECT
Preferimos comer aquí.   *We prefer to eat here.*
SUBJUNCTIVE—DIFFERENT SUBJECTS
Preferimos que coma aquí.   *We prefer that he eat here.*

INFINITIVE—SAME SUBJECT
(Ella) espera ser médico.   *She hopes to be a doctor.*
SUBJUNCTIVE—DIFFERENT SUBJECTS
(Ella) espera que (él) sea médico.   *She hopes he will be a doctor.*

INFINITIVE—SAME SUBJECT
Espero poder ir a la fiesta.   *I hope I can go to the party.*
SUBJUNCTIVE—DIFFERENT SUBJECTS
Espero que puedas ir a la fiesta.   *I hope you can go to the party.*

AVOID THE *Blunder*

✗ Ella espera que (ella misma) pueda ser médico.
✗ Preferimos que (él) come aquí.

Expressing Attempt to Control an Action

The present subjunctive is used to indicate an attempt to control the actions of others.

ENGLISH PATTERN   subject + verb + direct object + infinitive

SPANISH PATTERN   (subject) + indirect object + verb + *que*
                          + subjunctive verb

The subject has one of several different intentions:

- To make a request

Te pido que me acompañes.   *I'm asking you to go with me.*
Les ruego que me dejen ir.   *I beg you all to let me go.*
Me suplica que lo perdone.   *He begs me to forgive him.*
Le implora que tenga paciencia.   *He begs her to be patient.*

- To give advice

El consejero me recomienda   *The counselor recommends that*
    que estudie un idioma.   *I study a language.*
Yo te sugiero que vayas a casa.   *I suggest that you go home.*
El médico le aconseja que pierda   *The doctor advises her to lose*
    peso.   *weight.*

AVOID THE *Blunder*

Do not use the infinitive to indicate requests or to give advice.

✗ Pido a ti acompañarme.
✗ Sugiero a ti ir a casa.

- To make a demand

El jefe nos exige que trabajemos.	*The boss demands that we work.*
La maestra le manda a él que se siente.	*The teacher orders him to sit down.*
El oficial les ordena a ellos que marchen.	*The officer orders them to march.*
Mi madre me dice que la ayude.	*My mother tells me to help her.*

This construction is an alternative to the infinitive construction described on pages 99–100. Both patterns are correct.

AVOID THE *Blunder*

Do not leave out the indirect object pronoun.

✗ El jefe exige que trabajemos.
✗ La maestra manda a él que se siente.
✗ El oficial ordena a ellos que marchen.

- To prohibit an action

Sus padres les prohíben que se casen.	*Their parents forbid them to marry.*
El guardia nos impide que entremos.	*The guard stops us from entering.*

This construction is an alternative to the infinitive construction described on pages 99–100. Both patterns are correct.

AVOID THE *Blunder*

Do not leave out the indirect object pronoun.

✗ Sus padres prohíben que se casen.
✗ El guardia impide que entremos.

Expressing Feelings About a Fact

The subjunctive is used when there is an expression of personal feeling or emotion about a fact.

Es fantástico que estés aquí conmigo.	*It's fantastic that you're here with me.*
Es una lástima que te vayas.	*It's a shame that you're leaving.*
Me alegro mucho de que te sientas mejor.	*I'm so glad you feel better.*
Siento mucho que no te guste.	*I'm sorry you don't like it.*

When expressing emotion, if the second verb indicates an action performed by the subject of the first verb, an infinitive construction after a preposition is used instead of the subjunctive after *que* (see page 97).

INFINITIVE—SAME SUBJECT

Estoy contenta de estar aquí.	*I'm glad I'm here.*

SUBJUNCTIVE—DIFFERENT SUBJECTS

Estoy contenta que estés aquí.	*I'm glad you're here.*

INFINITIVE—SAME SUBJECT

Siento no poder visitarte.	*I'm sorry I can't visit you.*

SUBJUNCTIVE—DIFFERENT SUBJECTS

Siento que no puedas visitarme.	*I'm sorry you can't visit me.*

AVOID THE *Blunder*

✗ Estoy contenta que estoy aquí.
✗ Siento que no puedo visitarte.

Expressing Doubt

The subjunctive is used when there is an expression of doubt, possibility, impossibility, probability, or improbability in the present or future.

INDICATIVE

Creo que Julia viene mañana.	*I think Julia is coming tomorrow.*

SUBJUNCTIVE

No creo que Julia venga mañana.	*I don't think Julia is coming tomorrow.*

INDICATIVE

Estoy segura de que es Martín.	*I'm sure it's Martín.*

SUBJUNCTIVE

No estoy segura de que sea Martín.	*I'm not sure it's Martín.*

INDICATIVE

Es cierto que es su novio.
It's certain that he's her boyfriend.

SUBJUNCTIVE

Es imposible que sea su novio.
It's not possible that he's her boyfriend.

INDICATIVE

No hay duda de que es un buen curso.
There's no doubt that it's a good course.

SUBJUNCTIVE

Dudo que sea buen curso.
I doubt it's a good course.

INDICATIVE

Sé que está en su casa.
I know she's at home.

SUBJUNCTIVE

Tal vez/Quizá(s) no esté en su casa.
Maybe she's not at home.

AVOID THE *Blunder*

Use the indicative to indicate certainty, the subjunctive to indicate uncertainty.

✗ No creo que Julia viene mañana.
✗ Creo que Julia venga mañana.

Expressing the Time of a Future Action

The subjunctive is used after certain expressions that indicate the time of future action.

- *cuando* and *mientras* when they refer to a future action

Te llamo/Te voy a llamar/ Te llamaré cuando no estés ocupada.
I'll call you when you're not busy.

Te lo digo cuando llegues a casa.
I'll tell you when you get home.

Mis primos visitarán todos los museos mientras estén aquí.
My cousins will go to all the museums while they're here.

When *cuando* or *mientras* indicates simultaneous action, it is followed by a verb in the indicative.

Siempre me llamas cuando estoy ocupada.
You always call me when I'm busy.

En la mañana, mientras Claudio prepara el desayuno, Natalia lee el periódico.
In the morning, while Claudio prepares breakfast, Natalia reads the newspaper.

✗ Te lo digo cuando llegas a casa.
✗ Siempre me llamas cuando esté ocupada.

- *en cuanto* and *tan pronto como*

Vamos a empezar en cuanto vengan los otros.	*We're going to start as soon as the others get here.*
Ella se casará tan pronto como se gradúe.	*She will get married as soon as she graduates.*

- *antes que* and *después que*

Ricardo se graduará antes que su hermana empiece a estudiar.	*Ricardo will graduate before his sister begins her studies.*
Vamos de vacaciones después que Ricardo se gradúe.	*We're going on vacation after Ricardo graduates.*

When expressing "before" or "after," if the second verb indicates action to be performed by the subject of the first verb, an infinitive construction after a preposition is used instead of the subjunctive after *que* (see page 97).

INFINITIVE—SAME SUBJECT (*antes de*)
Comeremos antes de irnos.   *We'll eat before we leave.*
SUBJUNCTIVE—DIFFERENT SUBJECTS (*antes que*)
Comeremos antes que se vaya él.   *We'll eat before he leaves.*

INFINITIVE—SAME SUBJECT (*después de*)
Ella va a lavar los platos después de comer.   *She's going to wash the dishes after she eats.*
SUBJUNCTIVE—DIFFERENT SUBJECTS (*después que*)
Ella va a lavar los platos después que comamos.   *She's going to wash the dishes after we eat.*

✗ Comeremos antes que nos vamos.
✗ Comeremos antes que se va él.

- *hasta que*

Margarita va a estudiar hasta que tenga su doctorado.	*Margarita is going to study until she gets her doctorate.*

Expressing Conditions Required for the Occurrence of an Action

The subjunctive is used after certain expressions that indicate the conditions necessary for the occurrence of some other action.

- *siempre y cuando*

  Nos pagarán siempre y cuando terminemos el trabajo.

  They'll pay us if and when we finish the job.

- *siempre que*

  El niño puede ver televisión siempre que haga sus tareas primero.

  The boy can watch television as long as he does his homework first.

- *con tal (de) que*

  Te enseño a tocar la guitarra con tal de que me ayudes con la computadora.

  I'll teach you to play the guitar provided you help me with the computer.

When using *con tal*, if the second verb indicates action to be performed by the subject of the first verb, an infinitive construction is used after a preposition instead of the subjunctive after *que* (see page 97).

INFINITIVE—SAME SUBJECT (*con tal de*)

Iré contigo con tal de no tener que volver sola.

I'll go with you as long as I don't have to come back alone.

SUBJUNCTIVE—DIFFERENT SUBJECTS (*con tal (de) que*)

Iré contigo con tal de que vuelvas conmigo.

I'll go with you as long as you come back with me.

AVOID THE *Blunder*

✗ Nos pagarán siempre y cuando terminamos.
✗ El niño puede ver televisión siempre que hace sus tareas.
✗ Iré contigo con tal que no tengo que volver sola.

- *a menos que*

  Te llamaré a menos que no funcione mi celular.

  I'll call you unless my cell phone doesn't work.

- *en caso (de) que*

  Llévate el paraguas en caso de que llueva.

  Take your umbrella in case it rains.

Les voy a dar mi número en caso
de que necesiten algo.

*I'm going to give you all my
number in case you need
anything.*

Expressing Avoidance of Interference

The present subjunctive is used after *sin que* to indicate the avoidance
of interference with the action of the first verb.

Voy a leer la novela en clase sin
que la maestra se dé cuenta.

*I'm going to read the novel in
class without the teacher
noticing it.*

Ella va a salir con el chico sin que
su madre lo sepa.

*She's going to go out with the guy
without her mother knowing
about it.*

When using *sin*, if the second verb indicates action performed by the
subject of the first verb, an infinitive construction is used instead of the
subjunctive (see page 97).

INFINITIVE—SAME SUBJECT (*sin*)

Quiero practicar sin molestar
a nadie.

*I want to practice without
bothering anyone.*

SUBJUNCTIVE—DIFFERENT SUBJECTS (*sin que*)

Quiero practicar sin que nadie
me escuche.

*I want to practice without
anybody listening to me.*

Expressing Purpose of Action

The present subjunctive is used after *para que* and *a fin de que* to indicate the purpose of the action of the first verb.

Felipe le va a mandar un boleto
a su madre para que ella lo
visite.

*Felipe is going to send a ticket
to his mother so she can visit
him.*

Te doy la dirección de mi amigo
a fin de que puedas localizarlo
cuando llegues.

*I'll give you my friend's address
so that you can contact him
when you arrive.*

When expressing purpose, if the second verb indicates action performed by the subject of the first verb, an infinitive construction is used
instead of the subjunctive.

INFINITIVE—SAME SUBJECT (*para*)

Su mamá trabaja para poder
estudiar.

*His mother works so she can
study.*

SUBJUNCTIVE—DIFFERENT SUBJECTS (*para que*)

Su mamá trabaja para que él
pueda estudiar.

His mother works so he can study.

AVOID THE

✗ Su mamá trabaja para que (ella misma) pueda estudiar.
✗ Su mamá trabaja para que él puede estudiar.

Commands

The present subjunctive is used in the formation of some commands.

Review the forms in the chart on page 163.

Object pronouns are attached to the end of affirmative commands. An accent mark must be added to the stressed syllable of the verb.

Cómalo.	*Eat it.*
Abríguese.	*Put your coat on. (Wrap yourself up.)*
Dígaselo.	*Tell it to him.*
Váyanse de aquí.	*Get out of here.*

AVOID THE *Blunder*

Do not attach object pronouns to the verb in negative commands.

✗ no cómalo
✗ no siéntense
✗ no déselo

Affirmative commands of the verbs *ir* and *irse* in the *nosotros* form use the indicative instead of the subjunctive.

Vamos al cine.	*Let's go to the movies.*
Vámonos.	*Let's go./Let's leave.*

As an alternative to the *nosotros* command for other verbs, *vamos a* plus the infinitive can be used.

Comamos.
Vamos a comer. } *Let's eat.*

Sentémonos aquí.
Vamos a sentarnos aquí. } *Let's sit here.*

Negative commands of the verbs *ir* and *irse* use the subjunctive.

No vayamos al cine.	*Let's not go to the movies.*
No nos vayamos.	*Let's not leave.*

Exercises

A *Write the appropriate form—infinitive, indicative, or subjunctive—of the verb in parentheses.*

1. Buscamos una casa que _____ (tener) cuatro dormitorios.

2. Conozco a una persona que _____ (hablar) cinco idiomas.

3. No hay ningún postre que le _____ (gustar) a él.

4. El profesor nos exige que _____ (escribir) en español.

5. Por favor, no me _____ (llamar, tú) por la mañana.

6. Voy a buscar trabajo tan pronto como _____ (llegar) a la ciudad.

7. Estoy segura que _____ (venir, ellos) mañana.

8. Jaime no cree que lo _____ (aceptar, ellos) en la universidad.

9. Esperamos _____ (ir) a la reunión.

10. Esperamos que _____ (ir, ustedes) a la reunión.

B *Express the following in Spanish.*

1. *There's nobody who cooks like my mother.*

   _____

2. *We're looking for a manager who speaks Spanish.*

   _____

3. *I hope you come to the party.*

   _____

4. *She advises you to work harder.*

   _____

5. *It's wonderful that you're here!*

   _____

6. *He doubts that I can do it.*

   _____

7. *I'll call you as soon as I know the news.*

   _____

8. *I'll pick you up unless I have to work.*

_____

9. *She goes out without his knowing it.*

_____

10. *They'll save money so they can travel.*

_____

C *Write commands for the following situations.*

1. *Tell a child to come with you.*

_____ (venir)

2. *Tell someone you hardly know to please sit down.*

_____ (sentarse)

3. *Tell a group of people to stand up.*

_____ (levantarse)

4. *Suggest to your friends that you go to the movies.*

_____ (ir)

D *Now write the commands in Exercise C as negative commands.*

1. _____

2. _____

3. _____

4. _____

VERBS
the preterite perfect subjunctive

Formation

Present subjunctive of *haber* + past participle

The Present Subjunctive of *haber*

yo	haya	nosotros(-as)	hayamos
tú	hayas	vosotros(-as)	hayáis
usted/él/ella	haya		
ustedes/ellos/ellas	hayan		

Past Participle Formation

	-*ar* verbs	-*er* verbs	-*ir* verbs
Verb stem (infinitive minus -*ar*,/ -*er*,/ -*ir*) +	ado	-ido	-ido
	hablar	comer	vivir
	hablado	comido	vivido

IRREGULAR PARTICIPLES

abrir	abierto	**poner**	puesto
cubrir	cubierto	**oponer**	opuesto
descubrir	descubierto	**proponer**	propuesto
decir	dicho	**ver**	visto
predecir	predicho	**prever**	previsto
escribir	escrito	**volver**	vuelto
describir	descrito	**devolver**	devuelto
prescribir	prescrito	**revolver**	revuelto
hacer	hecho	**resolver**	resuelto
morir	muerto	**romper**	roto

Review the forms in the chart on the preceding page.

Note that the present subjunctive tense of *haber* is irregular. Be sure to learn the irregular past participle forms.

✗ que yo ha decido
✗ que él ha escribido

Uses of the Preterite Perfect Subjunctive

The preterite perfect subjunctive is used to express present or future emotion, doubt, hope, and other feelings about what may or may not have occurred in the past. It follows a "subjunctive signal" that is expressed in the present or future tense.

Expressing What Seems Not to Have Existed

The subjunctive is used to express what—at least for the speaker or writer—doesn't exist. The preterite perfect subjunctive describes that person or thing according to something that may or may not have occurred in the past.

No veo a nadie que haya estudiado conmigo el año pasado.

I don't see anybody who studied with me last year.

No hay ninguna receta aquí que haya sido comprobada en la cocina.

There isn't a single recipe here that's been kitchen-tested.

Do not forget the "personal *a*" before *nadie*.

✗ No veo nadie que haya estudiado conmigo.
✗ No conozco nadie que haya vivido aquí.

Expressing Desired Characteristics Based on Experience

Contrary to English usage, the subjunctive is used in Spanish to refer to someone who is needed by the subject, but who is as yet unknown to him or her. The preterite perfect subjunctive describes what kind of person this could be by telling what he or she has already done.

Necesito a alguien que haya vivido en ese pueblo.	*I need someone who has lived in that town.*
Busco un asistente que haya estudiado español.	*I'm looking for an assistant who has studied Spanish.*
Quiero un novio que haya empezado su carrera.	*I want a boyfriend who has already started his career.*

AVOID THE *Blunder*

Do not forget the "personal *a*" before *alguien*.

✗ Necesito alguien que haya vivido allí.

Do not use an indicative form, as you would in English. Use the subjunctive instead.

✗ Busco un asistente que ha estudiado español.
✗ Quiero un novio que ha empezado su carrera.

Expressing Other Desired Characteristics

The subjunctive in Spanish is also used to refer to something that is needed by the subject, but is as yet unknown to him or her. A passive construction in the preterite perfect subjunctive is used to describe what is desired according to what has been done to it.

Queremos un apartamento que haya sido pintado recientemente.	*We want an apartment that has been painted recently.*
Busco los exámenes que no hayan sido corregidos.	*I'm looking for the exams that haven't been corrected.*

AVOID THE *Blunder*

✗ Queremos un apartamento que ha sido pintado.
✗ Busco los exámenes que no han sido corregidos.

Expressing Hopes About a Past Event

The preterite perfect subjunctive is used when the subject indicates a hope or wish about a past event.

Esperamos que no hayan llegado tarde.	*We hope they didn't arrive late.*
Ojalá que no haya llovido.	*I hope it didn't rain.*

> **AVOID THE** *Blunder*
>
> Do not use a past indicative tense, as you would in English.
>
> ✗ Esperamos que no llegaron tarde.
> ✗ Ojalá que no llovió.

Expressing Present Feelings About the Past

The preterite perfect subjunctive is used when there is an expression of present feeling or emotion about a past occurrence.

Es fantástico que hayas estado aquí conmigo.	*It's fantastic that you were here with me.*
Es una lástima que se haya ido.	*It's a shame that he left.*
Me alegro que te hayas mejorado.	*I'm glad you got better.*
Siento mucho que no te haya gustado.	*I'm very sorry you didn't like it.*

> **AVOID THE** *Blunder*
>
> ✗ Es una lástima que se fue.
> ✗ Me alegro que te mejoraste.

When the second verb expresses an action performed by the subject of the first verb, an infinitive construction (*haber* + past participle) is used instead of the subjunctive.

ONE PERSON

Ella está contenta de haber estado aquí.	*She's glad she was here.*

TWO DIFFERENT PEOPLE

Ella está contenta que hayas estado aquí.	*She's glad you were here.*

ONE PERSON

Siento no haber podido visitarte.	*I'm sorry I couldn't visit you.*

TWO DIFFERENT PEOPLE

Siento que no hayas podido visitarme.	*I'm sorry you couldn't visit me.*

Expressing Present Doubt About Past Action

The preterite perfect subjunctive is used when there is a present expression of doubt, possibility, impossibility, probability, or improbability about what occurred in the past.

No creo que Julia haya ido a la fiesta.	*I don't think Julia went to the party.*
No estoy segura que haya sido Martín.	*I'm not sure it was Martín.*
Es imposible que haya ocurrido eso.	*It's not possible that that happened.*
Dudo que haya sido muy buen curso.	*I doubt that it was a very good course.*

AVOID THE *Blunder*

When there is present doubt about a past occurrence, do not use a past indicative tense, as you would in English.

✗ No creo que Julia fue a la fiesta.
✗ No estoy segura que era Martín.

Expressing Possibility of Occurrence

The preterite perfect subjunctive is used after the following expressions to indicate what may or may not have happened at some future time.

- *siempre y cuando*

Nos pagarán siempre y cuando hayamos terminado el trabajo.	*They'll pay us only when we have finished the job.*

- *con tal (de) que*

El abogado lo va a ayudar con tal que le haya dicho toda la verdad.	*The lawyer is going to help him provided he has told him the whole truth.*

- *a menos que*

Puedes ver la televisión después de cenar a menos que no hayas hecho tus tareas.	*You can watch television after dinner unless you haven't done your homework.*

- *en caso de que*

He hecho una sopa en caso de que no hayas comido.	*I made soup in case you haven't eaten.*

- *hasta que*

Me quedaré en la casa de mis padres hasta que haya encontrado trabajo.	*I'll stay at my parents' house until I have found a job.*

Do not use the indicative with these expressions, as you would in English.

✗ Llámame cuando has solucionado el problema.
✗ Vamos a empezar en cuanto todos se han sentado.
✗ El abogado lo va a ayudar con tal que le ha dicho toda la verdad.
✗ Me quedaré en la casa de mis padres hasta que he encontrado trabajo.

Expressing Completion of Future Action

The preterite perfect subjunctive is used after *cuando, en cuanto,* and *tan pronto como* to indicate when future action will have been completed.

- *cuando*

Llámame cuando hayas solucionado el problema.	*Call me when you have solved the problem.*
Vamos a celebrar cuando ellas se hayan graduado.	*We'll celebrate when they have graduated.*

- *en cuanto*

Vamos a empezar en cuanto todos se hayan sentado.	*We're going to start as soon as everybody has sat down.*

- *tan pronto como*

Ella se casará tan pronto como su novio haya empezado a trabajar.	*She will get married as soon as her boyfriend has started to work.*

The preterite perfect subjunctive is used after the following expressions when the verb in the first clause expresses future action and the subject of the second clause is different from that of the first. When the action is to be performed by the subject of the first verb, there is no *que* and an infinitive construction (*haber* + past participle) is used instead.

INFINITIVE—ONE PERSON (*con tal de*)
Iré contigo al cine con tal de haber arreglado el coche. — *I'll go to the movies with you provided I have fixed the car.*

SUBJUNCTIVE—TWO DIFFERENT PEOPLE (*con tal (de) que*)
Iré contigo al cine con tal que hayas arreglado el coche. — *I'll go to the movies with you provided you have fixed the car.*

INFINITIVE—ONE PERSON (*antes de*)

Ella lo sabrá antes de haber salido.	*She'll find out before she has left.*

SUBJUNCTIVE—TWO DIFFERENT PEOPLE (*antes que*)

Lo sabremos antes que haya salido mi hermano.	*We'll find out before my brother has left.*

INFINITIVE—ONE PERSON (*después de*)

Ella va a lavar los platos después de haber terminado de comer.	*She's going to wash the dishes after she has finished eating.*

SUBJUNCTIVE—TWO DIFFERENT PEOPLE (*después que*)

Ella va a lavar los platos después que hayamos terminado de comer.	*She's going to wash the dishes after we have finished eating.*

AVOID THE *Blunder*

Use the infinitive when the subjects are the same. Use the subjunctive when they are different.

✗ Ella lo sabrá antes que ha salido.
✗ Lo sabremos antes que ha salido mi hermano.

Exercise

A Fill in the blanks with the correct form of the verb in parentheses.

1. Carmen busca una asistente que _____ (estudiar) español por más de dos años.

2. No hay nadie aquí que _____ (terminar) sus estudios.

3. Nos alegra que _____ (poder, tú) visitarnos la semana pasada.

4. Siento mucho no _____ (poder) atenderte ayer.

5. Iré de compras con tal que mi jefe me _____ (pagar).

VERBS
the imperfect subjunctive

Formation

Stem (*ellos* form of the preterite minus *-ron*) + endings

INFINITIVE	3PL. PRETERITE	IMPERFECT SUBJUNCTIVE STEM
hablar	hablaron	habla-
comer	comieron	comie-
escribir	escribieron	escribie-
dormir	durmieron	durmie-
tener	tuvieron	tuvie-
ir	fueron	fue-

Endings

yo	-ra	nosotros(-as)	-ramos
tú	-ras	vosotros(-as)	-rais
usted/él/ella	-ra		
ustedes/ellos/ellas	-ran		

ALTERNATIVE ENDINGS

yo	-se	nosotros(-as)	-semos
tú	-ses	vosotros(-as)	-seis
usted/él/clla	-se		
ustedes/ellos/ellas	-sen		

The Imperfect Subjunctive of Pattern 1 Verbs

-*ar* VERBS

hablar

hablara	habláramos	OR	hablase	hablásemos
hablaras	hablarais		hablases	hablaseis
hablara			hablase	
hablaran			hablasen	

184

-*er* VERBS

comer

comiera	comiéramos	OR	comiese	comiésemos
comieras	comierais		comieses	comiesen
comiera			comiese	
comieran			comiesen	

leer

leyera	leyéramos	OR	leyese	leyésemos
leyeras	leyerais		leyeses	leyeseis
leyera			leyese	
leyeran			leyesen	

-*ir* VERBS

escribir

escribiera	escribiéramos	OR	escribiese	escribiésemos
escribieras	escribierais		escribieses	escribieseis
escribiera			escribiese	
escribieran			escribiesen	

-*ir* STEM-CHANGING VERBS

dormir

durmiera	durmiéramos	OR	durmiese	durmiésemos
durmieras	durmierais		durmieses	durmieseis
durmiera			durmiese	
durmieran			durmiesen	

The Imperfect Subjunctive of Pattern 2 Verbs

tener

tuviera	tuviéramos	OR	tuviese	tuviésemos
tuvieras	tuvierais		tuvieses	tuvieseis
tuviera			tuviese	
tuvieran			tuviesen	

ir

fuera	fuéramos	OR	fuese	fuésemos
fueras	fuerais		fueses	fueseis
fuera			fuese	
fueran			fuesen	

Review the forms in the charts on the preceding pages.

To form the imperfect subjunctive in Spanish, begin with the third-person plural form of the preterite indicative tense, delete the *-ron* ending, and add the endings *-ra*, *-ras*, etc.

Keep in mind the various irregularities in the formation of the preterite tense.

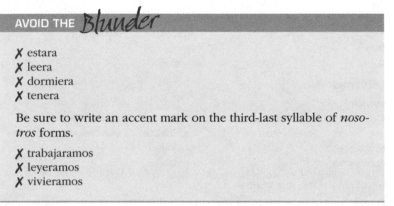

AVOID THE *Blunder*

✗ estara
✗ leera
✗ dormiera
✗ tenera

Be sure to write an accent mark on the third-last syllable of *nosotros* forms.

✗ trabajaramos
✗ leyeramos
✗ vivieramos

Uses of the Imperfect Subjunctive

Review expressions that trigger the use of the subjunctive (see pages 158–160).

A subjunctive signal expressed in the imperfect or preterite tense is followed by a clause in the imperfect subjunctive that refers to a past action or situation.

Expressing What Seemed Not to Exist

The imperfect subjunctive in Spanish is used to indicate that—for the speaker—something or someone did not exist.

No había ningún trabajo que me interesara.	*There was no job that interested me.*
No vi nada que me gustara.	*I didn't see anything I liked.*
No había nadie que me comprendiera.	*There was nobody who understood me.*
No existía nadie que cocinara mejor.	*There was nobody who cooked better.*

Expressing Desired Characteristics

The imperfect subjunctive is used to describe the characteristics that were desired in someone or something, but the actual person or object sought was as yet unknown.

Buscaba/Busqué un asistente que hablara español.	*I was looking for/looked for an assistant who spoke Spanish.*
Queríamos una casa que tuviera piscina.	*We wanted a house that had a swimming pool.*
Germán necesitaba un trabajo que le pagara bien.	*Germán needed a job that paid him well.*

AVOID THE *Blunder*

Do not use a past indicative tense in the second clause, as you would in English.

✗ Buscaba un asistente que hablaba español.
✗ Queríamos una casa que tenía piscina,

■ The "personal *a*," indicating that the direct object is a person, is not used when the person was as yet unknown.

INDICATIVE

Necesitaba a mi novio, quien me comprendía.	*I needed my boyfriend, who understood me.*

SUBJUNCTIVE

Necesitaba un novio que me comprendiera.	*I needed (to find) a boyfriend who understood me.*

Nevertheless, the "personal *a*" is used before *alguien* and *nadie* when they are direct objects, even if they were unknown.

Buscaba a alguien que me pudiera ayudar.	*I was looking for somebody who could help me.*
No encontré a nadie que supiera hacer esto.	*I didn't find anybody who knew how to do this.*

Expressing Desire for Action

The imperfect subjunctive is used when the subject expresses a past desire for action by another person or other people.

Yo quería que estudiaras.	*I wanted you to study.*
María prefería que te fueras.	*María wanted you to leave.*

| Esperábamos que no llegaran tarde. | *We hoped they wouldn't arrive late.* |
| Mis padres preferían que trabajara con ellos. | *My parents preferred that I work with them.* |

When the action of the second verb is to be performed by the subject of the first verb, an infinitive construction is used instead of the subjunctive.

INFINITIVE—SAME SUBJECT

| Quería estudiar. | *I wanted to study.* |

SUBJUNCTIVE—DIFFERENT SUBJECTS

| Quería que estudiaras. | *I wanted you to study.* |

INFINITIVE—SAME SUBJECT

| (Ella) esperaba ser médico. | *She hoped to be a doctor.* |

SUBJUNCTIVE—DIFFERENT SUBJECTS

| (Ella) esperaba que (él) fuera médico. | *She hoped he would be a doctor.* |

AVOID THE *Blunder*

✗ (Yo) quería que yo estudiara.
✗ Yo quería que tú estudiar.
✗ Ella esperaba que él sería médico.
✗ Ella esperaba que (ella misma) fuera médico.

Expressing Attempt to Control an Action

The imperfect subjunctive is used to indicate an attempt in the past to control the actions of others.

The subject has one of several different intentions:

- To report a past request

Te pedí que me acompañaras.	*I asked you to go with me.*
Les rogaba que me dejaran ir.	*I begged you all to let me go.*
Me suplicaba que lo perdonara.	*He begged me to forgive him.*
Le imploró que tuviera paciencia.	*He begged her to be patient.*

- To report past advice

El consejero me recomendó que estudiara un idioma.	*The counselor recommended that I study a language.*
Yo te sugerí que fueras a casa.	*I suggested that you go home.*
El médico le aconsejó que perdiera peso.	*The doctor advised her to lose weight.*

Do not use the infinitive to indicate requests or to give advice.

✗ Pedí a ti acompañarme.
✗ Sugerí a ti ir a casa.

- To report a past demand

El jefe nos exigió que trabajáramos.	*The boss demanded that we work.*
La maestra le mandó que se sentara.	*The teacher ordered him to sit down.*
El oficial les ordenó que marcharan.	*The officer ordered them to march.*
Mi madre me dijo que la ayudara.	*My mother told me to help her.*

This construction is an alternative to the infinitive construction described on page 99. Both patterns are correct.

- To report a past prohibition

ENGLISH PATTERN   subject + past tense verb + direct object
+ infinitive

SPANISH PATTERN   subject + indirect object
+ preterite or imperfect indicative verb
+ *que* + verb in imperfect subjunctive

Sus padres les prohibieron que se casaran.	*Their parents forbade them to marry.*
El guardia nos impedía que entráramos.	*The guard stopped us from entering.*

This construction is an alternative to the infinitive construction described on page 99. Both patterns are correct.

Expressing Past Feelings About Past Action

The imperfect subjunctive is used when there is an expression of past personal feeling or emotion about a fact.

Fue fantástico que estuvieras aquí conmigo.	*It was fantastic that you were here with me.*
Fue una lástima que se mudara.	*It was a shame that he moved away.*
Me alegraba mucho de que te sintieras mejor.	*I was so glad you felt better.*
Sentía mucho que no te gustara.	*I was sorry you didn't like it.*

When the second verb indicates an action performed by the subject of the first verb, an infinitive construction is used instead of the subjunctive.

INFINITIVE—SAME SUBJECT
Estaba contenta de estar allí. *I was glad to be there.*
SUBJUNCTIVE—DIFFERENT SUBJECTS
Estaba contenta que estuvieras allí. *I was glad you were there.*

INFINITIVE—SAME SUBJECT
Sentía no poder visitarte. *I was sorry I couldn't visit you.*
SUBJUNCTIVE—DIFFERENT SUBJECTS
Sentía que no vinieras a visitarme. *I was sorry you didn't come to visit me.*

AVOID THE *Blunder*

✗ (Yo) estaba contenta que yo estuviera allí.
✗ Yo sentía que no pudiera visitarte.

Expressing Past Doubt

The imperfect subjunctive is used to indicate doubt, possibility, impossibility, probability, or improbability in the past.

INDICATIVE
Creía que Julia venía mañana. *I thought Julia was coming tomorrow.*

SUBJUNCTIVE
No creía que Julia viniera. *I didn't think Julia was coming.*

INDICATIVE
Estaba segura de que era Martín. *I was sure it was Martín.*
SUBJUNCTIVE
No estaba segura de que fuera Martín. *I wasn't sure it was Martín.*

INDICATIVE
Fue cierto que era su novio. *It was certain that he was her boyfriend.*

SUBJUNCTIVE
Fue imposible que fuera su novio. *It wasn't possible that he was her boyfriend.*

INDICATIVE
No había duda de que fue un buen curso. *There was no doubt that it was a good course.*
SUBJUNCTIVE
Dudaba que fuera buen curso. *I doubted it was a good course.*

AVOID THE *Blunder*

Use the indicative to indicate certainty, the subjunctive to indicate uncertainty.

✗ Creía que Julia viniera mañana.
✗ Estaba segura que fuera Martín.
✗ No creía que Julia venía.
✗ No estaba segura de que fue Martín.

Expressing the Time of a Later Action

The imperfect subjunctive is used after certain expressions that indicate the time of later action.

- *cuando* when it refers to later action

Te iba a llamar cuando no estuvieras ocupada.	*I was going to call you when you weren't busy.*
Se lo iba a decir cuando llegara a casa.	*I was going to tell him when he got home.*

When *cuando* indicates simultaneous action in the past, it is followed by a verb in the imperfect indicative.

Siempre me llamabas cuando estaba ocupada.	*You always called me when I was busy.*
Ella siempre me traía flores cuando venía a mi casa.	*She always brought me flowers when she came to my house.*

AVOID THE *Blunder*

✗ Te iba a llamar cuando no estabas ocupada.
✗ Se lo iba a decir cuando llegaba a casa.
✗ Siempre me llamabas cuando estuviera ocupada.
✗ Ella siempre me traía flores cuando viniera a mi casa.

- *en cuanto* and *tan pronto como*

Íbamos a empezar en cuanto vinieran los otros.	*We were going to start as soon as the others got here.*
Ella se iba a casar tan pronto como se graduara.	*She was going to get married as soon as she graduated.*

- *antes que* and *después que*

Ricardo se graduó antes que su hermana empezara a estudiar.	*Ricardo graduated before his sister began her studies.*
Fuimos de vacaciones después que Ricardo se graduara.	*We went on vacation after Ricardo graduated.*

When expressing "before" or "after," if the second verb indicates action to be performed by the subject of the first verb, an infinitive construction is used instead of the subjunctive.

INFINITIVE—SAME SUBJECT (*antes de*)

Comimos antes de salir de casa.	*We ate before we left home.*

SUBJUNCTIVE—DIFFERENT SUBJECTS (*antes que*)

Comimos antes que se fuera mi hermano.	*We ate before my brother left.*

INFINITIVE—SAME SUBJECT (*después de*)

Ella lavó los platos después de comer.	*She washed the dishes after she ate.*

SUBJUNCTIVE—DIFFERENT SUBJECTS (*después que*)

Ella lavó los platos después que comiéramos.	*She washed the dishes after we ate.*

AVOID THE *Blunder*

✗ Comimos antes que salimos de casa.
✗ Ella lavó los platos después que comió.
✗ Comimos antes que se fue mi hermano.
✗ Ella lavó los platos después que comimos.

- *hasta que*

Ricardo estudió hasta que supiera todos los datos importantes.	*Ricardo studied until he knew all the important facts.*

Expressing Conditions Necessary for the Occurrence of an Action

The imperfect subjunctive is used to indicate the conditions that were necessary for the occurrence of some other action.

- *siempre y cuando*

Nos pagaban siempre y cuando termináramos el trabajo.	*They paid us if and when we finished the job.*

- *con tal (de) que*

Le enseñaba a tocar la guitarra con tal de que me ayudara con la computadora.	*I taught him to play the guitar on the condition that he help me with the computer.*

When using *con tal*, if the second verb indicates action to be performed by the subject of the first verb, an infinitive construction is used instead of the subjunctive.

INFINITIVE—SAME SUBJECT (*con tal de*)

La ayudaba con su tarea con tal de repasar un poco las lecciones.	*He helped her with her homework so he could review the lessons a bit.*

SUBJUNCTIVE—DIFFERENT SUBJECTS (*con tal (de) que*)

La ayudaba con su tarea con tal de que ella le prestara su coche.	*He helped her with her homework provided she would lend him her car.*

INFINITIVE—SAME SUBJECT (*con tal de*)

Trabajaba mucho con tal de ganar dinero.	*He worked a lot in order to earn money.*

SUBJUNCTIVE—DIFFERENT SUBJECTS (*con tal (de) que*)

Trabajaba mucho con tal de que su hija pudiera estudiar.	*He worked a lot so that his daughter could study.*

AVOID THE *Blunder*

✗ La ayudaba con su tarea con tal de que podía repasar las lecciones.
✗ Trabajaba mucho con tal de que podía ganar dinero.

- *a menos que*

Siempre me llamaba a las ocho a menos que no funcionara su celular.	*He always called me at eight unless his cell phone wasn't working.*

- *en caso (de) que*

Las chicas llevaron el paraguas en caso que lloviera.	*The girls took the umbrella in case it rained.*
Les di mi número en caso de que necesitaran algo.	*I gave them my number in case they needed something.*

Expressing Past Avoidance of Interference

The imperfect subjunctive is used after *sin que* to indicate the avoidance of interference with an action in the past.

Iba a leer la novela en clase sin que la maestra se diera cuenta.	*I was going to read the novel in class without the teacher noticing it.*
Ella salió con el chico sin que su madre lo supiera.	*She went out with the guy without her mother finding out.*

When using *sin*, if the second verb indicates action performed by the subject of the first verb, an infinitive construction is used instead of the subjunctive.

INFINITIVE—SAME SUBJECT (*sin*)

Quería practicar sin molestar a nadie.	*I wanted to practice without bothering anyone.*

SUBJUNCTIVE—DIFFERENT SUBJECTS (*sin que*)

Quería practicar sin que nadie me molestara.	*I wanted to practice without being bothered by anyone.*

AVOID THE *Blunder*

✗ Quería practicar sin molestando a nadie.

Expressing Past Purpose

The imperfect subjunctive is used after *para que* and *a fin de que* to indicate the purpose of the action of the first verb, which is in a past tense.

Felipe le mandó un boleto a su madre para que ella lo visitara.	*Felipe sent his mother a ticket so she could visit him.*
Te di la dirección de mi amigo a fin de que pudieras localizarlo cuando llegaras.	*I gave you my friend's address so you could contact him when you arrived.*

When expressing purpose, if the second verb indicates action performed by the subject of the first verb, an infinitive construction is used instead of the subjunctive.

INFINITIVE—SAME SUBJECT (*para*)

Su mamá trabajaba para poder estudiar.	*His mother worked so she could study.*

SUBJUNCTIVE—DIFFERENT SUBJECTS (*para que*)

Su mamá trabajaba para que él pudiera estudiar.	*His mother worked so he could study.*

AVOID THE *Blunder*

✗ Su mamá trabajaba para que (ella misma) podía estudiar.
✗ Su mamá trabajaba para que él podía estudiar.

Expressing What Appears to Be True

The imperfect subjunctive is used after *como si* to indicate an action or situation that appears to be true but isn't.

Ellos lo tratan como si fuera su hijo.	*They treat him as if he were their son.*
Habla de la actriz como si la conociera.	*He talks about the actress as if he knew her.*
La chica sonríe como si no tuviera tantos problemas.	*The girl smiles as if she didn't have so many problems.*

Expressing Wishes

The imperfect subjunctive is used after *ojalá (que)* to indicate a wish that something were true at the present time.

Ojalá que estuvieras aquí.	*I wish you were here.*
Ojalá no lloviera tanto.	*I wish it didn't rain so much.*

Expressing "If Only"

The imperfect subjunctive is used after *si* to express the notion "if something were true." A conditional clause, telling what would happen in such a case, usually accompanies this construction (see pages 153–154).

Si estuvieras aquí, nos divertiríamos.	*If you were here, we would have fun.*
Si tuviera un coche, iría a la playa.	*If I had a car, I would go to the beach.*
Si pudieras viajar a Sudamérica, ¿a qué país irías primero?	*If you could travel to South America, what country would you go to first?*
Si fueras rico, ¿qué harías con el dinero?	*If you were rich, what would you do with the money?*

AVOID THE *Blunder*

✗ Si podrías viajar...
✗ Si podías viajar...
✗ Si eras rico...

Expressing a Polite Request

The imperfect subjunctive of *querer* is used to make a polite request.

Quisiera hacerle una pregunta.	*I would like to ask you a question.*
Quisiéramos hablar con el médico.	*We would like to speak with the doctor.*

Exercises

 Circle the most appropriate form of the verb in each of the following sentences.

1. Mi hermana quería encontrar un hombre que **tuviera | tenía | haya tenido | tiene** buen trabajo.

2. Les pedí que me **acompañaron | acompañaran | acompañaban | hayan acompañado** a casa.

3. El gerente le sugirió a Antonio que **solicitaba | solicitó | haya solicitado | solicitara** un puesto en la compañía.

4. Íbamos a salir en cuanto nuestro amigo nos **llame | llamaba | llamara | haya llamado** por teléfono.

 Fill in the blanks with the appropriate form of the verb in parentheses.

1. Sus padres preferían que ella _____ (estudiar) medicina.

2. Pablo fue al cine para _____ (ver) la nueva película cubana.

3. Guardé el periódico para que tú _____ (leer) el artículo sobre tu amigo.

C *Write a sentence that indicates what would happen if the first sentence in each item below were true.*

> EXAMPLE   No tengo dinero. (compro un coche)
> *Si tuviera dinero, compraría un coche.*

1. No lo quiero. (me caso con él)

_____

2. Él no me llama todas las noches. (no contesto el teléfono)

_____

3. No quieres tocar el piano. (practicas todos los días)

_____

4. Mi papá no está aquí. (me ayuda)

_____

VERBS
the pluperfect subjunctive

Formation

Imperfect subjunctive of *haber* + past participle

The Pluperfect Subjunctive of *haber*

yo	hubiera	nosotros(-as)	hubiéramos
tú	hubieras	vosotros(-as)	hubierais
usted/él/ella	hubiera		
ustedes/ellos/ellas	hubieran		

Past Participle Formation

	-*ar* verbs	-*er* verbs	-*ir* verbs
Verb stem (infinitive minus -*ar*/-*er*/-*ir*) +	-ado	-ido	-ido
	hablar	**comer**	**vivir**
	hablado	comido	vivido

IRREGULAR PARTICIPLES

abrir	abierto	**poner**	puesto
cubrir	cubierto	**oponer**	opuesto
descubrir	descubierto	**proponer**	propuesto
decir	dicho	**ver**	visto
predecir	predicho	**prever**	previsto
escribir	escrito	**volver**	vuelto
describir	descrito	**devolver**	devuelto
prescribir	prescrito	**revolver**	revuelto
hacer	hecho	**resolver**	resuelto
morir	muerto	**romper**	roto

Review the forms in the chart on the preceding page.

AVOID THE *Blunder*

Be sure to learn the irregular past participle forms.

✗ hubiera oponido
✗ hubiéramos veído

Uses of the Pluperfect Subjunctive

Expressing "If Only" Concerning Past Action

The pluperfect subjunctive in Spanish is used to express "if something had been true" in the past. A clause with a verb in the conditional perfect, indicating what would have occurred in such a case, usually accompanies this construction. (See page 156.)

Si tú me hubieras llamado, yo te habría ayudado.	*If you had called me, I would have helped you.*
Si yo lo hubiera visto, lo habría saludado.	*If I had seen him, I would have said hello.*

AVOID THE *Blunder*

Do not use the pluperfect indicative tense, as you would in English.

✗ Si me habías llamado...
✗ Si lo había visto...

Using the Pluperfect Subjunctive as an Alternative to the Conditional Perfect

The pluperfect subjunctive can be used as an alternative to the conditional perfect.

Si tú me hubieras llamado, yo te hubiera ayudado.	*If you had called me, I would have helped you.*
Si yo lo hubiera visto, lo hubiera saludado.	*If I had seen him, I would have said hello.*

Expressing "Should Have"

The pluperfect subjunctive can be used to express "should have."

¡Hubieras visto lo que pasó!   *You should have seen what*
                                          happened!

Uds. hubieran estado en clase   *You guys should have been in*
  hoy.   *class today.*

Exercise

A   *Change the following sentences to indicate what would have happened if the first part had been true.*

1. No lo quería. (me casé con él)

_____

2. Él no me llamaba todas las noches. (no contestaba el teléfono)

_____

3. No quisiste tocar el piano. (practicabas todos los días)

_____

4. Mi papá no estuvo aquí. (me ayudó)

_____

REPORTED SPEECH

Reported-speech expressions are used to relate someone's words without using a direct quote.

Expressing "Say"

Decir without an indirect object usually means "to say." In Spanish, as in English, when reporting what someone "says," the tense used in the original statement is also used in the reported-speech expression. When reporting what someone "said," a past tense is used.

The indicative is used to report what someone says or said. The subjunctive is used to report what someone tells or told someone else to do.

TENSE OF ORIGINAL QUOTE	TENSE AFTER *dice que*	TENSE AFTER *dijo que*
INDICATIVE		
PRESENT	PRESENT	IMPERFECT
"Trabajo duro". *"I work hard."*	Dice que trabaja duro. *He says he works hard.*	Dijo que trabajaba duro. *He said he worked hard.*
"Voy a trabajar duro". *"I'm going to work hard."*	Dice que va a trabajar duro. *He says he's going to work hard.*	Dijo que iba a trabajar duro. *He said he was going to work hard.*
FUTURE	FUTURE	CONDITIONAL
"Trabajaré duro". *"I'll work hard."*	Dice que trabajará duro. *He says he will work hard.*	Dijo que trabajaría duro. *He said he would work hard.*
PRETERITE PERFECT	PRETERITE PERFECT	PLUPERFECT
"He trabajado duro". *"I worked hard."*	Dice que ha trabajado duro. *He says he has worked hard.*	Dijo que había trabajado duro. *He said he had worked hard.*

TENSE OF ORIGINAL QUOTE	TENSE AFTER *dice que*	TENSE AFTER *dijo que*
IMPERFECT	IMPERFECT	IMPERFECT
"Trabajaba duro". *"I worked hard."*	Dice que trabajaba duro. *He says he worked hard.*	Dijo que trabajaba duro. *He said he worked hard.*
PRETERITE	PRETERITE	PLUPERFECT
"Trabajé duro". *"I worked hard."*	Dice que trabajó duro. *He says he worked hard.*	Dijo que había trabajado duro. *He said he had worked hard.*
COMMAND		
IMPERATIVE	PRESENT SUBJUNCTIVE	IMPERFECT SUBJUNCTIVE
"¡Trabaje duro!" *"Work hard!"*	Me dice que trabaje duro. *He tells me to work hard.*	Me dijo que trabajara duro. *He told me to work hard.*

AVOID THE Blunder

In English, "that" is optional in reported speech: "He says he worked hard. / He says that he worked hard." In Spanish, *que* is not optional.

✗ Dice va a trabajar.
✗ Dijo trabajaba.

Remember that in Spanish, if the ending punctuation is a period or comma, it is placed after the quotation marks. In English it is enclosed within the quotation marks.

✗ "Trabajé duro."

Expressing "Ask"

Preguntar and *pedir* are both translated as "ask" and are both used with an indirect object pronoun. They follow the same patterns of reported speech as *decir*.

■ *Preguntar* is used to ask a question and is followed by a verb in the indicative.

□ Questions seeking information are expressed by using *preguntar* + question words (*qué, quién, dónde, cuánto, cuándo, cómo,* and *por qué*). (See pages 231–253.)

Me pregunta qué voy a hacer.	*He asks me what I'm going to do.*
Me preguntó qué iba a hacer.	*He asked me what I was going to do.*

Les pregunto dónde viven.	*I ask them where they live.*
Les pregunté dónde vivían.	*I asked them where they lived.*
Le pregunta cuánto costó.	*He asks her how much it cost.*
Le preguntó cuánto había costado.	*He asked her how much it (had) cost.*
Les preguntamos cuándo saldrán.	*We ask them when they'll leave.*
Les preguntamos cuándo saldrían.	*We asked them when they would leave.*
Me preguntan cómo lo hacía.	*They ask me how I did it.*
Me preguntaban cómo lo hacía.	*They asked me how I did it.*
Les pregunto por qué lo han hecho.	*I ask them why they did it.*
Les pregunté por qué lo habían hecho.	*I asked them why they had done it.*

AVOID THE *Blunder*

Do not forget the accent mark in the question word.

✗ Les pregunto donde viven.
✗ Me pregunta que voy a hacer.

☐ Yes-or-no questions are expressed by using *preguntar + si.*

Le pregunto si vive cerca.	*I ask him if he lives nearby.*
Le pregunté si vivía cerca.	*I asked him if he lived nearby.*
Me preguntan si hablo español.	*They ask me if I speak Spanish.*
Me preguntaron si hablaba español.	*They asked me if I spoke Spanish.*
Les pregunta si trabajarán allá.	*He asks them if they plan to work there.*
Les preguntó si trabajarían allá.	*He asked them if they would work there.*

AVOID THE *Blunder*

When reporting what someone "asks," use the same tense as in the original question. When reporting what someone "asked," use a past tense.

✗ Le pregunté si vive cerca.
✗ Me preguntaron si hablo español.

■ *Pedir* is used to ask a favor and is followed by *que* + a verb in the subjunctive.

Me pide que lo acompañe.	*He asks me to go with him.*
Me pidió que lo acompañara.	*He asked me to go with him.*
Les pido que me disculpen.	*I ask them to forgive me.*
Les pedí que me disculparan.	*I asked them to forgive me.*
Les pide que la corrijan.	*She asks them to correct her.*
Les pidió que la corrigieran.	*She asked them to correct her.*
Nos piden que no hablemos.	*They ask us not to talk.*
Nos pidieron que no habláramos.	*They asked us not to talk.*

AVOID THE *Blunder*

Do not confuse "ask a question" with "ask a favor."

✗ Te pedí dónde vives.
✗ Me pregunta acompañarlo.
✗ Les pregunto disculparme.

Exercise

A Change the following sentences from direct quotes to reported speech.

1. PACO: "Quiero ir al cine".

   Paco dice que _____.

   Paco dijo que _____.

2. MARÍA: "Fuimos al cine ayer".

   María dice que _____.

   María dijo que _____.

3. PACO: "Por favor, María, ayúdame con la computadora".

   Paco le pide a María que _____.

   Paco le pidió a María que _____.

4. MARÍA: "¿Vas a estar en casa esta tarde?"

   María le pregunta a Paco si _____.

   María le preguntó a Paco si _____.

SUBJECTS, OBJECTS, AND THEIR PRONOUNS

Subject Pronouns

I	yo	*we*	nosotros/nosotras
you	tú/usted	*you all*	vosotros/vosotras/ustedes
he	él	*they*	ellos/ellas
she	ella		
it	él/ella		

Object Pronouns

AFTER PREPOSITIONS

me	mí*	*us*	nosotros/nosotras
you	ti*/usted	*you all*	vosotros/vosotras/ustedes
him	él	*them*	ellos/ellas
her	ella		
it	él/ella	*conmigo; contigo.	

REFLEXIVE

me/myself	me	*us/ourselves*	nos
you/yourself	te/se	*you/yourselves*	os/se
him/himself	se	*them/themselves*	se
her/herself	se		
it/itself	se		

DIRECT OBJECT

me	me	*us*	nos
you	te/lo/la	*you all*	os/los/las
him	lo	*them*	los/las
her	la		
it	lo/la		

INDIRECT OBJECT

me	me	*us*	nos
you	te/le	*you all*	os/les
him	le	*them*	les
her	le		

Review the forms in the chart on the preceding page.

Subjects

■ Subjects can be nouns, pronouns, or infinitives.

In English and in Spanish, singular noun subjects, except for proper first names, are always preceded by an article or other determiner.

El libro está en la mesa.	*The book is on the table.*
La comida está lista.	*The meal is ready.*
María es simpática.	*María is nice.*
Mario está aquí.	*Mario is here.*

In Spanish, but not in English, names with a title are preceded by an article (see page 56).

El Sr. Gómez está aquí.	*Mr. Gómez is here.*
La señora Sánchez no está aquí.	*Mrs. Sánchez isn't here.*
La Dra. Campos es buena.	*Dr. Campos is good.*
La señorita Martínez es la jefa.	*Miss Martinez is the boss.*

AVOID THE *Blunder*

✗ Sr. Gómez está aquí.
✗ Señora Sánchez no está aquí.

In English, plural and noncount noun subjects are not preceded by "the" when all members of the noun class are intended. In Spanish, noun subjects are always preceded by an article or other determiner (see pages 53–79).

ENGLISH PATTERN — + plural or noncount noun

SPANISH PATTERN *el/la* + noncount noun
los/las + plural noun

La leche es buena fuente de calcio.	*Milk is a good source of calcium.*
El tiempo vuela.	*Time flies.*
Las ventanas son de vidrio.	*Windows are made of glass.*
Los hombres son todos iguales.	*Men are all alike.*

AVOID THE *Blunder*

✗ Leche es buena fuente de calcio.
✗ Tiempo vuela.
✗ Ventanas son de vidrio.

The definite article *el* is optional before an infinitive subject (see page 100).

(El) vivir aquí es difícil.	*Living here is hard.*
(El) saber español lo ayudará.	*Knowing Spanish will help him.*

In Spanish, pronouns are used as subjects only for emphasis or clarification. The subject of the sentence is expressed in the conjugated ending of the verb (see individual verb tenses).

■ To determine the subject of a sentence, first find the conjugated ending of the verb, then match it with the corresponding noun or pronoun, which may be in a previous sentence.

ENGLISH PATTERN   I/you/he/she/it/we/they + verb

SPANISH PATTERN   (subject pronoun) + verb with subject ending

NORMAL STATEMENT
Voy a pagar la cuenta.	*I'm going to pay the bill.*

STATEMENT WITH EMPHASIS ON THE SUBJECT
Yo voy a pagar la cuenta.	*I (not you) am going to pay the bill.*

NORMAL STATEMENT
Viene mañana.	*She's coming tomorrow.*

STATEMENT WITH EMPHASIS ON THE SUBJECT
Ella viene mañana.	*She (not someone else) is coming tomorrow.*

NORMAL STATEMENT
La visitamos con frecuencia.	*We visit her often.*

STATEMENT WITH EMPHASIS ON THE SUBJECT
Nosotros la visitamos con frecuencia.	*We (others may not) visit her often.*

AVOID THE *Blunder*

Do not keep repeating subject pronouns. Once it is established who you are talking about, use the pronoun only for emphasis— the equivalent in English of underlining the word or saying it louder.

✗ Yo soy Ana. Yo soy de Nueva York y ahora yo vivo en Chicago. Yo trabajo en un restaurante.

✗ Elena es mi amiga. Ella vive muy cerca de mi casa y ella trabaja en la misma parte de la ciudad que yo.

■ The Spanish subject is not necessarily at the beginning of a sentence.

| ENGLISH PATTERN | subject + verb + object + adverb |
| | John   calls   me   every day. |

| SPANISH PATTERN 1 | subject + object + verb + adverb |
| | *Juan   me   llama   todos los días.* |

| SPANISH PATTERN 2 | object + verb + subject + adverb |
| | *Me   llama   Juan   todos los días.* |

| SPANISH PATTERN 3 | adverb   + object + verb + subject |
| | *Todos los días   me   llama   Juan.* |

Objects

In English, object pronouns have only one form ("me," "you," "him," "her," "it," "us," "them") and are used to replace direct objects, indirect objects, and objects that follow prepositions. In Spanish, each type of object pronoun has its own set of forms, as well as different usage patterns.

Pronouns After Prepositions

In Spanish, the subject pronouns (except *yo* and *tú*) are used after prepositions.

Los regalos son para él.	*The presents are for him.*
Lo hicieron por ella.	*They did it because of her.*
Gracias a usted, estamos bien.	*Thanks to you, we're okay.*
¿Es la casa de ustedes?	*Is it your house?*
Fui al cine sin ellos.	*I went to the movies without them.*
Vamos con vosotros.	*We're going with you all.*

AVOID THE *Blunder*

Do not use direct object pronouns after prepositions.

✗ para lo
✗ para la
✗ de nos
✗ por los

The pronouns *mí* and *ti* are used for "me" and "you" after a preposition.

El regalo es para mí.	*The present is for me.*
Lo hicieron por ti.	*They did it because of you.*

AVOID THE *Blunder*

Do not use other object pronouns after prepositions.

✗ de me
✗ por te
✗ de yo
✗ para tú

There is an accent mark in *mí* to distinguish it from the possessive *mi*; there is no accent mark in *ti*.

✗ para mi
✗ para tí

Conmigo and *contigo* are used instead of *con* + *mí* and *con* + *ti*.

¿Vienes conmigo?	*Are you coming with me?*
Quiero hablar contigo.	*I want to talk to you.*

Consigo is used when the object of the preposition is the same person as the subject *él, ella, usted,* or *ustedes.*

Marcos llevó la maleta consigo.	*Marcos took the suitcase with him.*
¿Tiene usted los boletos consigo?	*Do you have the tickets with you?*
Ella trae la comida consigo.	*She's bringing the food with her.*
Traigan sus pasaportes consigo.	*Bring your passports with you.*

AVOID THE *Blunder*

Do not use *consigo* if the object of the preposition is a different person from the subject.

✗ Voy al cine consigo.
✗ ¿Vienes consigo?

Reflexive Pronouns

Reflexive pronouns indicate that the subject and the object are the same person or thing. They are placed before the conjugated verb.

Me miro en el espejo.	*I look at myself in the mirror.*
Ella se cuida.	*She takes care of herself.*

Los chicos se hieren.	*The kids hurt themselves.*
Nos servimos en estas fiestas.	*We serve ourselves at these parties.*

AVOID THE *Blunder*

Do not put the pronoun after the verb.

✗ Miro me.
✗ Ella cuida se.
✗ Los chicos hieren se.
✗ Servimos nos.

■ When an infinitive construction (see page 96) or gerund construction (see page 113) is used, the reflexive pronoun can be placed either before its corresponding conjugated verb or attached to the end of the infinitive or gerund.

INFINITIVE CONSTRUCTION
Me voy a mirar en el espejo.
Voy a mirarme en el espejo. } *I'm going to look at myself in the mirror.*
GERUND CONSTRUCTION
Me estoy mirando en el espejo.
Estoy mirándome en el espejo. } *I'm looking at myself in the mirror.*

INFINITIVE CONSTRUCTION
Ella se va a cuidar.
Ella va a cuidarse. } *She's going to take care of herself.*
GERUND CONSTRUCTION
Ella se está cuidando.
Ella está cuidándose. } *She's taking care of herself.*

INFINITIVE CONSTRUCTION
Los chicos se van a herir.
Los chicos van a herirse. } *The kids are going to hurt themselves.*
GERUND CONSTRUCTION
Los chicos se están hiriendo.
Los chicos están hiriéndose. } *The kids are hurting themselves.*

INFINITIVE CONSTRUCTION
Nos vamos a servir.
Vamos a servirnos. } *We're going to serve ourselves.*
GERUND CONSTRUCTION
Nos estamos sirviendo.
Estamos sirviéndonos. } *We're serving ourselves.*

AVOID THE *Blunder*

Do not forget to add an accent mark to the gerund if you have attached a reflexive pronoun.

✗ mirandome   ✗ cuidandose
✗ hiriendose   ✗ sirviendonos

Do not add an accent mark to the gerund if it does not have a pronoun attached.

✗ mirándo   ✗ cuidándo
✗ hiriéndo   ✗ sirviéndo

In affirmative commands (see page 163), the reflexive pronoun is attached to the end of the verb and an accent mark is added to the third-last syllable.

Siéntate aquí.	*Sit here.*
Cuídcse.	*Take care of yourself.*
Levántense, por favor.	*Please stand up.*

In negative commands (see page 163), the reflexive pronoun is placed between the *no* and the verb.

No te sientes aquí.	*Don't sit here.*
No se pierda.	*Don't get lost.*
No se levanten.	*Don't get up.*

■ Reflexive pronouns used with plural verbs can also indicate reciprocal action.

Los chicos se hieren (el uno al otro).	*The kids hurt each other.*
Nos servimos (el uno al otro).	*We serve each other.*

El uno al otro can be used to distinguish the reciprocal meaning from the reflexive meaning.

AVOID THE *Blunder*

Do not try to translate the words "each other." Use a plural reflexive pronoun (*nos* or *se*) (+ *el uno al otro*) to express this.

✗ Los chicos hieren cada otro.

■ Many reflexive expressions in Spanish have equivalents in English that are not expressed in reflexive terms. Following are some examples.

TRANSITIVE VERBS		REFLEXIVE VERBS	
VERB + DIRECT OBJECT NOUN OR PRONOUN		VERB + REFLEXIVE PRONOUN	
acostar (ue)	*put someone to bed*	acostarse (ue)	*lie down/ go to bed*
afeitar	*shave someone else*	afeitarse	*shave*
arreglar	*arrange something*	arreglarse	*freshen up*
bañar	*bathe someone else*	bañarse	*take a bath*
despertar (ie)	*wake someone up*	despertarse (ie)	*wake up*
divertir (ie, i)	*entertain someone*	divertirse (ie, i)	*have a good time*
levantar	*get someone up/ lift something*	levantarse	*get up*
llamar	*call someone*	llamarse	*be named*
preocupar	*worry someone*	preocuparse	*worry*
sentar (ie)	*seat someone*	sentarse (ie)	*sit down*
cansar	*tire someone out*	cansarse	*get tired*
emocionar	*excite someone*	emocionarse	*get excited*
enfadar	*make someone mad*	enfadarse	*get mad*
enfriar	*cool something*	enfriarse	*get cold*
enojar	*make someone mad*	enojarse	*get mad*
organizar	*organize something*	organizarse	*get organized*
vestir (i, i)	*dress someone else*	vestirse (i, i)	*get dressed*

Despertamos a los chicos
a las nueve.

We wake the kids up at nine.

Nos despertamos a las ocho.

We wake up at eight.

El payaso divierte a los niños.

The clown entertains the children.

Los niños se divierten en el
parque.

The children have fun (entertain themselves) at the park.

Su mamá lo llama todos los días.

His mother calls him every day.

El niño se llama Nicolás.

The child's name is Nicolás.

Mi prima me preocupa mucho.

My cousin worries me a lot.

Me preocupo mucho por mi
prima.

I worry a lot about my cousin.

El oficial me enfadó.

The officer made me mad.

Me enfadé con el oficial.

I got mad at the officer.

Note that in Spanish you do not say "I get dressed," but rather "I dress myself." Do not try to translate "up," "down," "get," "take," or "have" in this type of expression. Use the reflexive verb instead.

✗ Despertamos arriba a los niños.
✗ Los niños tienen diversión en el parque.
✗ Los niños tienen un buen tiempo en el parque.
✗ Conseguí enfadarme con el oficial.

In Spanish you can say *su nombre es* _____ or *mi nombre es* _____. To express the same meaning with *llamarse*, you must use the reflexive pattern.

(Yo) me llamo John.	(Nosotros) nos llamamos John y Sara.
¿(Tú) te llamas María?	¿(Vosotros) os llamáis María y Elena?
¿(Usted) se llama Eduardo?	¿(Ustedes) se llaman Eduardo y Javier?
(Él) se llama José.	(Ellos) se llaman José y Francisco.
(Ella) se llama Margarita.	(Ellas) se llaman Margarita y Julia.

✗ Su llamo es Nicolás.
✗ Mi llamo es John.

■ A reflexive construction is used when indicating action to or on one's own body. Unlike English, Spanish uses a definite article rather than a possessive (see page 59).

Me lavo la cara.	*I wash my face.*
Se lava los dientes.	*She brushes (washes) her teeth.*
Nos pintamos las uñas.	*We polish our nails.*
Se pintan el pelo.	*They color their hair.*

✗ Lavo mi cara.
✗ Se lava sus dientes.
✗ Pintan su pelo.

■ Certain verbs have different meanings when used with reflexive pronouns. Following are some examples.

acordar (ue)	*decide*	acordarse (ue) de	*remember*
aprovechar de	*take advantage of an opportunity*	aprovecharse de	*take advantage of a person*
burlar	*evade*	burlarse de	*make fun of*
comer	*eat*	comerse	*eat up*
despedir (i, i)	*fire someone*	despedirse (i, i) de	*say good-bye to*
dormir (ue, u)	*sleep*	dormirse (ue, u)	*fall asleep*
negar (ie)	*deny*	negarse a (ie)	*refuse to*
ofrecer	*offer something to someone*	ofrecerse a/para	*offer to do something*
quedar	*result in, fit, agree*	quedarse	*remain*
sentir (ie, i)	*be sorry*	sentirse (ie, i)	*feel*

El jefe despidió a tres empleados.	*The boss fired three employees.*
El jefe se despidió.	*The boss said good-bye.*
Duermo ocho horas.	*I sleep eight hours.*
Me duermo en el coche.	*I fall asleep in the car.*
Ese vestido te queda bien.	*That dress fits you well.*
Mi hermana se queda aquí.	*My sister is staying here.*
Quedamos en vernos esta tarde.	*We agreed to meet this afternoon.*
Nos quedamos con ustedes.	*We're staying with you all.*
Siento no poder acompañarte.	*I'm sorry I can't go with you.*
Me siento muy mal.	*I feel really bad.*

AVOID THE *Blunder*

Be sure you know the different meanings indicated by a reflexive pronoun.

✗ Mi hermana queda aquí.
✗ Siento muy mal.

■ A few verbs that do not have a reflexive meaning must nevertheless be used with reflexive pronouns. Following are some examples.

arrepentirse (ie, i)	*regret*
obstinarse en	*stand firm on, insist on*
quedarse	*remain, stay*
quejarse	*complain*
reírse (i, i)	*laugh*

Me arrepiento de haberlo dicho.	*I regret having said that.*
Los profesores se obstinan en no cambiar la fecha del examen.	*The professors stand firm on not changing the date of the exam.*
Me quedo aquí contigo.	*I'm staying here with you.*
Los alumnos se quejan de la comida.	*The students complain about the food.*
Nos reímos mucho anoche.	*We laughed a lot last night.*

AVOID THE *Blunder*

Do not try to find a reflexive meaning in these verbs, but do always use reflexive pronouns with them.

✗ Arrepiento de haberlo dicho.
✗ Los alumnos quejan.
✗ Reímos.

Direct Objects

A direct object can be a noun, a pronoun, or an infinitive (see page 99).

■ As in English, direct object nouns may follow the verb.

Compramos la casa.	*We bought the house.*
Juan perdió dinero.	*Juan lost money.*
Vi una película.	*I watched a movie.*
Ganaron el partido.	*They won the game.*

In contrast to English, direct object nouns may precede the verb in Spanish. This word order requires including a direct object pronoun as well as the direct object noun.

La casa la compramos ayer.	*We bought the house yesterday.*
El dinero lo perdió Juan.	*Juan lost the money.*
Esa película la vi anoche.	*I saw that movie last night.*
El partido lo ganaron los Tigres.	*The Tigers won the game.*

When the direct object is a person, the preposition *a* must precede the person's name or any other noun that refers to that person. This *a* has no English translation (see pages 261–262).

Miguel ayuda a María.	*Miguel helps María.*
Vimos a su hermano.	*We saw his brother.*
Reconozco al Sr. García.	*I recognize Mr. García.*
Visitaron a sus amigos.	*They visited their friends.*

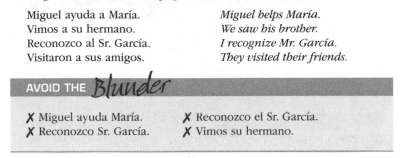

AVOID THE *Blunder*

✗ Miguel ayuda María. ✗ Reconozco el Sr. García.
✗ Reconozco Sr. García. ✗ Vimos su hermano.

Remember that *mirar* means "look at," *buscar* means "look for," and *esperar* means "wait for" (see page 104). No preposition is necessary unless the direct object is a person. The "personal *a*" is a signal that the direct object is a person. Compare the following sentences.

Carlos mira el coche.	*Carlos is looking at the car.*
Carlos mira a su papá.	*Carlos is looking at his dad.*
Busco un apartamento.	*I'm looking for an apartment.*
Busco a Pepe.	*I'm looking for Pepe.*
Espera un cheque.	*She's waiting for a check.*
Espera a su esposo.	*She's waiting for her husband.*

AVOID THE *Blunder*

✗ Carlos mira su papá.
✗ Busco por un apartamento.
✗ Espera por un cheque.

■ In contrast to English, direct object pronouns are placed immediately before the conjugated verb in Spanish.

Alberto come la tortilla.	*Alberto is eating the tortilla.*
La come.	*He is eating it.*
Luisa compra el periódico.	*Luisa buys the newspaper.*
Lo compra.	*She buys it.*
Susana lee las novelas.	*Susana reads the novels.*
Las lee.	*She reads them.*
Marta ve los programas.	*Marta watches the programs.*
Los ve.	*She watches them.*

AVOID THE *Blunder*

Remember that each noun is either masculine or feminine. The "it" or "them" denoted by the direct object pronoun must reflect the gender of the noun it replaces.

✗ Alberto lo come. (la tortilla)
✗ Luisa la compra. (el periódico)
✗ Marta las ve. (los programas)
✗ Susana los lee. (las novelas)

Direct object pronouns that refer to people follow the same pattern.

Mi amigo me llama.	*My friend calls me.*
Te llamo mañana.	*I'll call you tomorrow.*
Mis padres nos ayudan.	*My parents help us.*
José invita a Elena.	*José invites Elena.*
José la invita.	*José invites her.*
Elena mira a Alfredo.	*Elena is looking at Alfredo.*
Elena lo mira.	*Elena is looking at him.*
Visitamos a nuestros abuelos.	*We're visiting our grandparents.*
Los visitamos.	*We're visiting them.*

AVOID THE *Blunder*

Do not use a prepositional construction instead of the direct object pronoun.

✗ Mi amigo llama a mí.
✗ Llamo a ti.
✗ José invita a ella.
✗ Elena mira a él.
✗ Mis padres ayudan a nosotros.
✗ Visitamos a ellos.

In some parts of Spain, *le* and *les* are used as direct object pronouns in place of *lo, la, los,* and *las* when referring to people.

☐ In constructions with infinitives or gerunds, direct object pronouns can be placed either before the conjugated verb or attached to the end of the infinitive or gerund (see pages 96 and 113).

Tengo que ayudar a mi hermano.	*I have to help my brother.*
Tengo que ayudarlo. ⎫ Lo tengo que ayudar. ⎭	*I have to help him.*
Vamos a visitar a los abuelos.	*We're going to visit our grandparents.*
Vamos a visitarlos. ⎫ Los vamos a visitar. ⎭	*We're going to visit them.*
Está esperando a Pablo.	*She's waiting for Pablo.*
Está esperándolo. ⎫ Lo está esperando. ⎭	*She's waiting for him.*
Están buscando a las niñas.	*They're looking for the girls.*
Están buscándolas. ⎫ Las están buscando. ⎭	*They're looking for them.*

AVOID THE Blunder

Do not forget to use an accent mark when you attach the object pronoun to the gerund. Do not use an accent mark if the pronoun is placed before the conjugated verb.

✗ esperandolo
✗ esperándo

☐ In affirmative commands (see pages 163–164), the direct object pronoun is attached to the end of the verb and an accent mark is added to the third-last syllable.

Espérame aquí.	*Wait for me here.*
Búsquelo.	*Look for him.*
Mírenla.	*Look at her.*

☐ In negative commands (see pages 163–164), the direct object pronoun is placed between the *no* and the verb. No accent mark is added.

¡No me hables!	*Don't talk to me!*
¡No lo llame usted!	*Don't call him!*
¡No lo lean ustedes!	*Don't read it!*
¡No lo hagamos!	*Let's not do it!*

AVOID THE Blunder

✗ ¡No hábleme!
✗ ¡No llámelo!

Indirect Objects

The use of indirect objects is determined by the kind of verb used. Four types of verbs require indirect object pronouns—even when the indirect object is stated in noun or pronoun form after *a*.

VERBS THAT REQUIRE INDIRECT OBJECT PRONOUNS

■ Some verbs indicate a transfer of something (the direct object) from one person (the subject) to another (the indirect object). Following are some examples.

darle algo a alguien	*give something to somebody*
prestarle algo a alguien	*lend something to somebody*
comprarle algo a alguien	*buy something for somebody*
regalarle algo a alguien	*give a gift to somebody*
mandarle algo a alguien	*send something to somebody*
enviarle algo a alguien	*send something to somebody*
mostrarle algo a alguien	*show something to somebody*
demostrarle algo a alguien	*show something to somebody*
enseñarle algo a alguien	*teach something to somebody*
decirle algo a alguien	*tell something to somebody*
explicarle algo a alguien	*explain something to somebody*
creerle algo a alguien	*believe something of somebody (that he or she has said)*

Although the person who receives something may be indicated by *a* plus a noun or pronoun, this is optional. The indirect object pronoun, however, is always required with these verbs.

Le doy el dinero a Juan.	*I'm giving the money to Juan.*
Mi madre me manda los paquetes (a mí).	*My mother sends me the packages.*
A mis padres les mandó una tarjeta.	*He sent my parents a card.*
Nos enseña el baile (a nosotros).	*She teaches the dance to us.*
(A mí) me dijo la verdad.	*She told me the truth.*

AVOID THE *Blunder*

Do not leave out the indirect object pronoun that denotes the receiver, even when there is a prepositional phrase that tells who the receiver is.

✗ Mi madre manda los paquetes a mí.
✗ Doy el dinero a Juan.
✗ Enseña el baile a nosotros.
✗ Mandó una tarjeta a mis padres.
✗ Dijo la verdad a mí.

When the direct object is also expressed in pronoun form, it is placed between the indirect object pronoun and the conjugated verb.

María me muestra las manzanas.	*María is showing me the apples.*
María me las muestra.	*María is showing them to me.*
Él nos explicó la lección.	*He explained the lesson to us.*
Nos la explicó.	*He explained it to us.*

AVOID THE *Blunder*

✗ María me muestra las.
✗ María muestra me las.
✗ María las me muestra.
✗ María las muestra a mí.

When the indirect object pronoun *le* or *les* precedes a direct object pronoun, the indirect object pronoun changes to *se*.

María le muestra las manzanas a Pedro.	*María is showing the apples to Pedro.*
María se las muestra.	*María is showing them to him.*
Él les explicó la lección a ellos.	*He explained the lesson to them.*
Él se la explicó.	*He explained it to them.*

AVOID THE *Blunder*

✗ María le las muestra.
✗ María muestra le las.
✗ Él le la explicó.
✗ Él le explicó la.

Because *se* can refer to "you," "him," "her," "you all," and "them," it is helpful to add *a usted, a él, a ella, a ustedes,* or *a ellos* for clarification.

Remember that both the indirect object pronoun and the *a* + *mí/ti/ usted/él/ella/nosotros/vosotros/ustedes/ellos/ellas* constructions refer to the person who is the receiver of the direct object. The use of both objects in the same sentence is not considered redundant in Spanish, as it is in English.

Indirect and direct object pronouns may be attached to infinitives and gerunds (see pages 209 and 216–217).

María va a mostrármelas.
María me las va a mostrar. } *María is going to show them to me.*

Él va a explicárnosla.
Él nos la va a explicar. } *He is going to explain it to us.*

María va a mostrárselas.
María se las va a mostrar. } *María is going to show them to him.*

Él va a explicársela.
Él se la va a explicar. } *He is going to explain it to them.*

María está mostrándoselas.
María se las está mostrando. } *María is showing them to him.*

Él está explicándosela.
Él se la está explicando. } *He is explaining it to them.*

AVOID THE *Blunder*

Be sure to add an accent mark to the infinitive or gerund when two pronouns are attached.

✗ mostrarmelas
✗ mostrandoselas
✗ explicarnosla
✗ explicandosela

■ A number of verbs indicate a feeling imparted by the subject (a person or thing) to another person (the indirect object) (see page 106). There is no direct object in these constructions. Following are some examples.

parecerle _____ a alguien	_seem _____ to somebody_
caerle bien a alguien	_make a good impression on somebody_
interesarle a alguien	_interest somebody, be interesting to somebody_
importarle a alguien	_be important to somebody_
gustarle a alguien	_be pleasing to somebody, appeal to somebody, charm somebody_
fascinarle a alguien	_fascinate somebody, be fascinating to somebody_
encantar le a alguien	_be pleasing to somebody, appeal to somebody, charm somebody_
emocionarle a alguien	_excite somebody, be exciting to somebody_
caerle mal a alguien	_make a bad impression on somebody_
fastidiarle a alguien	_annoy somebody, be annoying to somebody_
molestarle a alguien	_bother somebody_
faltarle a alguien	_be lacking to somebody_
hacerle falta a alguien	_be lacking to somebody_

The English verbs "like," "love," "need," and "care about" are often translated with verbs from the above list. In English, however, these verbs are expressed as feelings of the subject. In Spanish, the subject is a person or thing that "imparts" a feeling to another person (the indirect object).

ENGLISH PATTERN
subject + verb + direct object (noun or pronoun)
You   like   Alex/him.
I   like   the house / it.

SPANISH PATTERN 1
subject + indirect object + verb
Alex   _te_   _gusta._
(Alex appeals to you.)
La casa   _me_   _gusta._
(The house appeals to me.)

SPANISH PATTERN 2
indirect object + verb + subject
_Te_   _gusta_   _Alex/él._
(Alex/He appeals to you.)
_Me_   _gusta_   _la casa._
(The house appeals to me.)

SPANISH PATTERN 3
indirect object + verb
_Te_   _gusta._ (He appeals to you.)
_Me_   _gusta._ (It appeals to me.)

A José le gusta el chocolate.	*José likes chocolate.* *(Chocolate appeals to José.)*
A José le gustan las enchiladas.	*José likes enchiladas.* *(Enchiladas appeal to José.)*
A las chicas les encanta el cine.	*The girls love the cinema.* *(The cinema enchants the girls.)*
A las chicas les encantan las películas.	*The girls love the movies.* *(Movies enchant the girls.)*
(Tú) me importas.	*I care about you.* *(You are important to me.)*
Me importan todos mis amigos.	*I care about all my friends.* *(All my friends are important to me.)*
Nos falta el dinero.	*We need money.* *(Money is lacking to us.)*
Nos faltan los recursos.	*We need resources.* *(Resources are lacking to us.)*
Tu novio me cae muy bien.	*I like your boyfriend very much.* *(Your boyfriend makes a very good impression on me.)*
Tus amigos me caen bien.	*I like your friends.* *(Your friends make a good impression on me.)*

AVOID THE *Blunder*

Do not try to translate English verbs of this type into Spanish. Rather, think about what feelings are being conveyed by the Spanish verbs. Make sure the subject and verb agree.

✗ Me gusto el chocolate.
✗ José le gusta las enchiladas.
✗ Nos faltamos los recursos.

The prepositional phrase *a* + noun or pronoun that indicates the person affected by the subject is optional. It is always the same person as the indirect object pronoun.

(A mí) me gusta el libro.	*I like the book.* *(The book appeals to me.)*
¿Qué te gusta (a ti)?	*What do you like?* *(What appeals to you?)*

Este libro le gusta mucho (a Juan/a él).	*Juan/He likes this book a lot. (This book appeals a lot to Juan/ to him.)*
(A Luisa/A ella) no le gusta.	*Luisa/She doesn't like it. (It doesn't appeal to Luisa/to her.)*
(A nosotros) nos gusta la clase.	*We like the class. (The class appeals to us.)*
No les gusta la clase (a María y a Susana/a ellas).	*María and Susana/They don't like the class. (The class doesn't appeal to María and Susana/to them.)*

AVOID THE *Blunder*

Do not forget the *a* before the noun or pronoun that indicates the person affected by the subject.

✗ Juan no le gusta este libro.
✗ Luisa no le gusta el libro.

Verbs of this type are always accompanied by indirect objects but do not have direct objects. The subjects "it" and "they" are expressed in the conjugation of the verb.

Me gusta el vestido.	*The dress appeals to me.*
Le encantan esos zapatos.	*Those shoes appeal to her.*
Me gusta.	*I like it. (It appeals to me.)*
Le encantan.	*She loves them. (They enchant her.)*

AVOID THE *Blunder*

Do not use *lo, la, los,* or *las* with these verbs.

✗ Me lo gusta.
✗ Se los encantan.
✗ Te la gusta.

■ In constructions with verbs that express requests, demands, or suggestions, indirect object pronouns are used with *que* + the subjunctive (see pages 167–168 and 188–189).

Te pido que me prestes dinero.	*I'm asking you to lend me money.*
Le ruega que lo llame.	*He begs her to call him.*
Nos recomienda que estudiemos.	*She recommends that we study.*
Les sugerimos que trabajen.	*We suggest that they work.*

■ Certain verbs combine a reflexive *se* with an indirect object to indicate accidental occurrences. In these constructions, the subject is a thing that has an accidental occurrence ("loses itself," "forgets itself," "breaks itself"), and in doing so it affects a person (the indirect object) (see page 108). Following are some typical verbs of this type.

acabársele a alguien	*run out of*
caérsele a alguien	*drop*
descomponérsele a alguien	*break*
olvidársele a alguien	*forget*
perdérsele a alguien	*lose*
quebrársele a alguien	*break*
quedársele a alguien en algún lugar	*leave by mistake*
quemársele a alguien	*burn*
rompérsele a alguien	*break*

Se le cayó la taza.	*He dropped the cup.* *(The cup fell from him.)*
Se le cayeron las tazas.	*He dropped the cups.* *(The cups fell from him.)*
La computadora se nos descompuso.	*The computer broke down on us.*
Las máquinas se nos descompusieron.	*The machines broke down on us.*
Se le olvidó el libro.	*He forgot the book.* *(The book got forgotten by him.)*
Se le olvidaron los libros.	*He forgot the books.* *(The books got forgotten by him.)*
Se me perdió la llave.	*I lost my key.* *(The key got lost from me.)*
Se me perdieron las llaves.	*I lost my keys.* *(The keys got lost from me.)*
Se les quedó el libro en el coche.	*They left the book in the car.* *(The book got left in the car by them.)*
Se les quedaron los libros en el coche.	*They left the books in the car.* *(The books got left in the car by them.)*
Se le quemó el dedo.	*She burned her finger.* *(The finger got burned on her.)*
Se le quemaron los dedos.	*She burned her fingers.* *(The fingers got burned on her.)*

Se me rompió el brazo.
I broke my arm.
(The arm got broken on me.)

Se me rompieron los brazos.
I broke my arms.
(The arms got broken on me.)

When the action is done on purpose, the subject takes the responsibility for the action.

Quemé los documentos.
I burned the documents.

El hombre rompió el contrato.
The man tore up the contract.

La mujer olvidó su triste pasado.
The woman forgot her sad past.

Dejamos los libros en el coche.
We left the books in the car.

AVOID THE *Blunder*

Do not attribute the action of breaking, forgetting, losing, dropping, or similar accidental occurrences to the subject, unless he or she does it on purpose. Do not use possessive pronouns with these constructions.

✗ Quemé mi dedo.
✗ Rompió su brazo.
✗ Olvidamos nuestros libros.

The Impersonal *se*

Se + a third-person singular verb is used to make a general observation that refers to everybody. This is often expressed in English with an impersonal "one," "you," "they," or "people."

Se siente en casa en ese hotel.
One feels at home at that hotel.

Se estudia más en la universidad.
You study more in college.

Se camina más rápido en la ciudad.
People walk faster in the city.

No se puede fumar en este edificio.
You can't smoke in this building.

Se + a third-person singular or plural verb + a noun can be used to make a passive statement, indicating a general custom. The verb is singular for a singular noun, plural for a plural noun. In English, "you," referring to everybody in general, is often used for this purpose.

¿Dónde se compra el pan?
Where do you buy bread?
(Where is bread bought?)

Se compra el pan en la panadería.
You buy bread at the bakery.
(Bread is bought at the bakery.)

¿Dónde se puede comprar el pan?
Where can you buy bread?

Se puede comprar el pan en la panadería.
You can buy bread at the bakery.

¿Dónde se reparan los zapatos?

Where do you get shoes repaired?
(Where are shoes repaired?)

Se reparan los zapatos en la
zapatería.

They repair shoes at the shoe store.
(Shoes are repaired at the shoe
store.)

AVOID THE *Blunder*

Do not use the personal pronoun to translate the English "you"
unless you are talking about the habits of a particular person.

✗ Tú estudias más en la universidad.
✗ Usted compra el pan en la panadería.
✗ Tú no fumas en este edificio.
✗ Dónde compras el pan?

The Pronoun *lo*

The pronoun *lo* has several uses (see page 86).

■ *Lo* can be used before the verbs *ser* and *estar* to refer to an adjective
in a previous statement.

—Ella es bonita.
—Sí, lo es.

"She's pretty."
"Yes, she is."

—¿Estás cansado?
—Sí, lo estoy.

"Are you tired?"
"Yes, I am."

■ An adjective can be used as a subject by placing *lo* before it.

Lo bueno del curso es que es
muy útil.
Lo malo es que la clase es a las
ocho.

The good thing about the course
is that it's very useful.
The bad thing is that the class
is at 8 o'clock.

AVOID THE *Blunder*

✗ la buena cosa es
✗ la mala parte es

■ *Lo* can refer to a masculine singular direct object, whether it is a person or a thing (see page 204).

Compré el libro.	*I bought the book.*
Lo compré en la librería.	*I bought it at the bookstore.*
Vi a tu hermano.	*I saw your brother.*
Lo vi en el parque.	*I saw him in the park.*

■ *Lo que* can refer to an object, an entire phrase, or an abstract idea.

Lo que ella compró no te importa.	*What she bought is none of your business.*
Lo que está haciendo es un secreto.	*What he's doing is a secret.*
Lo que él dice no es verdad.	*What he says isn't true.*
Lo que ustedes quieren es imposible.	*What you all want is impossible.*

■ *Lo cual* can follow an entire clause, adding a comment about it.

Ella compró un coche de lujo, lo cual nos sorprendió a todos.	*She bought a luxury car, which surprised everybody.*

el cual

■ *El cual/la cual/los cuales/las cuales* is used after prepositions to refer to a previously mentioned noun.

Me dio una cantidad de dinero, con el cual pagué mis estudios.	*He gave me some money, with which I paid for my education.*
Decidió comprar la casa, por la cual tuvo que pagar una fortuna.	*She decided to buy the house, for which she had to pay a fortune.*
Ella cuida a seis niños, cuatro de los cuales son de su hermana.	*She takes care of six children, four of whom are her sister's.*

AVOID THE *Blunder*

As in formal English, do not put a preposition at the end of the sentence. Place it before *el cual/la cual/los cuales/las cuales*.

✗ Compró la casa, que tenía que pagar una fortuna por.

Exercises

A *Circle the appropriate pronoun in the following sentences.*

1. Voy al cine con **la** | **lo** | **-tigo** | **ti**.

2. Ricardo llevó la maleta con **-sigo** | **si** | **él** | **ella**.

3. El regalo es para **-tigo** | **usted** | **lo** | **la**.

4. Sara hizo mucho por **mí** | **tú** | **yo** | **te**.

5. Van a salir sin **lo** | **la** | **les** | **mí**.

6. Ella piensa mucho en **tú** | **ti** | **lo** | **la**.

7. Sé que mi papá lo hizo por **sigo** | **las** | **nos** | **nosotros**.

8. A ella le gusta salir con **lo** | **la** | **él** | **le**.

B *Fill in the blanks with the appropriate reflexive pronoun.*

1. Generalmente _____ acostamos a las once de la noche.

2. Los niños _____ levantan temprano.

3. _____ voy a lavar el pelo.

4. Ese chico _____ queja de todo.

5. Mi hermana está divirtiéndo_____.

6. Por favor, siénta_____ aquí.

C *Circle the word or group of words that best completes each sentence.*

1. El estudiante **aprovechó** | **se aprovechó** de la beca.

2. Las chicas **quedaron** | **se quedaron** en salir juntas esta noche.

3. La niña **quedó** | **se quedó** toda la tarde sola en la casa.

4. No voy a la fiesta porque **siento** | **me siento** muy mal.

5. **Despedimos** | **Nos despedimos** a dos empleados.

D *Rewrite each of the following sentences, changing the underlined direct object to a pronoun.*

> EXAMPLE   Compramos <u>el periódico</u> todos los días.
>
> *Lo compramos todos los días.*

1. Juan no llamó <u>a María</u> esta tarde.

_____

2. Susana dejó <u>las uvas</u> en el mercado.

_____

3. Queremos mucho <u>a nuestros profesores</u>.

_____

E _Fill in the blanks with the appropriate indirect object pronoun._

1. A mí _____ regaló una pulsera preciosa.

2. Sandra _____ mostró las fotos a sus amigas.

3. Arturo y José _____ demostraron las nuevas computadoras a nosotros.

4. _____ enseñaré la cámara a ti más tarde.

F _Rewrite each of the following sentences, changing the underlined direct object to a pronoun._

EXAMPLE Le enseñaré <u>la cámara</u> a mi hermano mañana.

Se la enseñaré a mi hermano mañana.

1. Me va a enviar <u>una carta</u> la próxima semana.

_____

2. Ángela les dará <u>buenas noticias</u> muy pronto.

_____

3. ¿Te dijo Jorge <u>el secreto</u>?

_____

G _Express the following in Spanish._

EXAMPLE _I like the red dress. I like it a lot._

Me gusta el vestido rojo. Me gusta mucho.

1. _Victoria is interested in movies. She loves them._

_____

2. _Traffic annoys Roberto. It bothers him a lot._

_____

3. _Juan likes Inés. She fascinates him._

_____

H *Express the following in Spanish.*

EXAMPLE   *Pedro broke his arm.*

  A Pedro se le rompió el brazo.

1. *Mario left the keys in the car.*

_____

2. *We dropped the books.*

_____

3. *They forgot their homework.*

_____

I *Fill in the blanks with the correct form of the verb in parentheses.*

1. En la clase se _____ (hablar) español.

2. En esa escuela se _____ (enseñar) varios idiomas.

3. En el mercado se _____ (vender) varias frutas.

4. En ese restaurante se _____ (servir) la cocina peruana.

J *Fill in the blanks with the appropriate construction, using the English cues in parentheses.*

1. _____ es que hemos terminado. (*The good thing*)

2. A pesar de _____ que fue, me gustó el curso.
   (*how difficult*)

3. Este vestido, por _____ pagué $10, es el que me gusta más. (*which*)

4. Compré seis manzanas, cuatro _____ están podridas.
   (*of which*)

ADVERBS AND PREPOSITIONS WITH ADVERBIAL FUNCTIONS

Time Markers: To Answer *¿cuándo?*

GENERAL

de noche	*at night*
de día	*during the day*
al amanecer	*at dawn*
al anochecer	*at dusk*
a las diez	*at 10 o'clock*
a eso de las diez	*around 10 o'clock*
a principios de	*at the beginning of*
a mediados de	*in the middle of*
a fines de	*at the end of*
al principio	*in the beginning/at the beginning*
al final	*in the end/at the end*
temprano	*early*
tarde	*late*

PRESENT

ahora	*now*
en este momento	*at the moment*
hoy	*today*
esta mañana	*this morning*
esta tarde	*this afternoon*
esta noche	*tonight*
actualmente	*now*
estos días	*these days*
recientemente	*recently*

PAST

ayer	*yesterday*
anteayer	*the day before yesterday*
anoche	*last night*

hace unos minutos/días/años	*a few minutes/days/years ago*
hace unas horas/semanas	*a few hours/weeks ago*

la semana pasada	*last week*
el año pasado	*last year*

entonces, en aquel entonces	*back then*
en esos/aquellos días	*in those days*
en ese/aquel tiempo	*at that time*

a la una / a las dos	*at 1 o'clock / at 2 o'clock*

esta mañana	*this morning*
esta tarde	*this afternoon*

al día siguiente	*the next day*

FUTURE

mañana	*tomorrow*
pasado mañana	*the day after tomorrow*
el lunes / el martes	*on Monday / on Tuesday*

pronto	*soon*
más tarde	*later*
lo antes posible / lo más pronto posible	*as soon as possible*

después de + *infinitive*	*after (doing something)*
antes de + *infinitive*	*before (doing something)*

esta tarde	*this afternoon*
esta noche	*tonight*

antes que + *subjunctive*	*before (something happens)*
después que + *subjunctive*	*after (something happens)*
cuando _____	*when (something happens)*
en cuanto _____	
tan pronto } + *subjunctive*	*as soon as (something happens)*
como _____	

Order of Occurrence Markers

antes	*beforehand*
primero, en primer lugar	*first*
segundo, en segundo lugar	*second*
luego	*then*
después	*after that*
finalmente	*finally*

Frequency Markers: To Answer *¿con qué frecuencia?*

nunca	*never, the whole time*
casi nunca	*almost never*
poco, pocas veces	*seldom*
con poca frecuencia	*not very often*
de vez en cuando	*every once in a while*
alguna que otra vez	*every so often*
a veces	*sometimes*
generalmente	*usually*
a menudo	*often*
frecuentemente	*frequently*
un día sí, otro no	*every other day*
mucho	*a lot*
con mucha frecuencia	*very often*
casi siempre	*almost always*
siempre	*always, the whole time*

todos los días	*every day*
los lunes / los martes	*on Mondays / on Tuesdays*
los fines de semana	*on weekends*
una vez a la semana	*once a week*
dos veces al mes	*twice a month*

Place Markers: To Answer *¿dónde?*

ADVERBS

aquí/acá	*here*
ahí	*there*
allí/allá	*over there*

PREPOSITIONS

en	*in/on/at*
sobre	*on*
entre	*between/among*

ADVERBS

arriba	up there, on top
abajo	down there, below
adentro	inside
afuera	outside
adelante	ahead, forward
detrás	behind
atrás	back, in the back, behind, ago
enfrente	in front
al lado	on the side
a la derecha	on the right
a la izquierda	on the left
todo derecho	straight ahead
alrededor	all around
cerca	nearby
lejos	far away
a lo lejos	in the distance

PREPOSITIONS

encima de	on top of
debajo de	underneath (of)
dentro de	inside of
fuera de	outside of
delante de	ahead of
detrás de	behind
atrás de	behind
enfrente de / frente a	across from / facing
al lado de	next to
a la derecha de	to the right of
a la izquierda de	to the left of
alrededor de	around
cerca de	near, close to
lejos de	far from

Direction Markers: To Answer ¿adónde?

a	to
para	toward
hacia	toward
a través de	across
por	through, by, along
alrededor de	around
a la derecha	to the right
a la izquierda	to the left
adelante	straight ahead
recto	straight ahead
todo derecho	straight ahead

Adverbs of Manner: To Answer ¿cómo?

bien	well
mal	badly
(mucho) mejor	(much) better
(mucho) peor	(much) worse

ADVERBS ENDING IN -*mente*

FEMININE OR NEUTRAL FORM OF ADJECTIVE	+ -*mente*	
lenta	lentamente	*slowly*
rápida	rápidamente	*rapidly*
dulce	dulcemente	*sweetly*
alegre	alegremente	*joyously*
feliz	felizmente	*happily*
fácil	fácilmente	*easily*
difícil	difícilmente	*with difficulty*

MASCULINE OR NEUTRAL FORM OF ADJECTIVE USED AS ADVERB

fuerte	*strongly, tightly*	despacio	*slowly*
		lento	*slowly*
alto	*high, loud*	rápido	*rapidly, fast*
bajo	*low*		
claro	*clearly*	hondo	*deeply*
barato	*cheaply*	justo	*exactly, just*
caro	*expensively*		
		seguro	*definitely*
derecho	*straight*		
recto	*straight*		

Adverbs of Degree: To Answer ¿*cuánto*?

nada	*not at all*
poco	*hardly at all*
un poco	*slightly*
algo	*a bit*
bastante	*quite*
bien	*very*
muy	*very*
tan	*so*
más que	*more than*
menos que	*less than*
demasiado	*a lot, an extreme amount*

Review the forms in the charts on the preceding pages.

Adverbs give information about the time, place, direction, number of occasions, frequency, and manner of the action of verbs. They do not change in form. Often a longer expression or prepositional phrase functions as an adverb.

Adverbs can also modify the meaning of adjectives and other adverbs (see pages 89–90).

Time Markers

Review the time markers on pages 231–232.

Time markers can be placed at the beginning of a sentence, after a verb, or at the end of a sentence.

■ *Actualmente* is a false cognate, or *falso amigo* (see pages 303–305). It means "at present," "at this time," "right now." "Actually" is translated as *realmente* in Spanish.

AVOID THE *Blunder*

Do not use *actualmente* when you mean "actually."

✗ Actualmente, no es mi hermano.

■ The English word "last" is expressed in different ways in Spanish.

anoche   *last night*

● When it means "the period before this one," *pasado(-a)* is typically used.

el año pasado   *last year*
el viernes pasado   *last Friday*
la semana pasada   *last week*

AVOID THE *Blunder*

✗ la noche pasada   ✗ el día pasado

● When it means "the final period," *último(-a)* is used.

el último día   *the last day*
la última noche   *the last night*

la última semana de julio	*the last week of July*
las últimas semanas del verano	*the last weeks of summer*
los últimos días del año	*the last days of the year*

AVOID THE *Blunder*

✗ el pasado día
✗ la pasada noche

■ The English word "next" is expressed in two different ways in Spanish.

■ When it means "the period after this one," *próximo(-a)* is used.

la próxima semana	*next week*
el próximo mes	*next month*
el próximo año	*next year*

■ When it means "the period after that one," *siguiente* is used.

el día siguiente	*the next (following) day*
el mes siguiente	*the next (following) month*
el año siguiente	*the next (following) year*

AVOID THE *Blunder*

Do not use *próximo* to express "the next day" if the action has been completed. Use *siguiente* to express this meaning.

✗ Fuimos al cine el próximo día.

■ *Hace* is used to express the English "ago" (see page 123).

hace media hora	*a half hour ago*
hace diez días	*10 days ago*
hace catorce años	*14 years ago*

AVOID THE *Blunder*

✗ una media hora pasada
✗ diez días pasados

■ The English word "time" is expressed in several ways in Spanish.

■ To tell the current time, the pattern *es la una/son las dos* is used. To tell the time of an event or activity, the pattern *a la una/a las dos* is used (see page 261).

AVOID THE *Blunder*

✗ El concierto son las ocho.

■ The English adverb "again" can be expressed with *otra vez, de nuevo*, or *nuevamente*. It can also be expressed with the verb phrase *volver a* + infinitive.

Mañana nos vemos otra vez.	*Tomorrow we'll see each other again.*
Te vuelvo a llamar el viernes.	*I'll call you again on Friday.*

■ *Tiempo* is used to express time as a commodity.

No tengo mucho tiempo.	*I don't have much time.*
No hay tiempo para hacerlo.	*There's no time to do it.*
El tiempo vuela.	*Time flies.*
Salud, dinero, amor y tiempo para gastarlos.	*Health, money, love—and time to enjoy them.*

■ *Buen tiempo* means "good weather" in Spanish. To express "to have a good time," *pasarlo bien* or *divertirse* is used (see page 308).

Lo pasé muy bien en la Argentina.	*I had a good time in Argentina.*
¿Lo pasaste bien?	*Did you have a good time?*
Nos divertimos mucho en la fiesta.	*We had a good time at the party.*
Espero que se diviertan.	*I hope you all have a good time.*

AVOID THE *Blunder*

Don't confuse time with the weather!

✗ Tuve un buen tiempo en la Argentina.
✗ ¿Tuviste un buen tiempo?

■ In English, the markers "before" and "after" are followed by indicative constructions. In Spanish, there are two different patterns.

▪ When the subject of the first verb is the same person who performs the action of the second verb, the second verb is in the infinitive form after the preposition *de*.

Quiero estudiar antes de salir.	*I want to study before I go out.*
Fueron a casa después de hacer el examen.	*They went home after they took the exam.*
Voy a llamarte antes de hablar con ella.	*I'm going to call you before I talk to her.*
Vamos a jugar cartas después de comer.	*We're going to play cards after we eat.*

AVOID THE *Blunder*

✗ Quiero estudiar antes que hablo con ella.
✗ Fueron a casa después que hago el examen.

▪ When the subject of the first verb is a different person from the subject of the second verb, a subjunctive form is used after *antes que* or *después* (see page 171).

Quiero estudiar antes que regresen a casa los niños.	*I want to study before the children get home.*
La profesora fue a casa después que hicieran el examen los estudiantes.	*The teacher went home after the students took the exam.*
Voy a llamarte antes que salga mi esposo.	*I'm going to call you before my husband leaves.*
Vamos a comer después que hayan descansado un poco.	*We'll eat after you all have rested a bit.*

AVOID THE *Blunder*

Do not use the indicative after *antes que* or *después que*.

✗ Quiero estudiar antes que regresan los niños.
✗ Fue a casa después que hicieron el examen.
✗ Voy a llamarte antes que sale mi esposo.
✗ Vamos a comer después que han descansado.

Frequency Markers

Review the frequency markers in the chart on page 233.

■ To tell the number of times an activity takes place, expressions such as *una vez, dos veces,* and *muchas veces* are used.

Estuve en México una vez.	*I was in Mexico once.*
Mi tío hizo el examen dos veces.	*My uncle took the test two times.*
Ella bailó con Juan muchas veces.	*She danced with Juan many times.*
Quiero ver la película otra vez.	*I want to see the movie again.*

AVOID THE *Blunder*

✗ Estuve allí un tiempo.
✗ Comimos en ese restaurante muchos tiempos.

■ To modify a frequency expression, *más de* or *menos de* is used.

Mi tía come más de tres veces al día.	*My aunt eats more than three times a day.*
Voy al gimnasio menos de cuatro veces a la semana.	*I go to the gym less than four times a week.*

AVOID THE *Blunder*

Do not use *más que* before a number.

✗ Mi tía come más que tres veces al día.
✗ Tengo más que veinte dólares.

■ *A veces* is used to express "sometimes."

A veces estudiamos hasta muy tarde.	*Sometimes we study until very late.*
Ellos me ayudan a veces.	*They help me sometimes.*

AVOID THE *Blunder*

✗ algunos tiempos

■ The adverbs *siempre* and *nunca* can be used with both the imperfect and the preterite tenses, with slightly different meanings.

When used with the imperfect, *siempre* and *nunca* emphasize the meaning of the imperfect tense. They stress the fact that the verb describes a past period of time, and that the action occurred over and over in a general way (see pages 133–134).

Mi hermana siempre ayudaba a mi mamá.	*My sister would always help my mother.*
Siempre íbamos juntos al cine los sábados.	*We always used to go to the movies together on Saturdays.*
Su novio nunca se olvidaba de llamarla.	*Her boyfriend would never forget to call her.*
Nunca estábamos de acuerdo en nada.	*We used to never agree on anything.*

When used with the preterite, *siempre* and *nunca* refer to a whole period of time that is now over and that the speaker chooses not to describe any further (see page 130).

Mi hermana siempre lo quiso.	*My sister loved him the whole time.*
Siempre supimos la verdad.	*We knew the truth all along.*
Nunca pude olvidarte.	*I never managed to forget you.*
Nunca tuviste tiempo para mí.	*You didn't (even once) have time for me.*

AVOID THE *Blunder*

Do not assume that *siempre*, like "always" in English, refers only to a description of habitual past action.

■ To express action that occurs regularly on certain days, no preposition is used in Spanish. Also note that all the days whose names end in -*s* have only one form and do not change in the plural; *sábado* and *domingo* are the only days that add -*s* in the plural.

Tenemos clases los lunes.	*We have classes on Mondays.*
Salimos los viernes por la noche.	*We go out on Friday nights.*
¿Qué haces los fines de semana?	*What do you do on weekends?*
No trabaja los sábados.	*She doesn't work on Saturdays.*

AVOID THE *Blunder*

✗ en los lunes
✗ en los fines de semana

Place Markers

Review the place markers in the chart on pages 233–234.

■ The preposition *en* can indicate "in a place," "on a place," or "at a place."

Las cartas están en la caja.	*The letters are in the box.*
Los platos están en la mesa.	*The plates are on the table.*
Los niños están en la escuela.	*The children are at school.*
Comemos a menudo en este restaurante.	*We often eat at this restaurant.*

AVOID THE *Blunder*

✗ Está al aeropuerto.
✗ Comemos al restaurante.
✗ Ella está a casa.

■ The preposition *a* can indicate movement toward a place. When a verb that indicates movement toward a place (such as *ir*) is combined with another verb, *a* is used instead of *en* to indicate "in" or "at."

Vamos al aeropuerto.	*We're going to the airport.*
Vamos a comer al restaurante.	*We're going to eat at the restaurant./ We're going to the restaurant to eat.*

AVOID THE *Blunder*

✗ Voy a comer en el restaurante.

■ In many countries, *acá* is used instead of *aquí* when used with a verb of movement, such as *venir*. Likewise, *allá* is used instead of *allí* when used with a verb of movement, such as *ir*.

Estoy aquí.	*I'm here.*
Juana está allí.	*Juana is over there.*
Ven acá.	*Come here.*
Ve allá.	*Go over there.*

■ Certain adverbs of place are different from their prepositional counterparts.

Mis cosas están arriba.	*My things are up there.*
Mis cosas están encima de las tuyas.	*My things are on top of yours.*

Las maletas están abajo.	*The suitcases are down there.*
Las maletas están debajo de los libros.	*The suitcases are underneath the books.*
El dinero está adentro.	*The money is inside.*
El dinero está dentro de la maleta.	*The money is inside the suitcase.*
El coche está afuera.	*The car is outside.*
El coche está fuera del garaje.	*The car is outside (of) the garage.*
Tenemos que seguir adelante.	*We have to go forward.*
Hay muchas personas delante de nosotros.	*There are a lot of people ahead of us.*

AVOID THE *Blunder*

✗ adentro de la maleta
✗ afuera de la casa
✗ adelante de nosotros

■ *Delante de* and *enfrente de* both mean "in front of," but they do not express the same concept. *Delante de* expresses the concept "ahead of," as in a row or line. *Enfrente de* expresses the concept "facing."

Esta cola es muy larga y hay muchas personas delante de mí.	*This line is really long, and there are a lot of people in front of me.*
La maestra está enfrente de la clase.	*The teacher is in front of the class.*

Enfrente also translates into English as "across from."

La casa enfrente de mi casa es blanca.	*The house across (the street) from mine is white.*

AVOID THE *Blunder*

Do not use *enfrente de* to indicate someone or something whose back is in front of you.

✗ Él está enfrente de mí en la cola.

■ Prepositional phrases that indicate place include the word *de* (*adentro de, enfrente de*), with three exceptions: *en, sobre,* and *entre.*

Los documentos están en la mesa.	*The documents are on the table.*
He puesto las fotos sobre la mesa.	*I put the photographs on the table.*

El libro pequeño está entre dos
libros grandes.

*The little book is between two big
ones.*

Encontramos sus papeles entre
los de otras personas.

*We found your papers among
those of other people.*

AVOID THE *Blunder*

✗ El libro está sobre de la mesa.
✗ El libro pequeño está entre de dos libros grandes.

Adverbs of Manner

Adverbs of manner are formed by adding *-mente* to the feminine or
neutral form of an adjective. If there is an accent mark in the adjective,
it is retained in the adverb.

El chico corrió rápidamente.

The boy ran fast.

Ella pronunció cuidadosamente
cada palabra.

*She pronounced each word
carefully.*

■ When two or more adverbs of manner modify the same verb, *-mente*
is omitted from all but the last one.

Ella leyó lenta y cuidadosamente
cada palabra.

*She read each word slowly and
carefully.*

AVOID THE *Blunder*

✗ lentamente y cuidadosamente

■ When *recientemente* directly precedes a past participle (see page
87), it is shortened to *recién*.

Llevaron al niño recién nacido
a casa.

*They took the newborn child
home.*

Los recién casados están en
Madrid.

The newlyweds are in Madrid.

AVOID THE *Blunder*

✗ el niño recientemente nacido
✗ la mujer recientemente casada

■ Several masculine adjectives are used as adverbs of manner.

alto	*high*	derecho	*straight*
bajo	*low*	despacio	*slowly*
barato	*cheaply*	hondo	*deeply*
caro	*dearly, expensively*	recto	*straight*

Tiró la pelota muy alto.	*He threw the ball very high.*
Canta bajo.	*He sings low.*
Me costó muy caro.	*It cost me dearly.*
Siga derecho.	*Continue straight ahead.*
Caminaron despacio.	*They walked slowly.*
Respire hondo.	*Breathe deeply.*

■ Certain adverbs have two alternative forms: the masculine or neutral singular adjective form and the feminine or neutral singular adjective form + -*mente*.

claro/claramente	*clearly*
fuerte/fuertemente	*strongly, tightly*
justo/justamente	*exactly*
lento/lentamente	*slowly*
seguro/seguramente	*safely*

El profesor habló claro/claramente.	*The teacher spoke clearly.*
Sujétalo fuerte/fuertemente.	*Fasten it tightly.*
El chico corrió rápido/rápidamente.	*The boy ran fast.*

AVOID THE *Blunder*

Only certain adverbs have two alternative forms.

✗ altamente	✗ bajamente	✗ caramente
✗ baratamente	✗ hondamente	

■ Prepositional phrases are often used to express manner.

a ciegas	*blindly*
con calma	*calmly*
con cuidado	*carefully*
con esmero	*with care*

Tomó la decisión a ciegas.	*She made the decision blindly.*
Reportó las noticias con calma.	*He reported the news calmly.*

Ella pronunció cada palabra con cuidado.	*She pronounced each word carefully.*
Cocinó el plato con esmero.	*He prepared the dish with care.*

■ *Cada vez más* + an adverb of manner indicates steadily increasing intensity.

La chica corre cada vez más rápido.	*The girl runs faster and faster.*
Sus padres son cada vez más estrictos.	*His parents are getting stricter.*

Adverbs of Degree

Review the adverbs of degree in the chart on page 235.

■ The adverbs *un poco, bastante, muy, bien,* and *demasiado* can modify adjectives (see pages 89–91), as well as adverbs of manner.

Es un poco tarde.	*It's a little late.*
Está bastante lejos de aquí.	*It's pretty far from here.*
Ella maneja muy lentamente.	*She drives very slowly.*
Ella maneja bien lentamente.	*She drives really slowly.*
Él corre demasiado rápido.	*He runs extremely fast.*
Él corre rapidísimo.	*He runs extremely fast.*

AVOID THE *Blunder*

Demasiado is better translated as "extremely" rather than "too." "Too" indicates a negative consequence, while *demasiado* does not.

✗ Su casa está demasiado lejos.
  (meaning you are not going to go there)

■ Unlike "very" in English, the adverb *muy* cannot stand alone in answer to a question. *Mucho* is used instead.

—¿Estás cansado? —Sí, mucho.	*"Are you tired?" "Yes, very."*
—¿Es bonita? —Sí, mucho.	*"Is she pretty?" "Yes, very."*

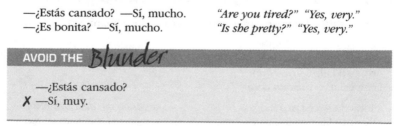

AVOID THE *Blunder*

  —¿Estás cansado?
✗ —Sí, muy.

■ To compare adverbs of manner, *tan* + adverb + *como* is used.

Ella cocina tan bien como su mamá.	*She cooks as well as her mother (does).*
Él canta tan dulcemente como su hermana.	*He sings as sweetly as his sister (does).*

To indicate "as much as," *tanto como* is used.

Susana habla tanto como su mamá.	*Susana talks as much as her mother (does).*
Roberto come tanto como su papá.	*Roberto eats as much as his father (does).*

AVOID THE *Blunder*

✗ tan bien que su mamá
✗ tanto que su papá

■ To indicate "to what extent," *lo* + adverb is used.

Es impresionante lo bien que canta.	*It's impressive how well she sings.*
Me preocupa lo rápido que maneja.	*It worries me how fast she drives.*

AVOID THE *Blunder*

✗ Es impresionante como bien canta.
✗ Me preocupa como rápido maneja.

■ When an adverbial comparison is made that involves two different subjects and verbs, *más/menos* + adverb + *de lo que* is used between the two clauses.

Ella trabaja más duro de lo que piensas.	*She works harder than you think (she does).*
Su hijo maneja más rápido de lo que ella quiere.	*Her son drives faster than she wants (him to).*

The adverb *apenas* is used to indicate "hardly" or "just barely."

Apenas tiene suficiente para comer.	*He hardly has enough to eat.*
Apenas podía verlos.	*I could barely see them.*

Questions

Questions are always preceded by an upside-down question mark and followed by a standard question mark. The question mark immediately precedes the question, even if the question does not begin the sentence. In this case, the first word of the question is not capitalized.

A propósito, ¿va Roberto a la reunión?	*By the way, is Roberto going to the meeting?*
Y tú, ¿qué vas a hacer?	*What about you? What are you going to do?*

AVOID THE *Blunder*

✗ ¿A propósito, va Roberto a la reunión?
✗ ¿Y tú, qué vas a hacer?
✗ Y tú, ¿Qué vas a hacer?

Questions are formed in several ways in Spanish.

■ Yes-or-no questions are usually formed by reversing the order of the subject and the verb, using question marks at the beginning and at the end of the question, or using rising intonation at the end.

¿Estudia Jaime?	*Does Jaime study?*
¿Eres (tú) de Lima?	*Are you from Lima?*
¿Viven ustedes aquí?	*Do you all live here?*
¿Trabajan tus hermanos?	*Do your brothers work?*

AVOID THE *Blunder*

There is no equivalent of "do you?"/"does he?"/"are they?" in Spanish. Do not try to translate these expressions.

✗ Hace Jaime estudiar?
✗ Hacen ustedes vivir aquí?

□ When the answer is "yes," it is expressed by *sí*. The following expressions may also be used.

Cómo no.	*Yes, indeed.*
Por supuesto.	*Yes, (naturally).*
Claro.	*Of course.*

To add another positive element, *también* may be used.

Sí, Jaime estudia, y yo también.	*Yes, Jaime studies, and so do I.*
Sí, soy de Lima, y mi papá también.	*Yes, I'm from Lima, and so is my dad.*

☐ When the answer is "no," it is expressed by *no*. The following expressions may also be used.

De ninguna manera.	*No way.*
Todavía no.	*Not yet.*
Hoy no.	*Not today.*
Ahora no.	*Not now.*
Mañana no.	*Not tomorrow.*

AVOID THE *Blunder*

In a short negative answer, put the *no* after the adverb.

—¿Vas a comprarlo?
✗   No hoy.
✗ —No ahora.
✗ —No mañana.

When a sentence contains a negative word in any position other than the first word in the sentence, the verb is preceded by *no*.

No tengo nada.	*I don't have anything.*
No vamos a ninguna parte.	*We're not going anywhere.*
No lo hace nunca.	*He never does it.*
No conozco a nadie.	*I don't know anybody.*
No hay ningún libro en la mesa.	*There's no book on the table./ There are no books on the table.*

AVOID THE *Blunder*

Double negatives are correct in Spanish.

✗ Tengo nada.
✗ No hay un libro en la mesa.

In the examples below, the first *no* answers a question; the second *no* is used before the verb to make the sentence negative.

No, Jaime no estudia.	*No, Jaime doesn't study.*
No, no soy de Lima.	*No, I'm not from Lima.*

To add an additional negative element, *tampoco* may be used.

No, Jaime no estudia, ni yo tampoco.	*No, Jaime doesn't study, and neither do I.*
No, no soy de Lima, ni mi papá tampoco.	*No, I'm not from Lima, and neither is my dad.*

■ Many questions can be formed with interrogative words.

An accent mark is used over the stressed vowel of an interrogative word in a question.

¿Quién es?	*Who is he?*
¿De dónde es?	*Where is he from?*
¿Hasta cuándo te quedas?	*How long are you staying?*

☐ Two interrogative words, *quién* and *cuánto*, can be either singular or plural.

If you are sure the answer is singular, or do not know if the answer is singular or plural, *quién* is used to ask "who."

¿Quién es ese chico?	*Who is that boy?*
¿Con quién estás?	*Who are you with?*

If you are pretty sure the answer is plural, *quiénes* is used to ask "who."

¿Quiénes son esos chicos?	*Who are those boys?*
¿Quiénes van a la fiesta?	*Who is going to the party?*

AVOID THE *Blunder*

Do not use *quién* if you expect the answer to be plural.

✗ ¿Quién va a la fiesta/a la reunión?

Cuánto is used to express "how much." *Cuántos* is used to express "how many."

¿Cuánto cuestan estos zapatos?	*How much do these shoes cost?*
¿Cuántas personas vienen esta noche?	*How many people are coming tonight?*

☐ Both *qué* and *cuál* can mean "what" and "which," but they are not interchangeable.

Qué can ask for an identification or a definition.

¿Qué es esto?	*What's this?*
¿Qué es eso?	*What's that?*
¿Qué es un abrelatas?	*What's an "abrelatas"?*

Qué followed by a noun asks "which one."

¿Qué vestido te gusta más?	*Which dress do you like best?*
¿Qué abrelatas vas a usar?	*Which can opener are you going to use?*

AVOID THE *Blunder*

✗ ¿Cuál vestido te gusta más?   ✗ ¿Cuál abrelatas vas a usar?

Cuál followed by a form of the verb *ser* asks "what" (which one of all the possibilities).

¿Cuál es su nombre?	*What's your name?*
¿Cuál es la fecha?	*What's the date?*
¿Cuál es su número de teléfono?	*What's your telephone number?*

Cuál + *de* + a plural noun asks "which" of two or more alternatives.

¿Cuál de los libros prefieres?	*Which book do you prefer?*
¿Cuál de las ideas te interesa más?	*Which idea interests you the most?*

AVOID THE *Blunder*

✗ ¿Qué es su nombre?   ✗ ¿Qué es su número de teléfono?

☐ In Spanish, prepositions precede a question word. They never go at the end of a question.

¿De qué hablas?	*What are you talking about?*
¿De dónde son ellos?	*Where are they from?*
¿Para quién es el regalo?	*Who is the present for?*
¿Con quién vas?	*Who are you going with?*
¿De quién es este suéter?	*Whose sweater is this?*
¿A quién llamas?	*Who are you calling?*

A dónde is usually contracted to *adónde*.

¿Adónde van Uds.?	*Where are you all going?*
¿Adónde quieren ir?	*Where do they want to go?*

AVOID THE *Blunder*

✗ ¿Qué hablas de?
✗ ¿Quién es el regalo para?
✗ ¿Dónde vas?

☐ *Por qué* is used to ask "why." It is two words, with an accent mark in *qué*. To answer "because," *porque* is used. It is one word and does not have an accent mark.

—¿Por qué no está trabajando   *"Why isn't your brother working*
    tu hermano hoy?   *today?"*
—Porque está enfermo.   *"Because he's sick."*

AVOID THE *Blunder*

✗ —¿Porque no trabaja?
✗ —Por que está enfermo.

■ Questions may be asked indirectly, following certain clauses. As in direct questions, the interrogative word has an accent mark.

José me preguntó qué hiciste   *José asked me what you did with*
    con el dinero.   *the money.*
Dime a qué hora quieres venir.   *Tell me what time you want to*
                                    come.

Lack of knowledge can also be expressed with a question word within a sentence. An accent mark is used in the question word.

No sé cómo lo hace.   *I don't know how he does it.*
Necesitamos saber adónde fue. *We need to know where she went.*

When there is no direct or indirect question, *que, cuando, como,* and *donde* do not have accent marks.

Pedro me dijo que quería   *Pedro told me (that) he wanted*
    acompañarnos.   *to go with us.*
Estoy contenta cuando estás aquí. *I'm happy when you're here.*
Corre como el viento.   *He runs like the wind.*
Vamos al restaurante donde   *Let's go to the restaurant where*
    comimos la semana pasada.   *we ate last week.*

Exclamations

Exclamations are preceded by an upside-down exclamation point and followed by a standard exclamation point. The exclamatory word has an accent mark. The following patterns are used.

■ *¡Qué* + noun + *más/tan* + adjective!

¡Qué niño más adorable!   *What an adorable child!*
¡Qué clase tan aburrida!   *What a boring class!*

- ¡*Qué* + adjective + noun!

¡Qué buena idea!	*What a good idea!*
¡Qué mala suerte!	*What bad luck!*

AVOID THE *Blunder*

✗ ¡Qué un adorable niño!
✗ ¡Qué una clase aburrida!

- ¡*Qué* + adjective/adverb + verb!

¡Qué bonita estás!	*How pretty you look!*
¡Qué bien hablas español!	*How well you speak Spanish!*
¡Qué rápido corre!	*How fast he runs!*

AVOID THE *Blunder*

✗ ¡Cómo bonita estás!
✗ ¡Cómo bien hablas!

- ¡*Cómo* + verb!

¡Cómo habla!	*How she talks!/The way she talks!*
¡Cómo corre!	*How he runs!/The way he runs!*

- ¡*Cuánto* + (object) + verb!

¡Cuánto te quiero!	*I love you so much!*
¡Cuánto gastas!	*You spend so much!*

- ¡(object) + verb + *tanto*!

¡Te quiero tanto!	*I love you so much!*
¡Gastas tanto!	*You spend so much!*

Exercises

A *Fill in the blanks with the Spanish equivalent of the English expression in parentheses.*

1. Ella fue a Chile la semana _____ (*last*).

2. ¿Te llamó Santiago _____ (*last night*)?

3. La _____ (*last*) vez que lo vi fue

   _____ (*two weeks ago*).

4. Siempre nos divertimos durante las _____ (*last*) semanas del año.

5. Ramón vio dos películas el sábado y vio otras dos el día

   _____ (*next*).

6. Nos vamos a ver el _____ (*next*) viernes.

7. Tuvimos muy _____ (*good weather*).

8. Mi hijo vio esa película tres _____ (*times*).

9. ¿_____? (*Did you have a good time?*)

10. El _____ (*time*) es oro.

11. Por favor, toca esa canción _____ (*again*).

12. _____ (*Sometimes*) camina al trabajo y vuelve en el metro.

B *Fill in the blanks with the infinitive or subjunctive form of the verb in parentheses, as appropriate.*

1. El profesor fue a casa después de _____ (*leer*) los exámenes.

2. Ella va a pintar la sala antes que _____ (*regresar*) su esposo.

3. Vamos a descansar después que _____ (*volver*) los otros.

4. Ana siempre hace ejercicio antes de _____ (*vestirse*).

C *Fill in the blanks with the appropriate Spanish expressions.*

1. En mi oficina siempre nos reunimos _____ (*on Mondays*) a las diez de la mañana.

2. No voy a estar aquí _____ (*on Monday*), pues tengo una cita con el médico.

3. _____ (*The whole time*) estuve de acuerdo contigo.

4. Su novio la llama _____ (*more than*) dos veces cada día.

5. Siempre estudiamos _____ (*at*) la biblioteca.

D *Circle the expression that best completes each sentence.*

1. Hay tres personas **delante de | enfrente de | adelante** mí en la cola.

2. Los niños están jugando **fuera | afuera**.

3. Hay más de diez personas **dentro de | dentro | adentro** la casa.

4. Entramos en el segundo piso y los cuartos de los niños están **debajo de | debajo | abajo**.

E *Fill in the blanks with the appropriate Spanish adverbs.*

1. Alejandra cantó _____ (*softly and sweetly*).

2. Los _____ (*recently*) casados ya volvieron de su luna de miel.

3. Ella recibió la noticia _____ (*calmly*).

4. Yo corro _____ (*slowly*).

F *Match each English expression in the left column with a Spanish expression in the right column.*

_____ 1. *as much as*   a. tantos como

_____ 2. *more than you think* b. tanto como

_____ 3. *as well as*   c. tan bien como

_____ 4. *as many as*   d. lo bien que

_____ 5. *how well*   e. más de lo que piensas

G *Express each of the following questions in Spanish.*

1. *Where are you going?*

_____

2. *What are you all talking about?*

_____

3. *Who are you going to the movies with?*

_____

4. *When are you all coming back?*

_____

H *Now write negative responses to the questions in Exercise G.*

1. _____

2. _____

3. _____

4. _____

I *Match each English expression in the left column with a Spanish expression in the right column.*

_____ 1. *How talkative she is!*   a. ¡Cómo habla!

_____ 2. *How does he speak?*   b. No sabes lo mucho que habla.

_____ 3. *Because he talks so much.*   c. ¡Habla tanto!

_____ 4. *Why does he talk so much?*   d. ¡Qué habladora es!

_____ 5. *How he talks!*   e. ¿Por qué habla tanto?

_____ 6. *She talks so much!*   f. Porque habla tanto.

_____ 7. *You don't know how much he talks.*   g. ¿Cómo habla?

OTHER PREPOSITIONS

a	to, for, indicator of personal direct object	entre	between/among
		hacia	toward
ante	before (in the presence of)	hasta	until
bajo	under	para	destined for, for
con	with	por	by, along, for
contra	against	según	according to
de	from, of	sin	without
salvo, excepto	except	sobre	over, about, on
desde	since, from	tras	behind
en	in, on, at		

Review the prepositions in the chart above.

Form and Function of Prepositions

Prepositions are invariable in form. They often have no exact English equivalents.

■ When the prepositions *a* and *de* are used immediately before the masculine definite article *el*, the two words are contracted to *al* and *del*, unless the *el* is part of a proper name.

Vamos al mercado.	*We're going to the market.*
Ya salieron del edificio.	*They already left the building.*
Eduardo va a El Salvador la próxima semana.	*Eduardo is going to El Salvador next week.*

AVOID THE *Blunder*

✗ Vamos a el mercado.
✗ Ya salieron de el edificio.

257

■ Pronouns that follow prepositions have several variations.

■ In Spanish the subject pronouns *él, ella, usted, ustedes, ellos, ellas, nosotros,* and *vosotros* are used after prepositions, unlike English where the object pronouns ("him," "her," "you," "you all," "them," and "us") are used.

Voy con ella.	*I'm going with her.*
Lo hice por él.	*I did it because of him.*
El regalo es para nosotros.	*The present is for us.*
La carta es de ellos.	*The letter is from them.*

AVOID THE *Blunder*

Do not use the direct and indirect object pronouns *le, lo, la, les, los, las, nos,* and *os* after prepositions.

✗ Lo hice por lo.
✗ La carta es de los.

■ The subject pronouns *yo* and *tú* are used after the prepositions *entre, según, salvo,* and *excepto.*

El asunto es entre tú y yo.	*The matter is between you and me.*
Según tú, todo el mundo está loco.	*According to you, everyone is crazy.*
Todo el mundo salvo yo se va.	*Everybody except me is leaving.*

■ The object pronouns *mí* and *ti* are used after other prepositions.

Lo hizo por mí.	*He did it because of me.*
Tienes que ir sin mí.	*You have to go without me.*
El regalo es para ti.	*The present is for you.*
Estoy pensando en ti.	*I'm thinking about you.*

AVOID THE *Blunder*

Mí after a preposition has an accent mark to distinguish it from the possessive *mi. Ti* does not have an accent mark.

✗ por mi   ✗ para mi   ✗ mí casa   ✗ para tí

■ When the preposition *con* is followed by the pronoun *mí, ti,* or *si* ("me," "you," "himself," "herself," "themselves"), *-go* is added to form one word. The accent mark in *mí* is dropped (see page 14).

Puedes ir conmigo.	*You can go with me.*
No quiero hablar contigo.	*I don't want to talk to you.*

Rubén trajo sus libros consigo.
Los chicos se fueron, y se
llevaron la pizza consigo.

Rubén brought his books with him.
The boys left and took the pizza
with them.

AVOID THE *Blunder*

Do not use *él, ella, ellos,* or *ellas* to express "himself," "herself," or
"themselves."

✗ con mí	✗ con ti	✗ con sí
✗ con él	✗ con ella	
✗ con ellos	✗ con ellas	

- In Spanish, the preposition is usually repeated when there is more
than one object.

El regalo es para ti y para Carlos.
Lo hizo por mí y por ti.
Estoy pensando en ti y en él.
Vive lejos de mí y de mis
hermanos.

The present is for you and Carlos.
He did it because of me and you.
I'm thinking about you and him.
She lives far away from me and
my brothers.

AVOID THE *Blunder*

✗ El regalo es para ti y Carlos.
✗ Lo hizo por mí y ti.
✗ Estoy pensando en ti y él.
✗ Vive lejos de mí y mis hermanos.

■ A verb that directly follows a preposition is in the infinitive form (see
page 97).

Voy a llamarlo antes de salir.
Van al mercado a comprar pan.

I'm going to call him before I leave.
They're going to the market to
buy bread.

Vimos la película después de
comer.
Come menos para perder peso.

We watched the movie after we
ate.
She eats less in order to lose weight.

AVOID THE *Blunder*

✗ Voy a llamarlo antes de yo salgo.
✗ Vimos la película después que comimos.

■ In Spanish, a sentence never ends with a preposition. In both direct and indirect questions the preposition goes before the interrogative word.

¿De qué se queja?	*What is she complaining about?*
¿En quién piensas?	*Who are you thinking about?*
¿Desde cuándo están aquí?	*How long have you been here?*
¿Hasta cuándo se queda?	*How long is he staying?*
No sé con quién fue.	*I don't know who he went with.*
Díganos de quién es esta carta.	*Tell us who this letter is from.*

AVOID THE *Blunder*

✗ ¿Qué se queja de?   ✗ No sé quien fue con.
✗ ¿Quién piensas de?

■ Certain verb + preposition combinations in English are translated into Spanish using a verb without a preposition. The following verbs are some common examples (see page 104).

agradecer	*be grateful for*	escuchar	*listen to*
buscar	*look for*	llorar	*cry over*
esperar	*wait for*		
pagar	*pay for*	mirar	*look at*
pedir (i, i)	*ask for*		
votar	*vote for (something)*	padecer	*suffer from*
atender (ie)	*wait on, take care of*		
comentar	*comment on*		

Te agradezco tus consejos.	*I'm grateful for your advice.*
Estoy buscando mis lentes.	*I'm looking for my glasses.*
Espérame aquí.	*Wait for me here.*
Tenemos que pagar la luz.	*We have to pay for the electricity.*
Tienes que pedirle un cupón.	*You have to ask him for a coupon.*
¿Qué miras?	*What are you looking at?*

AVOID THE *Blunder*

✗ Estoy buscando para mis lentes.
✗ Tienes que pedirle por un cupón.
✗ Espera por mí aquí.
✗ ¿A qué miras?

Usage of Common Prepositions

Individual prepositions have a variety of uses.

a

The preposition *a* has specific uses and is sometimes required in set phrases.

■ *A* is used after *ir* and other verbs that indicate movement to another place.

Voy a la universidad.	*I'm going to the university.*
La chica corrió a la casa.	*The girl ran to the house.*
Nos mudamos a la ciudad.	*We moved to the city.*
Caminaron al mercado.	*They walked to the market.*

■ In only a few instances is *a* translated into English as "at" (see pages 272–273).

■ With the verb *ir* to indicate the activity intended.

Voy a estudiar a la universidad.	*I'm going to study at the university. (I'm going to the university to study.)*
Fueron a comer a un restaurante.	*They went to eat at a restaurant. (They went to a restaurant to eat.)*

■ With the verb *sentar* to indicate "facing."

La familia estaba sentada a la mesa.	*The family was seated at the table.*
La mujer se sentaba a la ventana y miraba a la gente.	*The woman used to sit at the window and watch people.*

■ To ask for and to indicate the time of an event.

¿A qué hora es la reunión?	*(At) what time is the meeting?*
Es a las diez.	*It's at 10 o'clock.*
Es a mediodía.	*It's at noon.*

■ The personal "*a*" is used before a direct object noun that refers to a person or a pet (see page 215).

Llamo a mi mamá todos los días.	*I call my mother every day.*
Vio a su amiga en la tienda.	*He saw his friend at the store.*
¿Cuándo visitan a su abuela?	*When do you visit your grandmother?*
¿Encontró al señor Sánchez?	*Did you find Mr. Sánchez?*

AVOID THE *Blunder*

Do not forget the *a*, even though it is not translated.

✗ Llamo mi mamá.   ✗ Vio su amiga.

The "personal *a*" is typically not used after the verb *tener.*

Tengo tres primos en California.	*I have three cousins in California.*
Tienen un hijo.	*They have one child.*

■ *A* is used before an indefinite pronoun that refers to an unidentified person.

—¿Conoces a alguien que hable italiano?	*"Do you know anyone who speaks Italian?"*
—No, no conozco a nadie aquí.	*"No, I don't know anybody here."*
—¿Ves a algún chico de nuestro colegio?	*"Do you see any boys from our school?"*
—No, no veo a ninguno.	*"No, I don't see any (not a single one)."*

■ *A* is used with exchange-type verbs that indicate something taken from another person or something done to or for another person (see pages 105–106 and 218–219).

Raúl le compró un coche a ese tipo.	*Raúl bought a car from that guy.*
A mí me robaron la cartera.	*They stole my purse (from me).*
Ana le regaló una corbata a su hijo.	*Ana gave her son a necktie.*
Miguel le mandó la carta a Pedro.	*Miguel sent the letter to Pedro.*

AVOID THE *Blunder*

✗ Robaron mi cartera de mí.
✗ Ana regaló su hijo una corbata.

■ *A* is used before indirect object nouns and the pronouns that refer to them.

A mí me gustan las telenovelas.	*I like soap operas. (They appeal to me.)*
A Juan no le molesta el ruido.	*The noise doesn't bother Juan.*
A nosotros no nos gusta el frío.	*We don't like the cold. (It doesn't please us.)*
Y a ti, ¿qué te interesa?	*And you, what are you interested in? (What is interesting to you?)*

■ *A* is used after certain verbs and is followed by another verb in the infinitive form (see page 97). Following are some common examples.

aprender a	*learn to*	invitar a	*invite to*
atreverse a	*dare to*	negarse a	*refuse to*
ayudar a	*help (do)*	obligar a	*make (someone) do*
comenzar a	*begin to*	ofrecerse a	*offer to*
decidirse a	*decide to*	oponerse a	*be opposed to*
detenerse a	*stop to*	ponerse a	*begin, set out to*
empezar a	*begin to*	resolverse a	*make up one's mind to*
enseñar a	*teach (to)*	volver a	*(do) again*

Aprendí a manejar el año pasado.   *I learned to drive last year.*
Se atrevió a decirme eso.   *He dared to tell me that.*
Empezó a llover.   *It started to rain.*
Volvió a llamarme.   *She called me again.*

AVOID THE *Blunder*

Do not forget the *a*, even though the English infinitive begins with "to."

✗ Aprendí manejar.
✗ Empezó llover.

■ *A* is used after certain verbs and is followed by a noun.

acercarse a	*approach*	condenar a	*condemn to*
acostumbrarse a	*get used to*	dar a	*have a view of*
asistir a	*attend*	dirigirse a	*head toward*
asomarse a	*lean out of*	jugar a	*play*

La chica asiste a todas sus clases.   *The girl attends all her classes.*
Mi habitación da a la plaza.   *My room overlooks the plaza.*

VERBS RELATED TO THE SENSES

oler a	*smell like*	saber a	*taste like*
parecerse a	*look like*	sonar a	*sound like*

La casa olía a humo.   *The house smelled like smoke.*
Ella se parece a su mamá.   *She looks like her mother.*

AVOID THE

Do not use a different preposition, and do not leave the preposition out.

✗ Asiste las clases.
✗ La casa olía como humo.

■ *A* is used before certain nouns to indicate the manner in which something is done.

La blusa fue bordada a mano.	*The blouse was embroidered by hand.*
Escribe el trabajo a máquina.	*Type the paper.* ✗
Invirtió en la empresa a ciegas.	*He invested in the firm blindly.*
Fue a la estación a pie.	*He went to the station on foot.*

AVOID THE

✗ bordar por mano   ✗ ir en pie
✗ escribir por máquina   ✗ lavar por mano

■ *A* is used to express certain measurements.

El coche corre a 70 millas por hora.	*The car is going 70 miles an hour.* ✗
Se venden las galletas a tres dólares la docena.	*The cookies are on sale for three dollars a dozen.* ✗

■ *A* is used to express that something happens a certain number of times in a given period of time.

Comemos tres veces al día.	*We eat three times a day.*
La llamo una vez a la semana.	*I call her once a week.*
Lo visita varias veces al año.	*She visits him several times a year.*
Van al cine una vez al mes.	*They go to the movies once a month.*

■ *A* is used to express distance.

Su casa está a 50 kilómetros de la ciudad.	*Their house is 50 kilometers from the city.* ✗

quedo? too?

■ *A* is used to express "style."

Celebramos a la española.	*We celebrated Spanish style.*
Preparó los frijoles a la mexicana.	*She prepared the beans Mexican style.*
Vamos a cocinar las papas al estilo peruano.	*We're going to cook the potatoes Peruvian style.*

? spain?

■ *A* is used to indicate musical accompaniment.

Bailamos al son cubano.	*We danced to the Cuban beat.*
Marcharon al compás de los tambores.	*They marched to the beat of the drums.*

■ *A* can be used to give an order or exhortation.

¡A trabajar!	*Get to work!/Let's get to work!*
¡A comer!	*Eat!/Let's eat!*

■ *A* is used before *qué* to express "I'll bet."

¡A qué no sabes quién es ese chico!	*I'll bet you don't know who that boy is!*

■ *A* is used in certain set phrases.

a base de	*based on*	a lo mejor	*most likely*
a caballo	*on horseback*	a menudo	*often*
a causa de	*because of*	a partir de	*beginning from (a time)*
a consecuencia de	*because of*		
		a pesar de	*in spite of*
a costa de	*at the expense of*	a propósito	*on purpose, by the way*
a diferencia de	*compared to*		
a duras penas	*with difficulty*	a saber	*namely*
a escondidas	*secretly*	a salvo	*unharmed*
a eso de	*approximately*	a solas	*all alone*
a espaldas de	*behind (some-one's) back*	a tiempo	*on time*
		a través de	*by means of*
a favor de	*in favor of*	a veces	*sometimes*
a fin de cuentas	*after all*	al contrario	*quite the opposite*
a gusto	*according to taste*	al principio	*at first*
a la larga	*in the long run*	al revés	*backwards*
a lo largo de	*along (a path)*		

con

The preposition *con* has specific uses and is sometimes required after certain verbs.

- *Con* is often used like "with" in English.

Ven conmigo.	*Come with me.*
Voy contigo.	*I'm going with you.*
Nos reunimos con los nuevos empleados.	*We met with the new employees.* ✗

- *Con* can indicate a way of doing something.

Caminó al trabajo con dificultad.	*He walked to work with difficulty.* ✗
Hay que tomar las cosas con calma.	*One must accept things calmly.* ✗
Nos ayudó con mucho gusto.	*She helped us with pleasure.*

- Following are some common verbs that are followed by *con*.

acabar con	*finish off*	encontrarse con	*run into* ✗
casarse con	*marry*	hablar con	*talk to*
coincidir con	*agree with*	meterse con	*challenge*
contar con	*count on*	poder con	*be able to deal with*
contentar con	*be satisfied with* ✓		
cumplir con	*fulfill*	soñar con	*dream about*
dar con	*run into* ✓		

Julia se casa con Martín muy pronto.	*Julia is marrying Martín soon.* ✗
Coincido contigo en eso.	*I agree with you on that.* ✗
Cuenta conmigo.	*Count on me.*
Voy a hablar con el profesor mañana.	*I'm going to talk to the professor tomorrow.*
No puedo con ese tipo.	*I can't deal with that guy.*
Estoy soñando contigo.	*I'm dreaming about you.* ✗

AVOID THE *Blunder*

Do not try to translate the English prepositions.

✗ Julia se casa a Martín.
✗ Cuenta en mí.
✗ Voy a hablar al profesor.
✗ Estoy soñando de ti.

sin

The preposition *sin* has several uses.

■ *Sin* generally corresponds to English "without."

Salió sin dinero.	*She left without money.*
No puedo vivir sin ti.	*I can't live without you.*
Se fue sin despedirse.	*He left without saying good-bye.* X
Lo llamé sin darme cuenta.	*I called him without realizing it.* ⊘

■ *Sin* occurs after the verb *llevar* and is followed by a verb in infinitive form to indicate how long it has been since something has occurred (see pages 116–117).

Llevamos veinte años sin vernos.	*We haven't seen each other for* ⊘ *twenty years.*
Lleva seis meses sin hablar español.	*He hasn't spoken Spanish for six months.*

AVOID THE *Blunder*

X No nos hemos visto por veinte años.
X No ha hablado español por seis meses.

■ *Sin* is followed by a verb in the infinitive form to indicate a condition that exists because an action has not occurred.

Hay problemas sin resolver.	*There are unsolved problems.* X
El dormitorio todavía está sin pintar.	*The bedroom is still unpainted.* x

de

The preposition *de* has specific uses and is sometimes required in set phrases.

■ *De* can indicate origin and is used in other expressions translated as "from."

—¿De dónde es Sara?	*"Where is Sara from?"*
—Es de Chicago.	*"She's from Chicago."*
Lo sé de memoria.	*I know it from memory.* O
Voy a Nueva York de vez en cuando.	*I go to New York from time to time.*
De ahora en adelante vamos a tener más cuidado.	*From now on we're going to* ⊘ *be more careful.*

■ *De... en...* indicates a repetitive activity, translated as "from ... to ..." in English.

El príncipe fue de casa en casa en busca de la princesa.	*The prince went from house to house looking for the princess.*

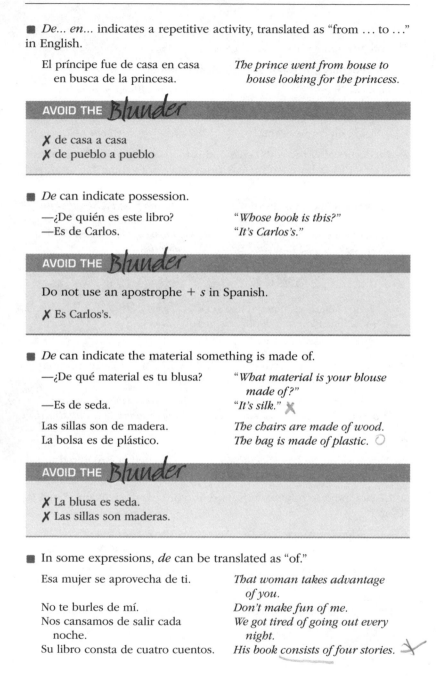

AVOID THE *Blunder*

✗ de casa a casa
✗ de pueblo a pueblo

■ *De* can indicate possession.

—¿De quién es este libro?	*"Whose book is this?"*
—Es de Carlos.	*"It's Carlos's."*

AVOID THE *Blunder*

Do not use an apostrophe + *s* in Spanish.

✗ Es Carlos's.

■ *De* can indicate the material something is made of.

—¿De qué material es tu blusa?	*"What material is your blouse made of?"*
—Es de seda.	*"It's silk."*
Las sillas son de madera.	*The chairs are made of wood.*
La bolsa es de plástico.	*The bag is made of plastic.*

AVOID THE *Blunder*

✗ La blusa es seda.
✗ Las sillas son maderas.

■ In some expressions, *de* can be translated as "of."

Esa mujer se aprovecha de ti.	*That woman takes advantage of you.*
No te burles de mí.	*Don't make fun of me.*
Nos cansamos de salir cada noche.	*We got tired of going out every night.*
Su libro consta de cuatro cuentos.	*His book consists of four stories.*

■ In some expressions, *de* can be translated as "about."

Se alegra de las noticias.	*He is happy about the news.*
Nos enteramos de su visita.	*We found out about her visit.*
Me olvidé de llamarte.	*I forgot about calling you.*
Se rieron de los fracasos.	*They laughed about the failures.*

■ *De* can be used after *estar* to indicate a current state.

de acuerdo	*in agreement*
de buen humor	*in a good mood*
de caza	*(in the act of) hunting*
de mal humor	*in a bad mood*
de merienda	*having a snack*
de moda	*in style*
de mudanza	*(in the process of) moving*
de pie	*standing*
de prisa	*in a hurry*
de visita	*visiting*

Los hombres están de caza.	*The men are out hunting.*
Estamos de merienda.	*We're having a snack.*
Las faldas cortas están de moda.	*Short skirts are in style.*
Están de mudanza.	*They're in the process of moving.*
Las chicas están de pie.	*The girls are standing up.*
¿Están de visita?	*Are you visiting?*

AVOID THE *Blunder*

Do not use *en* with these expressions to translate "in."

✗ en acuerdo   ✗ en un buen humor   ✗ en moda

■ *De* is used to express the appropriate time for an activity.

Es la hora de descansar.	*It's time to rest.*
No es hora de comer.	*It's not time to eat.*

AVOID THE *Blunder*

Do not leave out the preposition, even though "to" is expressed in the English infinitive.

✗ Es la hora descansar.
✗ No es hora comer.

■ *De* is used to express a type of activity or temporary job.

María trabaja de niñera.	*María works as a babysitter.*
Mi hermana hace de cocinera.	*My sister is doing the cooking.*

■ *De* is used to define certain objects according to their use.

Chicle es otro nombre por goma de mascar.	*"Chicle" is another word for chewing gum (gum used for chewing).*
Las computadoras han reemplazado a las máquinas de escribir.	*Computers have replaced typewriters (machines used for writing).*

■ *De* is used in comparisons.

Mateo es el mejor de la clase.	*Mateo is the best in the class.*
Eres el chico más simpático del mundo.	*You are the nicest guy in the world.*

AVOID THE *Blunder*

✗ el mejor en la clase
✗ el más simpático en el mundo

■ *De* is used after *ser* to express desired or suggested activity.

Es de desear que terminemos temprano.	*It is to be desired that we finish early.*
Ese grupo es de temer.	*That group is to be feared.*
Lo que dice es de creer.	*What he says should be believed.*

■ *De* can be used to express "if" before a conditional statement.

De no haber visto a tu hermana, me habría olvidado de llamarte.	*If I hadn't seen your sister, I would have forgotten to call you.*

■ *De* is used after a conjugated form of *acabar* to indicate action that has just been completed (see pages 119–120).

Acabo de comer.	*I have just eaten./I just ate.*
Acaban de hacer el examen.	*They have just taken the test./ They just took the test.*

AVOID THE *Blunder*

✗ acabo de comido
✗ acaban de hecho el examen

■ *De* is used after a conjugated form of *haber* to indicate an obligation.

He de hacerlo por mi familia.	*I must do it for my family.*
La carta ha de ser firmada.	*The letter has to be signed.*

■ When *de* is used after certain verbs, it is followed by another verb in the infinitive form.

acordarse de	*remember to*	parar de	*stop (doing)*
cesar de	*stop (doing)*	tener ganas de	*want to*
dejar de	*stop (doing)*	terminar de	*finish (doing)*
ocuparse de	*deal with*	tratar de	*try to*

Quiere dejar de fumar.	*He wants to stop smoking.*
Ella no para de hablar.	*She doesn't stop talking.*
Tengo ganas de conocerlo.	*I want to meet him.*
Trata de comprenderla.	*Try to understand her.*

AVOID THE *Blunder*

Do not omit the preposition *de*, even though "to" is part of the English infinitive.

✗ Quiere dejar fumar.
✗ Trata comprenderla.

Do not use a gerund construction, as you would in English.

✗ Quiere dejar fumando.

■ *De* is used after certain verbs and is followed by a noun or pronoun.

abusar de	*abuse, rape*	disfrutar de	*enjoy*
cambiar de	*change*	enamorarse de	*fall in love with*
carecer de	*lack*	gozar de	*enjoy*
constar de	*consist of*	ocuparse de	*deal with*
cuidar de	*be careful of*	preocuparse de	*worry about*
depender de	*depend on*	quejarse de	*complain about*
despedirse (i, i) de	*say good-bye to*	servir (i, i) de	*serve as*
		tratarse de	*be about*

La familia depende del hijo mayor.	*The family depends on the oldest son.*
Vamos a despedirnos de Carmen.	*We're going to say good-bye to Carmen.*

María se enamoró de Pedro.	*María fell in love with Pedro.*
El libro se trata de una familia pobre.	*The book is about a poor family.*

■ *De* is the first word in a number of set expressions.

de buena gana / de mala gana	*gladly/unwillingly*
de cena / de almuerzo	*for dinner/for lunch*
de día / de noche	*during the day/at night*
de la misma manera	*in the same way*
de nada, no hay de qué	*you're welcome*
de ninguna manera	*in no way*
de nuevo	*again*
de pronto	*suddenly*
de repente	*suddenly*
de todo corazón	*sincerely*
de verdad	*really, truly*

¿Qué hay de cena?	*What's for dinner?*
Trabaja de día y estudia de noche.	*She works during the day and studies at night.*
Por favor, toca la canción de nuevo.	*Please play the song again.*
Es un amigo de verdad.	*He's truly a good friend.*

AVOID THE *Blunder*

Do not try to translate these expressions that use the Spanish *de* word for word. Learn the entire expression as a unit.

✗ a noche
✗ en ninguna manera
✗ por cena

en

The preposition *en* has specific uses and is sometimes required in set phrases.

■ *En* corresponds to the English "in," "on," and "at" to indicate place.

¿Qué tienes en la mano?	*What do you have in your hand?*
El gato está en el techo.	*The cat is on the roof.*
Mi esposo está en el aeropuerto.	*My husband is at the airport.*
Vivimos en el tercer piso.	*We live on the third floor.*

The definite article is omitted after *en* in several expressions.

Estoy en casa.	*I'm at home.*
Los niños están en clase.	*The children are in class.*

■ *En* indicates occurrence within a certain period of time.

Vamos a la playa en el verano.	*We go to the beach in summer.*
Su cumpleaños es en julio.	*Her birthday is in July.*
Fueron a España en 2002.	*They went to Spain in 2002.*
Se reúnen en la mañana.	*They meet in the morning.*
Descanso en la tarde.	*I rest in the afternoon.*
Sale en la noche.	*He goes out at night.*
No lo he visto en todo el día.	*I haven't seen him all day.*
Hay siete días en una semana.	*There are seven days in a week.*

En is not used with days of the week (see page 232).

Te veo el miércoles.	*I'll see you on Wednesday.*
Nos reunimos los viernes.	*We meet on Fridays.*

AVOID THE *Blunder*

✗ en miércoles   ✗ en los viernes

En is not used with specific times of the morning, afternoon, evening, or night (see page 48).

Nos reunimos en la mañana.	*We meet in the morning.*
Nos reunimos a las 10 de la mañana.	*We meet at 10 o'clock in the morning.*
Te veo en la tarde.	*I'll see you in the afternoon.*
Te veo a las cuatro de la tarde.	*I'll see you at 4 o'clock in the afternoon.*

AVOID THE *Blunder*

✗ a las 10 en la mañana   ✗ a las cuatro en la tarde

■ *En* indicates the length of time spent on an activity.

Pintó la casa en tres días.	*He painted the house in three days.*
Completamos el curso en dos semanas.	*We finished the course in two weeks.*

■ *En* indicates how someone is dressed.

Ella llegó en pantalones.	*She arrived in pants.*
Vino a la fiesta en disfraz.	*He came to the party in a costume.*

■ *En* indicates certain methods of transportation.

Fui en tren.	*I went on the train.*
Deberían ir en taxi.	*You all should take a taxi.*
¿Van Uds. en coche?	*Are you going by car?*
Hay que ir en avión.	*You have to go by plane.*
Quiero ir en bicicleta.	*I want to go on a bicycle.*
Van a Australia en barco.	*They're going to Australia by ship.*

AVOID THE Blunder

✗ Voy por tren.
✗ Vamos por coche.

■ *De... en...* indicates a repetitive activity, translated as "from ... to ..." in English.

Los chicos fueron de casa en casa vendiendo revistas.	*The children went from door to door selling magazines.*

AVOID THE Blunder

✗ Los chicos fueron de puerta a puerta.

■ When used after *el primero* and *el último* to indicate an activity performed by someone, *en* is followed by a verb in the infinitive form.

Fui el primero en levantar la mano.	*I was the first to raise my hand.*
Fue la última en salir.	*She was the last to leave.*

AVOID THE Blunder

Do not try to translate English prepositions for these functions.

✗ Fui el primero a levantar la mano.
✗ Fue la última a salir.

■ *En* is used in certain negative expressions.

En mi vida he visto tanta gente.	*I've never seen so many people in all my life.*

—¿Me vas a dejar ir?　　　　*"Are you going to let me go?"*
—En absoluto.　　　　　　*"No way!"*

AVOID THE *Blunder*

Do not add *no* to *en mi vida.*

✗ En mi vida no he visto _____.

Do not use *en absoluto* if you mean "yes." Do not confuse *en absoluto*, which means "absolutely not," with *absolutamente*, which means "yes, indeed."

✗ Sí, en absoluto.

■ *En* is used in certain set expressions.

en balde	*in vain*	en llamas	*in flames*
en broma	*as a joke*	en lugar de	*instead of*
en casa	*at home*	en mi opinión	*in my opinion*
en construcción	*under construction*	en obras	*under construction*
en contra de	*opposed to*	en punto	*on the dot*
en cuanto a	*as for*	en seguida	*right away*
en cuanto	*as soon as*	en suma	*in short*
en efectivo	*in cash*	en venta	*on sale*
en este momento	*at the moment*	en vez de	*instead of*
en flor	*in bloom*	no en balde	*no wonder*

Seguro que lo dijo en broma.　　*Surely he said it as a joke.*
En cuanto a mí, estoy en contra　*As for me, I'm against the idea.*
　de la idea.
El puente está en obras.　　　*The bridge is under construction.*
En este momento estoy ocupada.　*I'm busy at the moment.*

■ *En* is used after certain verbs.

coincidir en	*be similar to*	fijarse en	*take notice of*
confiar en	*trust*	insistir en	*emphasize*
consentir en	*consent to*	meterse en	*meddle with*
convenir en	*agree on*	pensar en	*think about*
convertir en	*become, turn into*	quedar en	*agree to*
dudar en	*hesitate to*	tardar (una	*take (an hour)*
empeñarse en	*be determined to*	hora) en	*to*
entrar en	*enter*		

Coinciden en sus ideas.	*They have the same ideas.*
No dudes en llamarme.	*Don't hesitate to call me.*
Entramos en la casa a las ocho.	*We entered the house at 8 o'clock.*
Insistió en la importancia de ahorrar dinero.	*She stressed the importance of saving money.*
Pienso en ti todo el día.	*I think about you all day.*
Quedamos en comer juntos.	*We agreed to eat together.*

AVOID THE *Blunder*

Do not try to translate English prepositions. Learn these expressions as units.

✗ Entramos la casa.
✗ Consiente a ir.
✗ Tarda una hora a llegar.

para

The preposition *para* has specific uses and is sometimes required in set phrases.

■ *Para* can indicate purpose.

▪ *Para* can be followed by a noun to indicate a specific purpose.

Esta es ropa para niños.	*This is children's clothing.*
Ella preparó comida para todos.	*She fixed food for everybody.*
Estos asientos son reservados para un grupo.	*These seats are reserved for a group.*
Tengo que estudiar para un examen.	*I have to study for an exam.*

▪ *Para* can be followed by a verb in the infinitive form to indicate purpose.

Vamos a casa para descansar.	*Let's go home to rest.*
Jorge fue al mercado para comprar uvas.	*Jorge went to the market to buy grapes.*

AVOID THE *Blunder*

Rather than translate *para* as "to" or "for," think of its function as an indicator of purpose.

✗ Tengo que estudiar por un examen.
✗ Vamos a casa por descansar.

- *Para* can be followed by *que* + a verb in the subjunctive to indicate the purpose of the action of the first verb. The subject of the second clause must be different from the subject of the first clause.

Vamos a casa para que los niños descansen.	*Let's go home so the children can rest.*
Jorge fue al parque con los niños para que su esposa pudiera descansar.	*Jorge went to the park with the children so that his wife could rest.*

- *Para* can indicate destination.

Salieron para la estación.	*They left for the station.*
Voy para tu casa esta tarde.	*I'm coming to your house this afternoon.*
Estos chocolates son para ti.	*These chocolates are for you.*

AVOID THE *Blunder*

Rather than translate *para* as "to," "toward," or "for," think of its function as an indicator of destination.

✗ Salieron por la estación.
✗ Voy por tu casa.
✗ Estos chocolates son por ti.

- *Para* can indicate future time.

Termínalo para el 15 de septiembre.	*Finish it by September 15.*
Tenemos que escribir el ensayo para el lunes.	*We have to write the essay for Monday.*
No dejes para mañana lo que puedes hacer hoy.	*Don't put off until tomorrow what you can do today.*
Faltan tres semanas para el receso de verano.	*There are three more weeks until summer break.*

AVOID THE *Blunder*

Rather than translate *para* as "for," "by," or "until," think of its function as an indicator of future time.

✗ Tenemos que escribir el ensayo por lunes.

■ *Para* is used to indicate a characteristic, ability, or opinion that distinguishes one person, group, or thing from others.

Ella es muy joven para manejar un coche.	*She is too young to drive a car.*
Este problema es muy difícil para mí.	*This problem is very difficult for me.*

■ *Para* is used to compare someone or something with others of its type.

Para un chico de cuatro años, es muy alto.	*For a four-year-old boy, he is very tall.*
Para ser una chica tan joven, es muy madura.	*For such a young girl, she's very mature.*
Para un extranjero, hablas español muy bien.	*For a foreigner, you speak Spanish very well.*
Para ser recién llegado a este país, ese niño se ha adaptado muy bien.	*For someone who has just arrived in this country, that child has adapted very well.*

■ *Para* is used to indicate someone's opinion.

Para ella, él es rey del mundo.	*She thinks he's the best man on earth.*
Para mí, es un ladrón y debemos despedirlo.	*In my opinion, he's a thief and we should fire him.*

■ *Para* is used in certain set expressions.

estar para	*be about to (do)*
leer para sí	*read silently*
nacer para	*be born to (do)*
no ser para tanto	*not be such a big deal*

Estamos para salir.	*We're about to leave.*
El niño tiene que aprender a leer para sí.	*The boy has to learn to read silently.*
Nació para ser cantante.	*She was born to be a singer.*
No te preocupes. No es para tanto.	*Don't worry. It's not such a big deal.*

para serte sincero	*to tell you the truth*
para servirle	*at your service*
para colmo	*to top it all off*
para mi gran sorpresa	*to my surprise*
para siempre	*forever*
para su desgracia	*unfortunately for him/her*

Estoy resfriada, tengo dolor de cabeza y para colmo, tengo que estar en una reunión a las ocho de la mañana.	*I have a cold, my head aches, and to top it all off, I have to be at a meeting at 8 A.M.*
Para su gran sorpresa, le ascendieron de puesto.	*To his great surprise, they promoted him.*
Te amaré para siempre.	*I'll love you forever.*
Mi hermano, para su desgracia, tuvo que trabajar diez años en ese lugar.	*My brother, unfortunately for him, had to work in that place for 10 years.*

AVOID THE *Blunder*

Rather than translate word for word, think of set expressions as complete units.

✗ a mi sorpresa   ✗ por colmo   ✗ por su desgracia

para que te enteres / para que lo sepas para variar	*for your information / just so you know for a change*

—Cenicienta, eres muy poca cosa. Nadie se casará contigo.	*"Cinderella, you're a nobody. No one will marry you."*
—Pues, para que te enteres, el príncipe me propuso matrimonio anoche.	*"Well, for your information, the prince proposed to me last night."*
Esteban no vino a clase hoy, ¡para variar!	*Esteban didn't come to class today, for a change!*

AVOID THE *Blunder*

These expressions are used sarcastically; do not use them if you want to express a sincere feeling.

por

The preposition *por* has specific uses and is sometimes required in set phrases.

■ *Por* can indicate the agent or means of the action of the verb.

La novela fue escrito por su abuela.	*The novel was written by his grandmother.*

| Anoche hablamos por teléfono. | *We talked on the phone last night.* |
| Le mandé el paquete por correo aéreo. | *I sent him the package via air mail.* |

■ *Por* can indicate a route or vague location.

Caminaron por el parque.	*They walked through the park.*
Anda por el jardín, viendo las flores.	*He's walking around the garden, looking at the flowers.*
Está por aquí.	*It's near here.*

| —¿Dónde estabas? | *"Where were you?"* |
| —Por ahí. | *"Not too far away."* |

■ *Por* can indicate time, as an alternative to *en.*

| Tenemos clases por la mañana, descansamos por la tarde y estudiamos por la noche. | *We have classes in the morning, we rest in the afternoon, and we study at night.* |

AVOID THE *Blunder*

When an actual time is expressed, use the pattern *a las diez de la mañana, a las cuatro de la tarde.*

✗ a las diez por la mañana
✗ a las cuatro por la tarde

■ *Por* can indicate the duration of planned future action.

| Van a Guatemala por dos años. | *They're going to Guatemala for two years.* |
| Voy a estudiar por cinco horas. | *I'm going to study for five hours.* |

When indicating the duration of past action, *por* is not necessary.

| Estuvimos dos años en Guatemala. | *We were in Guatemala for two years.* |
| Estudié cinco horas anoche. | *I studied (for) five hours last night.* |

When the duration of planned future action is indicated after the verb *estar, por* is not necessary.

Vamos a estar dos años en Guatemala.	*We're going to be in Guatemala for two years.*
Voy a estar cinco horas en la biblioteca.	*I'm going to be at the library for five hours.*
Vamos a estar en Guatemala dos años.	*We're going to be in Guatemala for two years.*

Por can indicate an exchange of one thing for another.

Quiero cambiar esta camisa por la otra.	*I want to exchange this shirt for the other one.*
Pagó $20 por el libro.	*He paid $20 for the book.*

Por can indicate a substitution of one thing for another.

Ella va a asistir al congreso por su jefe.	*She's going to attend the conference in place of her boss.*
Ana trabaja por mí mañana.	*Ana is substituting for me tomorrow.*

AVOID THE *Blunder*

Do not confuse "work in my place" (*por mí*) with "work for me" (*para mí*).

■ *Por* can indicate the motive, reason, or cause of an action.

Lo hizo por amor.	*She did it out of love.*
Vendió su coche por necesidad.	*He sold his car out of necessity.*
—¿Por qué te vas?	*"Why are you leaving?"*
—Porque no me gusta el trabajo.	*"Because I don't like the job."*
Ella se perdió por mi culpa.	*She got lost because of me.*
Él se mudó a otro país por ella.	*He moved to another country for her.*
Por ser de Canadá, hablaba inglés con fluidez.	*Since he was from Canada, he spoke English fluently.*

■ There is a distinction between *por ser*, which explains a reason for something being as it is, and *para ser*, which compares something or someone with others of its type (see page 278).

Por ser de Londres, habla inglés con fluidez.	*Since he's from London, he speaks English fluently.*
Para ser angloparlante, habla español muy bien.	*For a native speaker of English, he speaks Spanish very well.*

■ *Por* indicates a more dramatic motive than *para*.

Su esposo compró la casa por ella.	*Her husband bought the house for her (because of her needs).*
Su esposo compró la casa para ella.	*Her husband bought the house for her (as a gift).*

AVOID THE *Blunder*

Do not confuse *¿por qué?* "for what reason?" with *¿para qué?* "for what purpose?"

■ *Por* can indicate the benefactor of an action.

¡Brindemos por la salud de nuestro gran amigo!	*Let's drink to the health of our great friend!*
Voy a votar por la maestra, porque conoce los problemas de las escuelas.	*I'm going to vote for the teacher, because she knows the problems with the schools.*

■ *Por* can be used after *ir* to mean "to go get."

Fueron al centro por pan.	*They went to town for bread.*
Voy a la biblioteca por un libro.	*I'm going to the library to get a book.*

■ *Por* can indicate action yet to be done.

Tengo tres trabajos por terminar.	*I still have three papers to finish.*
Tiene dos coches por reparar.	*He still has two cars to repair.*

■ *Por* can indicate a lack of purpose.

Este político habla por hablar.	*This politician talks just for the sake of talking.*

■ *Por* can mean "per."

Pagamos casi dos dólares por galón.	*We paid almost two dollars per gallon.*
Ahorró el 10 por ciento de su sueldo.	*She saved 10 percent of her salary.*

■ *Por* can mean "times" in multiplication.

—¿Cuánto es tres por tres?	*"How much is three times three?"*
—Tres por tres es nueve.	*"Three times three is nine."*

■ *Por* is used in certain set expressions.

por adelantado	*in advance*	por escrito	*in writing*
por ahora	*for the time being*	por favor	*please*
por cierto	*by the way*	por la fuerza	*by force*
por desgracia	*unfortunately*	por lo menos	*at least*
por Dios	*For heaven's sake!*	por medio de	*by means of*
por ejemplo	*for example*	por parejas	*in pairs*
por el presente	*for the time being*	por si acaso	*just in case*
por encima de	*over the top of*	por supuesto	*naturally*

Por ahora, me quedo en casa.	*For the time being, I'm staying home.*
Por favor, mándame tus ideas por escrito.	*Please send me your ideas in writing.*
Dejaré mi número de teléfono, por si acaso necesitas algo.	*I'll leave my telephone number just in case you need anything.*

AVOID THE *Blunder*

✗ para desgracia   ✗ para si acaso   ✗ para supuesto

contra

The preposition *contra* has several different uses.

■ *Contra* is used to indicate odds.

| Las posibilidades son una contra un millón que ganes la lotería. | *Your chances of winning the lottery are one in a million.* |

■ *Contra* is used to indicate a remedy.

| El médico me dio un medicamento contra los dolores. | *The doctor gave me some medicine for the pain.* |

■ *Contra* is used to indicate "against" a thing or a person.

| Vamos a poner la mesa contra la pared. | *We're going to put the table against the wall.* |
| Ramón boxea contra el campeón esta noche. | *Ramón is boxing against the champion tonight.* |

■ The phrase *en contra de* is used to indicate "not in favor of" or "against" an idea.

| Se manifestaron en contra de la guerra. | *They demonstrated against the war.* |
| El estudiante se expresó en contra de las ideas del profesor. | *The student spoke against the professor's ideas.* |

desde

The preposition *desde* has several different uses.

■ *Desde* is used to indicate time (see page 257).

El semestre es desde el 12 de enero hasta el 5 de mayo.	*The semester is from January 12 to May 5.*
—¿Desde cuándo estás aquí?	*"How long have you been here?" ("Since when are you here?")*
—Estoy aquí desde hace cuatro semanas.	*"I've been here for four weeks."*

AVOID THE *Blunder*

Do not translate the English expressions word for word.

✗ ¿Cuánto tiempo has estado aquí?
✗ He estado aquí por cuatro semanas.

■ *Desde* is used to indicate a starting point leading to a destination.

Viajó desde Europa a California en un día.	*She traveled from Europe to California in one day.*
Me llamó desde su hotel en San José.	*He called me from his hotel in San José.*

ante

The preposition *ante* has several uses.

■ *Ante* indicates "in the presence of" with a certain solemnity not implied by *delante de* (see page 234).

Tuvo que presentar su versión de los hechos ante el juez.	*She had to present her version of the story before the judge.*

■ *Ante* is used in a figurative sense to indicate reason or motive.

Está emocionado ante la posibilidad de estudiar en el extranjero.	*He's excited about the possibility of studying abroad.*
Ante los problemas que tenía en casa, tuvo que dejar de trabajar.	*Because of the problems she had at home, she had to stop working.*

■ *Ante* is used in the expression *ante todo* to indicate "above all," "most importantly."

Ante todo, quiero graduarme de enfermera.	*Most importantly, I want to get my nursing degree.*
Ante todo cuida tu salud.	*Above all, take care of your health.*

hacia

The preposition *hacia* is used to indicate "toward."

Ustedes van hacia el norte.	*You all are headed north.*
Sintió mucho cariño hacia su padre.	*She felt a lot of affection for her father.*

sobre

The preposition *sobre* has several uses.

■ *Sobre* is an alternative for *en, encima de,* and *por encima de* to indicate place.

El libro está sobre la mesa.   *The book is on the table.*
Puse las llaves sobre el libro.   *I put the keys on top of the book.*

■ *Sobre* can indicate "above" or "higher than."

La ciudad está a 5.000 metros   *The city is 5,000 meters above*
sobre el nivel del mar.   *sea level.*

■ *Sobre* can indicate a topic.

Tengo un libro sobre las flores   *I have a book about the*
silvestres de esta región.   *wildflowers in this area.*

■ *Sobre* can indicate approximation.

Tenemos que leer sobre cien   *We have to read about a*
páginas.   *hundred pages.*

■ *Sobre* can indicate the addition of more of the same.

Sobre los problemas que ya   *On top of the problems she*
tiene, ahora viene esto.   *already has, now this.*
En ese pueblo, ocurre tragedia   *In that town, one tragedy*
sobre tragedia.   *happens on top of another.*

■ *Sobre* can indicate close observation.

El jefe está siempre sobre sus   *The boss is always watching*
empleados.   *what his employees do.*

bajo

The preposition *bajo* has several uses.

■ *Bajo* can indicate "below" or "lower than."

Hace muchísimo frío. Está en   *It's freezing. It's five degrees*
cinco grados bajo cero.   *below zero.*

■ *Bajo* can indicate "under the power/influence/protection of."

La gente sufrió muchas desgracias   *The people suffered great*
bajo su gobierno.   *misfortune during (under the*
    power of) his government.

No debió manejar cuando estaba   *He shouldn't have been driving*
bajo la influencia de los   *under the influence of the*
medicamentos.   *medicine.*
Por fin estamos bajo techo.   *We're finally indoors (under the*
    protection of the roof).

■ *Bajo* can indicate presence in certain natural settings.

Caminamos bajo la lluvia.	*We walked in the rain.*
Se sentaron bajo la sombra de un árbol.	*They sat in the shade of a tree.*
Se besaron bajo las estrellas.	*They kissed under the stars.*
Se puede ver bajo la luz de la luna.	*You can see by the light of the moon.*

■ *Bajo* is used in certain expressions.

bajo cuerda	*under the counter/table*
bajo juramento	*under oath*
bajo llave	*under lock and key*
bajo mano	*on the quiet*
bajo techo	*under cover*

Hicieron algunos pagos bajo cuerda.	*They made several under-the-counter payments.*
Las joyas están bajo llave.	*The jewelry is under lock and key.*

AVOID THE *Blunder*

✗ Caminamos en la lluvia.
✗ Se puede ver en la luz de la luna.

tras

The preposition *tras* has several uses.

■ *Tras* can indicate "following."

Tras los acontecimientos de ayer, ella toma más precauciones.	*Following yesterday's events, she is being more careful.*

■ *Tras* can indicate pursuit.

Todos los chicos andan tras ella.	*All the boys are after her.*

■ *Tras* can indicate tedious repetition.

Día tras día, trabajaba doce horas y volvía a casa en la noche.	*Day after day, he worked 12 hours and came back home at night.*

entre

The preposition *entre* has several uses.

■ *Entre* indicates both "between" and "among."

En la clase, me siento entre Juan y Miguel.	*In the class I sit between Juan and Miguel.*
Aquí estoy, entre gente de todas partes del mundo.	*Here I am among people from all over the world.*

AVOID THE *Blunder*

Do not use the preposition *de* after *entre*.

✗ Me siento entre de Juan y Miguel.
✗ Estoy entre de gente de todas partes.

■ Unlike most prepositions, *entre* is followed by the subject pronouns *yo* and *tú*, rather than *mí* and *ti*.

Esto es entre tú y yo.	*This is between you and me.*
¿Juan se sentó entre tu hermana y tú?	*Did Juan sit between you and your sister?*

AVOID THE *Blunder*

✗ Esto es entre ti y mí.
✗ Juan se sentó entre ti y ella.

■ *Entre* is used in division to mean "divided by."

Dieciséis entre dos son ocho.	*Sixteen divided by two is eight.*

según

The preposition *según* generally corresponds to English "according to."

Hicimos el trabajo según nos indicó.	*We did the job according to his instructions.*
Según el periódico, hoy va a llover.	*According to the paper, it's going to rain today.*

Unlike most prepositions, *según* is followed by the subject pronouns *yo* and *tú*, rather than *mí* and *ti*.

Según tú, tenemos un examen mañana, pero yo no estoy tan seguro de eso.	*According to you, we have an exam tomorrow, but I'm not so sure about that.*

salvo and *excepto*

The prepositions *salvo* and *excepto* indicate exception.

Todos los chicos, salvo mi   *All the boys except my brother*
   hermano, estaban contentos.   *were happy.*

Unlike most prepositions, *salvo* and *excepto* are followed by the subject pronouns *yo* and *tú*, rather than *mí* and *ti*.

Toda la familia, excepto yo,   *The whole family went to the*
   fue al campo.   *country, except for me.*

AVOID THE *Blunder*

✗ según mí
✗ según ti
✗ salvo mí
✗ salvo ti

Exercises

A *Circle the correct pronouns to complete the following sentences.*

1. Este asunto es entre **ti y mí | él y mí | tú y yo | ti y él**.

2. Voy al mercado con **-tigo | -sigo | nosotros | ti**.

3. Ella no conoce **al | la | a la | el** Sra. Rodríguez.

4. Este regalo es para **la | lo | ella | yo | tú**.

5. Mi papá lo hizo por **mí y ti | mí y ella | ella y él | ella y por él**.

B *Express the following English questions in Spanish.*

1. *What are you thinking about?* _____

2. *Who is he looking for?* _____

3. *Who is she going with?* _____

4. *What are we waiting for?* _____

5. *What are you looking at?* _____

6. *Who is the letter from?* _____

7. *How long have you been here?* _____

8. *How often do you visit your grandmother?*

_____

C *Circle the appropriate prepositions to complete the following sentences.*

1. La casa huele **como** | **de** | **a** pan.

2. Fuimos a la escuela **en** | **por** | **a** pie.

3. Carmen se va a casar **con** | **a** | **contra** Pablo.

4. Él está soñando **de** | **a** | **con** | **en** ella.

5. Él está pensando **de** | **a** | **con** | **en** ella.

6. Ella es la mejor **de** | **entre** | **en** | **por** la clase.

7. Ella se enamoró **de** | **con** | **en** | **para** él.

8. Nos vemos a las 10 **en** | **de** | **por** | **para** la mañana.

9. Nos vemos **de** | **para** | **por** | **después** la mañana.

10. Quedamos **a** | **en** | **por** | **con** encontrarnos aquí a las nueve.

D *Fill in the blanks with por or para.*

1. Julio fue al mercado _____ leche

2. Esteban compró una casa _____ su familia.

3. Pasamos _____ el parque en camino a la biblioteca.

4. Estos regalos son _____ mis primos.

5. _____ ser extranjera en los Estados Unidos, habla inglés muy bien.

6. Esa pregunta es muy fácil _____ mí

7. Estaba _____ abrir la botella.

8. Ya he leído este libro. Voy a cambiarlo _____ otro.

9. Pagó diez dólares _____ la camiseta.

CONJUNCTIONS

y/e	*and*
o/u	*or*
pues	*for*
pero	*but*

CORRELATIVE CONJUNCTIONS

o... o...	*either ... or ...*
ni... ni...	*neither ... nor ...*
apenas... cuando...	*hardly ... when ...*

OTHER CONJUNCTIONS

aunque	*although, even if*
de modo que	*so*
mientras que	*while* (in a comparison)
puesto que	*since (because)*

Review the conjunctions in the chart above.

The basic conjunctions are similar to, but not always equivalent to, their English counterparts.

y

The conjunction *y*, like the English "and," is used to connect similar parts of speech.

Roberto y Ricardo estudian.	*Roberto and Ricardo are studying.*
Ana estudia y trabaja.	*Ana studies and works.*
Vamos a estudiar y trabajar.	*We're going to study and work.*
Ana es inteligente y trabajadora.	*Ana is smart and hardworking.*

When two or more adverbs of manner are connected by *y*, only the last one mentioned includes the suffix -*mente* (see page 244).

Roberto lee lenta y cuidadosamente.	*Roberto reads slowly and carefully.*

AVOID THE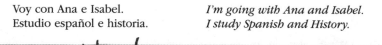

✗ lentamente y cuidadosamente

When the word following *y* begins with the letter *i-* or the letters *hi-*, *y* changes to *e.*

Voy con Ana e Isabel.	*I'm going with Ana and Isabel.*
Estudio español e historia.	*I study Spanish and History.*

AVOID THE

✗ España y Inglaterra   ✗ islamismo y hinduismo

Y expressed as a question is used to ask for a response to an understood or assumed request for information

SITUATION A young woman returns home after an important job
interview.

HER FATHER	—¿Y?	*"So?"*
THE YOUNG WOMAN	—¡Me contrataron!	*"They hired me!"*

AVOID THE

Do not assume that *y* is always translated as "and."

The English correlative conjunctions "both ... and ..." can be expressed with *tanto... como...* in Spanish.

Tanto la madre como el hijo estudian español.	*Both the mother and the son are studying Spanish.*

AVOID THE

Do not assume that "and" is always translated as *y.*

o

The conjunction *o,* like the English "or," is used to indicate an option of one thing rather than another.

—¿Quieres helado de chocolate o de vainilla?	*"Do you want chocolate or vanilla ice cream?"*

—No sé si quiero helado o no.   *"I don't know whether I want ice cream or not."*

The correlative conjunctions *o... o...* are used to present an ultimatum or to offer a choice.

¡O te portas bien, o te marchas!   *Either you behave yourself, or you leave!*

La reunión tiene que ser esta semana, o el martes o el miércoles.   *The meeting has to be this week, on either Tuesday or Wednesday.*

Usually only one *o* is used to translate "either ... or ..." in other contexts.

No sé qué voy a hacer. Iré al concierto o al cine.   *I don't know what I'm going to do. I'll go to either the concert or the movies.*

Ella no está conmigo. Está con su hermano o con su novio.   *She isn't with me. She's with either her brother or her boyfriend.*

When the word following *o* begins with the letter *o-* or the letters *ho-*, *o* changes to *u*.

Puedes usar esa palabra u otra.   *You can use that word or another one.*

No sé si la cita es mañana u hoy.   *I don't know if the appointment is tomorrow or today.*

AVOID THE *Blunder*

✗ ayer o hoy   ✗ esta o otra   ✗ Francia o Holanda

When the conjunction *o* is used between numbers, it is written with an accent mark.

Seremos unos 20 ó 30 personas.   *We'll be about 20 or 30 people./ There'll be about 20 or 30 of us.*

The expression *o sea* is used to signal a clarification, like the English "in other words" or "I mean."

No fue como tú imaginas, o sea, no fue tan dramático.   *It wasn't what you think, I mean, it wasn't that dramatic.*

AVOID THE *Blunder*

Do not assume that *o* is always translated as "or."

ni, ni siquiera, and *ni... ni...*

The conjunction *ni* has several uses.

Ni or *ni siquiera* can express "not even."

Ni (siquiera) su esposa lo sabe.	*Not even his wife knows.*
No ha visto ni (siquiera) a su mejor amigo.	*He hasn't seen even his best friend.*

The correlative conjunctions *ni... ni...* are used to express the lack of an alternative.

No viene ni Carlos ni Ricardo.	*Neither Carlos nor Ricardo is coming.*
Esos chicos ni trabajan ni estudian.	*Those boys don't work or study.*

AVOID THE *Blunder*

Do not leave out the first *ni*.

✗ No viene Carlos ni Ricardo

pues

The conjunction *pues* indicates a reason for the previous statement.

Ernesto no comprende la lección, pues no estuvo en clase ayer.	*Ernesto doesn't understand the lesson because he wasn't in class yesterday.*
Voy a invitar a Paco, pues es mi mejor amigo.	*I'm going to invite Paco, since he's my best friend.*

AVOID THE *Blunder*

The word *pues* has other meanings and can also be used as an adverb. Do not assume that it always has the same translation into English.

pero

The conjunction *pero*, like the English "but," indicates a contrast with the previous statement.

La lección parece difícil, pero no lo es.	*The lesson looks hard, but it isn't.*
Tino no va a la fiesta, pero yo sí.	*Tino isn't going to the party, but I am.*

no... sino (que)...

The expressions *no... sino...* and *no... sino que...* are used to correct a previous statement.

Sino is used to correct any sentence element, with the exception of a conjugated verb.

No canta Julio, sino Enrique.	*Julio isn't singing; Enrique is.*
No quieren bailar, sino cantar.	*They don't want to dance; they want to sing.*
No vamos al cine, sino al teatro.	*We're not going to the movies; we're going to the theater.*
No voy con Juan, sino con Mario.	*I'm not going with Juan; I'm going with Mario.*

AVOID THE *Blunder*

Be sure to repeat any preposition that occurs between *sino* and the correcting item.

✗ No vamos al cine, sino teatro.
✗ No voy con Juan, sino Mario.

Sino que is used to correct a previous statement when the conjugated verb is repeated or changed.

No vamos al cine, sino que vamos al teatro.	*We're not going to the movies; we're going to the theater.*
Ellos no alquilaron la casa, sino que la compraron.	*They didn't rent the house; they bought it.*

AVOID THE *Blunder*

Do not omit the *que* when there is a conjugated verb in the correction.

✗ No vamos al cine, sino vamos al teatro.
✗ No alquilaron la casa, sino la compraron.

---

apenas

The conjunction *apenas* refers to action that occurs immediately before new action (see page 247).

When *apenas* introduces a past action, it is followed by a verb in the indicative.

| Apenas lo vio, corrió a ayudarlo. | *As soon as she saw him, she ran to help him.* |

When *apenas* introduces an action that has not yet taken place, it is followed by a verb in the subjunctive. It is an alternative to *en cuanto*.

| Apenas lo sepa, te llamaré. | *As soon as I find out, I'll call you.* |
| Me dijo que apenas lo supiera, me llamaría. | *He told me that as soon as he found out, he would call me.* |

The correlatives *apenas... cuando...* are used to express action that follows immediately.

| Apenas empecé a leer cuando sonó el teléfono. | *I had just begun to read when the phone rang.* |

AVOID THE *Blunder*

Do not confuse the conjunction *apenas* with the adverb *apenas*, which indicates a less than adequate amount or degree.

Other Common Conjunctions

There are many other connective words and expressions. Following are some of the most common.

■ The conjunction *aunque* expresses the meaning "although" or "in spite of the fact that."

When *aunque* introduces information that is new to the hearer, it is followed by a verb in the indicative mood.

| Aunque mi hermano no durmió bien anoche, está listo para el examen. | *Even though my brother didn't sleep well last night, he's ready for the test.* |
| Aunque se discutieron ayer, hoy están de acuerdo. | *Even though they argued yesterday, they are in agreement today.* |

When *aunque* precedes a fact that is already known to the hearer, it is followed by a verb in the subjunctive mood.

—¡Su novio es muy rico!	*"Her boyfriend is rich!"*
—Aunque su novio tenga mucho dinero, es muy tacaño.	*"Even though her boyfriend has a lot of money, he's very stingy."*
—No dormí ni una hora anoche.	*"I didn't get even an hour's sleep last night."*

—Aunque no durmieras anoche, pareces estar listo para el examen.

"Even if you didn't sleep last night, you seem to be ready for the test."

■ *De modo que* indicates a consequence.

Estaba muy alterado, de modo que lo llevaron a su casa para que se tranquilizara.

He was very upset, so they took him home to calm him down.

■ *Mientras que* is used in a comparison.

Yo trabajo todo el día, todos los días, mientras que tú te quedas en casa viendo la televisión.

I work all day every day, while you stay home watching TV.

■ *Puesto que* introduces a reason.

Tengo que volver a mi país, puesto que se me ha acabado el dinero.

I have to go back to my country, since I've run out of money.

Exercise

A *Fill in the blanks with the appropriate conjunction.*

1. Estudio latín _____ inglés.

2. No viene Andrés, _____ su hermano.

3. Alfredo es inteligente _____ Ricardo también.

4. Patricia no es simpática _____ su hermana tampoco.

5. ¿Prefieres ir al campo _____ quedarte en la ciudad?

6. Tengo que estudiar _____ mañana es el examen final.

7. _____ Adriana _____ Paula pasaron el verano en Europa.

8. ¡_____ te callas _____ te echo de la clase!

9. No sabe si la fiesta es hoy _____ otro día.

10. No quiere mostrarle la foto a nadie, _____ a su mejor amigo.

VOCABULARY

WORDS

Cognates

Cognates are words that have a similar spelling and similar meaning in two languages. English and Spanish share many cognates, which are an enormous help in developing a working vocabulary. Following are a few examples of cognates.

Nouns

actor	capital	director	menú
alcohol	cereal	error	mineral
ángel	chocolate	favor	mosquito
animal	club	gas	motor
área	color	general	ópera
arquitecto	control	hotel	piano
banana	criminal	humor	profesor
cable	debate	idea	radio

■ Many nouns that end in "-ion" in English end in *-ción, -sión,* or *-xión* in Spanish. These nouns are always feminine (see page 31). Following are some examples.

información	televisión
solución	
satisfacción	conexión

Just because a Spanish word is a cognate does not mean that it is always used exactly like it is in English. *La televisión*, for example, refers to TV programming, and *el televisor* is the TV set.

Quiero ver la televisión a las ocho.	*I want to watch TV at eight.*
Ayer compramos un televisor nuevo.	*Yesterday we bought a new TV.*

■ A few masculine nouns end in *-ión* and do not have cognates in English.

el avión	*the airplane*	el guión	*the script*
el camión	*the truck*	el sarampión	*the measles*

■ Many nouns that end in "-ity" in English end in *-dad* in Spanish. These nouns are always feminine (see page 31).

cualidad	honestidad	seguridad
especialidad	posibilidad	sociedad
felicidad	responsabilidad	

AVOID THE

Be careful spelling cognates that contain "qu" in English.

✗ qualidad

Add *e-* before English words beginning with *sp-, st-,* and *sc-.*

✗ specialidad

Be careful not to use a double *s* in *posibilidad.*

✗ possibilidad

Note the spelling difference in *responsabilidad.*

✗ responsibilidad

■ The names of most academic subjects in English have cognates in Spanish. Many nouns of this type that end in "-y" or "-ology" in English end in *-ía* or *-ología* in Spanish.

anatomía	psicología*
biología	sociología
filosofía	

*Also spelled *sicología.*

AVOID THE *Blunder*

Equivalent usage often differs. In English, "science" is singular, but Spanish *ciencias* is plural. Also, in English, "physics" is plural, but Spanish *física* is singular.

✗ Estudia ciencia y físicas.

■ Many noun cognates that end in "-nt" in English end in *-nte* in Spanish.

adolescente	inmigrante	restaurante
delincuente	paciente	sirviente
estudiante	presidente	

■ Certain nouns that end in "-ment" in English have cognates ending in -*mento* in Spanish.

argumento	pavimento
documento	suplemento
fragmento	

AVOID THE *Blunder*

Some of these cognates can be very tricky. *Argumento* means "argument" in the sense of "presentation of a case," but not "a heated discussion." "Government" is *gobierno,* and "disappointment" is *desilusión.* Also, *medicamento* is "medication." Check these words in a dictionary before trusting them as cognates.

■ Other noun cognates that end in "-ment" in English end in -*miento* in Spanish.

comportamiento	*comportment (behavior)*
entretenimiento	*entertainment*
sentimiento	*sentiment*

AVOID THE *Blunder*

This group of cognates can also be tricky. *Entrenamiento* means "training" as in sports, while *adiestramiento* means "training" as in learning skills. *Conocimiento* is "knowledge," and *pimiento* is "pepper." Check these words in a dictionary before trusting them as cognates.

■ Many English words that end in "-ance" or "-ence" have cognates that end in -*ancia* or -*encia* in Spanish. They are always feminine.

abundancia	emergencia	referencia
arrogancia	existencia	repugnancia
correspondencia	presencia	

■ Many English words that end in "-ist" have counterparts in Spanish that end in -*ista* for both males and females.

artista*	materialista	racista
feminista	optimista	socialista
lingüista	pesimista	

*Artista refers to any creative person, not just a painter. An *artista* can be a *pintor, músico,* or *actor,* among other creative professions.

Verbs

Following is a sample of the many Spanish verbs that have English cognates.

demostrar (ue)	imitar	liberar	practicar
fascinar	iniciar	manipular	servir (i, i)
finalizar	insistir	necesitar	solucionar
ilustrar	inventar	obtener	visitar

Adjectives

Following is a sample of the many Spanish adjectives that have English cognates.

artístico	envidioso	liberal	quieto
decente	generoso	necesario	reciente
difícil	honesto	obvio	reservado
eficiente	inocente	popular	sincero

AVOID THE *Blunder*

Do not use *celoso* if you want to say that you are "envious." *Envidioso* means "envious" or "jealous" of someone because he or she has what you want. *Celoso* means "jealous" of someone because of another interest he or she has in someone or something else. A person who is *celoso* wants to have control over another person's feelings.

✗ Estoy celosa de ella porque ganó el premio.

Adverbs

Many adverbs that end in " ly" in English have cognates that end in *-mente* in Spanish (see pages 244–246). Following are a few examples.

artísticamente	inocentemente	probablemente
eficientemente	naturalmente	rápidamente
especialmente	obviamente	recientemente
generosamente	perfectamente	responsablemente
honestamente	posiblemente	sinceramente

AVOID THE *Blunder*

Even though cognates may convey similar meanings, they are not necessarily used in exactly the same way. For example, *sinceramente* means "sincerely," but it is not used as the closing of a friendly letter, as is its English counterpart. A better closing in Spanish would be *Afectuosamente* or *Cordialmente*.

Falsos amigos

False cognates, often called *falsos amigos*, are words that look so similar in two languages that we expect them to have the same meaning in both—but they don't! Because there are so many true cognates in English and Spanish, it is no wonder that these words have been labeled "false friends." Following are the most common ones.

Nouns

SPANISH NOUN	ENGLISH MEANING	ENGLISH NOUN	SPANISH MEANING
apología	*eulogy*	*apology*	disculpa
arena	*sand*	*arena*	estadio
campo	*field, countryside*	*camp*	campamento
carpeta	*folder*	*carpet*	alfombra
carta	*letter, playing card*	*card*	tarjeta
colegio	*high school*	*college*	universidad
collar	*necklace*	*collar*	cuello (de camisa)
competencia	*competition*	*competence*	capacidad
complexión	*temperament*	*complexion*	tez
compromiso	*commitment*	*compromise*	término medio
concurso	*contest*	*concourse*	explanada
confección	*handiwork*	*confection*	pastel
conferencia	*lecture*	*conference*	congreso, reunión
coraje	*anger*	*courage*	valor
costumbre	*custom*	*costume*	disfraz
decepción	*disappointment*	*deception*	engaño
delito	*crime*	*delight*	alegría
desgracia	*bad luck*	*disgrace*	vergüenza
dirección	*address*	*direction*	rumbo
discusión	*argument*	*discussion*	conversación
disgusto	*argument*	*disgust*	asco, repugnancia
dormitorio	*bedroom*	*dormitory*	residencia de estudiantes

SPANISH NOUN	ENGLISH MEANING	ENGLISH NOUN	SPANISH MEANING
educación	manners, education	education	instrucción formal
éxito	success	exit	salida
fábrica	factory	fabric	tela
falta	lack, error, absence, foul	fault	culpa
idioma	language	idiom	modismo
injuria	injustice, harm	injury	herida, daño
lectura	reading selection	lecture	discurso
librería	bookstore	library	biblioteca
manifestación	protest, demonstration	manifestation	señal, síntoma
parientes	relatives, kinfolk	parents	padres
pena	embarrassment, punishment, sadness	pain	dolor, molestia
recolección	compilation	recollection	recuerdo
sentencia	verdict, sentence	sentence	frase, oración, veredicto
suceso	event	success	éxito
trampa	trick, trap	tramp	vagabundo, mujerzuela
vaso	glass	vase	florero

Verbs

SPANISH VERB	ENGLISH MEANING	ENGLISH VERB	SPANISH MEANING
abusar	molest	abuse	maltratar
advertir (ie, i)	warn	advertise	anunciar
apuntar	write down	appoint	nombrar
argüir	present a case	argue	discutir
asistir	attend	assist	ayudar
atender (ie)	pay attention to	attend	asistir
avisar	inform	advise	aconsejar
demandar	sue	demand	exigir
discutir	argue	discuss	hablar, conversar
explanar	level	explain	explicar
fabricar	make, craft	fabricate	mentir (ie, i)
ignorar	be unaware of	ignore	no hacer caso
molestar	bother	molest	abusar
pretender	aspire to, try to, court	pretend	fingir

SPANISH VERB	ENGLISH MEANING	ENGLISH VERB	SPANISH MEANING
realizar	*achieve, effect*	*realize*	darse cuenta de
recordar (ue)	*remember*	*record*	grabar, inscribir
resistir	*tolerate*	*resist*	tener fuerzas
restar	*subtract*	*rest*	descansar
revisar	*review*	*revise*	enmendar
solicitar	*apply (submit an application)*	*solicit*	pedir, buscar
soportar	*tolerate*	*support*	mantener, apoyar

Adjectives

SPANISH ADJECTIVE	ENGLISH MEANING	ENGLISH ADJECTIVE	SPANISH MEANING
actual	*current*	*actual*	verdadero
bizarro	*gallant*	*bizarre*	extraño
bravo	*angry*	*brave*	valiente
casual	*unexpected*	*casual*	informal
constipado	*having a bad cold*	*constipated*	estreñido
conveniente	*advantageous*	*convenient*	cómodo, oportuno
corriente	*ordinary*	*current*	actual
distinto	*different*	*distinct*	visible
egoísta	*selfish*	*egotistical*	presumido
embarazada	*pregnant*	*embarrassed*	avergonzado
exitoso	*successful*	*exciting*	emocionante
fastidioso	*annoying*	*fastidious*	detallado
gracioso	*funny*	*gracious*	gentil
largo	*long*	*large*	grande
ordinario	*vulgar*	*ordinary*	común, corriente
particular	*private*	*particular*	especial, cierto
real	*royal*	*real*	verdadero
sano	*healthy*	*sane*	cuerdo, sensato
sensible	*sensitive*	*sensible*	sensato, juicioso
simpático	*nice*	*sympathetic*	compasivo

Adverbs

One adverb is a common *falso amigo*.

SPANISH ADVERB	ENGLISH MEANING	ENGLISH ADVERB	SPANISH MEANING
actualmente	*currently*	*actually*	realmente

English Words with More Than One Spanish Meaning

Many words in English have two or more noninterchangeable translations in Spanish. Following are some common examples.

Nouns

character
el personaje	*part in a movie or play*
el carácter	*a person's moral makeup*
el tipo	*unusual type of person*
un cómico	*comedian*

El personaje de la pieza que me gustó más es la hermana mayor.	*The character that I liked best in the play is the older sister.*
Ella demostró que tenía muy buen carácter.	*She showed that she had great strength of character.*
Ese tipo apareció en la fiesta sin invitación.	*That character showed up uninvited at the party.*
El hermano de Jaime es un cómico de verdad.	*Jaime's brother is a real character.*

corner
el rincón	*corner indoors (one you can stand in)*
la esquina	*corner outdoors (one you can stand on)*

Ella puso la lámpara en un rincón de la sala.	*She put the lamp in a corner of the living room.*
Lo vi en la esquina buscando un taxi.	*I saw him on the corner looking for a taxi.*

country
el país	*independent nation*
la patria	*native land*
el campo	*farmland, land outside the city*

Brasil es el país más grande de Sudamérica.	*Brazil is the biggest country in South America.*
Murieron por la patria.	*They died for their country.*
Ellos viven en Madrid pero tienen otra casa en el campo.	*They live in Madrid, but they have another house in the country.*

paper
el papel	*material used for writing and drawing*
el informe	*informative document, report*
el trabajo	*academic theme or term paper*
el documento	*official document*

La niña necesita papel para escribir su carta.	*The child needs paper to write her letter on.*

El comité mandó su informe al gobierno.	*The committee sent its paper to the government.*
Eduardo escribió un trabajo de cincuenta páginas sobre ese tema.	*Eduardo wrote a 50-page paper on that subject.*
Su hermano llegó al país sin documentos.	*Her brother arrived in the country without papers.*

party

la fiesta	*friendly get-together*
el partido	*political group*
el cómplice	*co-conspirator*
el grupo	*a group of people to be seated together*

Al final del curso hicimos una fiesta.	*We had a party when the course was over.*
¿De qué partido es tu candidato preferido?	*What party is your favorite candidate a member of?*
Creo que ella fue cómplice en el crimen.	*I think she was a party to the crime.*
Tengo un grupo de tres para la mesa número 4.	*I have a party of three for table 4.*

people

la gente	*men, women, and children*
el pueblo	*a specific community*
las personas	*human beings*

La amabilidad de la gente es lo que me gustó más del país.	*The kindness of the people is what I liked best about the country.*
Este candidato es el mejor representante del pueblo.	*This candidate is the best representative of the people.*
Había más de cien personas en la fiesta.	*There were more than a hundred people at the party.*

AVOID THE *Blunder*

La gente is a singular noun that refers to all the people. Use *las gentes* only if you are referring to various tribes or other populations.

✗ las gentes

right el derecho *a just claim*
(see also pages 311 and 320)

Este grupo ha luchado por los derechos humanos.	*This group has worked hard for human rights.*

time	la vez	*an individual occasion*
	el tiempo	*the past, the present, and the future*
	la hora	*a point in time indicated by the clock*
	divertirse (ie, i)	*have a good time*
	pasarlo bien	*have a good time*

Él la llamó tres veces.	*He called her three times.*
Hemos perdido mucho tiempo discutiendo.	*We wasted a lot of time arguing.*
¿Qué hora es?	*What time is it?*
—¿Se divirtieron?	*"Did you have a good time?"*
—Sí, lo pasamos muy bien.	*"Yes, we had a very good time."*

AVOID THE *Blunder*

El tiempo also refers to the weather. *Tener buen tiempo* means "have good weather."

✗ La llamó tres tiempos.
✗ ¿Qué tiempo es?
✗ Tuvimos un buen tiempo.

Verbs

| **appear** | aparecer | *show up* |
| | parecer | *seem to be* |

Su nombre apareció tres veces en el artículo.	*His name appeared in the article three times.*
Parece que no va a venir.	*It appears that he's not coming.*

ask	pedirle a uno	*make a request of someone*
	preguntarle a uno	*make a query to someone*
	hacerle una pregunta a uno	*pose a question to someone*

(see also pages 167 and 201–202)

Ella nos pidió que la lleváramos a su casa.	*She asked us to take her home.*
Le preguntamos dónde vivía.	*We asked her where she lived.*
¿Puedo hacerte una pregunta?	*Can I ask you a question?*

be (see pages 87–89)

■ *Ser* is used to indicate origin, nationality, religion, profession, civil status, ownership, composition, and descriptive characteristics of people and things.

Ramón es de México. Es católico.	*Ramón is from Mexico.*
Es médico. Es soltero.	*He's a Catholic. He's a doctor.*
Es simpático.	*He's single. He's nice.*
Esta chaqueta es de Guatemala.	*This jacket is from Guatemala.*
Es de algodón. Es roja. Es mía.	*It's cotton. It's red. It's mine.*

Ser is used to tell the current time and date, as well as the time, date, and location of events.

Hoy es miércoles, 12 de enero.	*Today is Wednesday, January 12.*
La reunión es mañana. Es a las	*The meeting is tomorrow.*
diez. Es en la oficina del jefe.	*It's at 10 o'clock. It's in the boss's office.*

AVOID THE *Blunder*

Forget the misleading rule that *ser* indicates permanence. Many uses of *ser* are not necessarily permanent: *es joven, soltero, gordo, pequeño, pobre, de Ramón.*

■ *Haber* is used to state the existence of something. In all tenses, it is used only in the third-person singular, even when it is followed by a plural noun.

Hay una persona en la cocina.	*There is one person in the kitchen.*
Hay diez personas en la cocina.	*There are ten people in the kitchen.*
No había nada que leer.	*There was nothing to read.*
Había tres libros en la mesa.	*There were three books on the table.*
Hubo un accidente ayer.	*There was an accident yesterday.*
Hubo dos accidentes ayer.	*There were two accidents yesterday.*

AVOID THE *Blunder*

✗ Habían tres libros.　　✗ Hubieron dos accidentes.

■ *Estar* is used to tell the current condition of a person or thing.

Sara está enferma.	*Sara is sick.*
El dormitorio está sucio.	*The bedroom is dirty.*
Su tío está muerto.	*His uncle is dead.*
La máquina está rota.	*The machine is broken.*

Estar is used to tell the location of people and things.

Ana María no está en clase hoy porque está enferma.	*Ana María isn't in class today because she's sick.*
La Argentina está en el sur de Sudamérica.	*Argentina is in the southern part of South America.*
La oficina está en el tercer piso.	*The office is on the third floor.*
Todos estamos aquí para la reunión.	*We're all here for the meeting.*

Estar is used with a gerund to indicate ongoing activity (see page 115).

Mis amigos están estudiando en la biblioteca.	*My friends are studying at the library.*

Estar is used with a past participle to indicate a current condition (see page 87).

Las ventanas están abiertas.	*The windows are open.*
La puerta está cerrada.	*The door is closed.*

AVOID THE *Blunder*

Forget the misleading rule that *estar* indicates temporary meaning. Many uses of *estar* are not temporary.

✗ La Argentina es en Sudamérica.
✗ Su tío es muerto.

■ *Tener* is used to tell age. The word *años* is usually stated, and the word "old" is not translated. Since age is a characteristic, it answers the question *¿cómo es?*

El muchacho tiene diez años.	*The boy is ten.*
Esta casa tiene cien años.	*This house is a hundred years old.*

AVOID THE *Blunder*

✗ El muchacho es diez.
✗ El muchacho tiene diez.
✗ Esta casa es cien años viejo.

Tener is used with certain nouns to indicate a current condition. It answers the question *¿cómo está?*

tener (mucho) calor	be (very) hot
tener (mucho) frío	be (very) cold
tener (mucha) hambre	be (very) hungry
tener (mucho) miedo	be (very) afraid
tener (mucha) sed	be (very) thirsty
tener (mucho) sueño	be (very) sleepy

AVOID THE *Blunder*

✗ Estoy hambre.
✗ Estoy sed.
✗ Estoy frío.

■ *Muy* used after *ser* and *estar* means "very." *Mucho(-a)* is used after *tener*.

AVOID THE *Blunder*

✗ Tengo muy hambre.   ✗ Tiene muy sueño.

be right   tener razón   *make sense*
ser correcto   *be the truth, behave appropriately*
estar correcto *be a correct response on a test*

Su madre dice que debe hacer las tareas antes de ver la televisión. Su madre tiene razón.	*His mother says he has to do his homework before watching TV. His mother is right.*
El mensaje es correcto.	*The message is true.*
Ese señor es muy correcto.	*That man is very well mannered.*
Espero que todas las respuestas en el examen estén correctas.	*I hope all the answers on the test are right.*

become   hacerse   *change over the course of time*
ponerse   *experience a sudden change in condition*
convertirse *transform completely, turn into*
llegar a ser *achieve a change*

Piensa hacerse abogado, por lo tanto, estudia mucho.	*He wants to become a lawyer, so he studies a lot.*
El abogado se puso bravo cuando oyó el veredicto.	*The lawyer became angry when he heard the verdict.*

La niña se convirtió en una   *The little girl became a great*
belleza.   *beauty.*
Ella se dedicó a cantar y llegó   *She devoted her life to singing*
a ser famosa.   *and became famous.*

can   poder + *infinitive*   *be able to* (because the possibility exists)
            saber + *infinitive*   *know how to*

Sé manejar, pero hoy no puedo   *I can drive, but I can't drive today*
manejar porque no tengo coche.   *because I don't have a car.*

eat   comer   *eat*
            desayunar   *eat breakfast*
            almorzar   *eat lunch*
            cenar   *eat dinner*

Vamos a comer a las ocho.   *We're going to eat at eight.*
¿A qué hora desayunan ustedes?   *What time do you all eat*
                                     breakfast?
No almuerzan hasta las dos.   *They don't eat lunch until two.*
¿Dónde quieres cenar?   *Where do you want to eat dinner?*

AVOID THE *Blunder*

El desayuno, el almuerzo, and *la cena* are meals that can be
prepared, served, or enjoyed. But in Spanish, you "breakfast,"
"lunch," and "dine."

✗ Voy a comer desayuno.
✗ Va comer almuerzo.
✗ Vamos a comer la cena.

go   ir   *move from one place to another*
            irse   *leave, go away*
            subir   *go up*
            bajar   *go down*
            volverse loco(-a)   *go crazy*

Tenemos que ir al mercado por   *We have to go to the store for*
leche.   *milk.*
Tengo que irme. Se me hace tarde.   *I have to go. I'm late.*
El ascensor subió al séptimo piso.   *The elevator went up to the*
                                     seventh floor.
Queremos bajar al sótano.   *We want to go down to the*
                                     basement.
Me estoy volviendo loca con   *I'm going crazy with so much*
tanto trabajo.   *work.*

AVOID THE *Blunder*

Do not confuse *ir* and *irse*.

✗ El ascensor fue arriba al séptimo piso.
✗ Tengo que ir.
✗ Tenemos que irnos al mercado.

| **go** and **come** | ir | *go to another place (there)* |
| | venir | *come to where the speaker is (here)* |

| Voy a tu casa mañana. | *I'm coming to your house tomorrow.* |
| Por favor, ven a mi oficina a las once. | *Please come to my office at 11 o'clock.* |

AVOID THE *Blunder*

In English, it is possible to "come there," when "there" means where the person you are talking to is or expects to be at the time of your arrival. In Spanish, this is not possible.

✗ Vengo a tu casa mañana.
✗ Venimos a tu fiesta el sábado.

| **have** | hacer una fiesta | *organize a party* |
| | tener una fiesta | *be invited to a party* |

| ¡Vamos a hacer una fiesta! | *Let's have a party!* |
| Tenemos una fiesta el viernes. | *We have a party to go to on Friday.* |

| **have to** | deber + *infinitive* | *be obligated to* |
| | tener que + *infinitive* | *need to* |

| Debemos pagar los impuestos cada año. | *We have to pay our taxes every year.* |
| Me duele mucho el diente. Tengo que ir al dentista ahora mismo. | *My tooth really hurts. I have to go to the dentist right away.* |

| **know** | conocer | *be acquainted with a person, have visited a place* |
| | saber | *be aware of information* |

| No conozco Bolivia, pero conozco a muchos bolivianos. | *I've never been to Bolivia, but I know a lot of Bolivians.* |

—¿Sabes tú dónde está Bolivia?   *"Do you know where Bolivia is?"*
—Claro, sé que está al este del   *"Of course, I know that it's east*
  Perú.   *of Peru."*

leave   salir   *go out of a place*
                 dejar   *not bring something with you, leave something behind*

Humberto sale de su casa a las   *Humberto leaves home at 8 A.M.*
  ocho de la mañana.
Dejó su maletín en su casa.   *He left his briefcase at home.*

like   apreciar/estimar   *hold in high esteem*
                 caerle bien a uno   *have a good impression of*
                 gustarle a uno   *be pleased by the company of a person,*
                                          be attracted to a person, be delighted
                                          by a thing

Aprecia mucho a sus colegas.   *She likes her colleagues.*
Su novio me cae muy bien.   *I like her boyfriend.*
A Alejandro le gusta mucho   *Alejandro really likes Cristina.*
  Cristina.
Le gustan todas sus clases.   *She likes all her classes.*
A mí me gusta mucho el   *I like chocolate a lot.*
  chocolate.

AVOID THE *Blunder*

Keep in mind that in these constructions the person with the feeling is the indirect object, and the person or thing that causes the feeling is the subject.

✗ Su novio me caigo bien.
✗ Le gusta sus clases.
✗ Me gusto el chocolate.

AVOID THE *Blunder*

Gustar usually implies "attracted to." Use *querer* to express "liking" family members or those in platonic relationships.

✗ Me gusta mi hermana.
✗ Le gusta mucho su abuelo.

---

love   querer   *care for someone, love*
                 amar   *love unconditionally*
                 encantarle a uno   *be really delighted by a person or thing*

Ella quiere mucho a sus padres.	*She loves her parents a lot.*
Te amo. Quiero casarme contigo.	*I love you. I want to marry you.*
Tú me encantas.	*You enchant me.*
Me encanta tu nuevo vestido.	*I love your new dress. Where did*
¿Dónde lo compraste?	*you buy it?*

AVOID THE *Blunder*

Querer means "love" or "care for" when referring to people, but "want" when referring to things. *Encantar* means "love" when referring to things, but "entice," "enchant," or "delight" when referring to people.

✗ Amo el chocolate.

make	hacer	*construct*
	hacer un ruido	*make a noise*
	hacer/tender (ie) la cama	*make the bed*
	anotar algo	*make a note of something*
	cometer un error	*make a mistake*
	ganar dinero	*make money*

Voy a hacerme un vestido nuevo.	*I'm going to make a new dress.*
¡No hagas tanto ruido!	*Don't make so much noise!*
Hoy ni quiero tender la cama.	*Today I don't even want to make my bed.*
Anota esa dirección, por favor.	*Please make note of that address.*
Todos cometemos errores.	*We all make mistakes.*
Su hijo gana bastante dinero.	*His son makes a lot of money.*

meet	conocer	*get acquainted with, be introduced to for the first time*
	encontrarse	*run into someone you already know*

Conocí a Josefina en la clase de español.	*I met Josefina in Spanish class.*
Ayer nos encontramos en la cafetería.	*We met in the cafeteria yesterday.*

miss	echar de menos, extrañar	*feel nostalgic for*
	perder, faltar a	*not attend an event*
	perder	*be late for (a bus or train)*
	pasar por alto	*overlook*

Me gusta estar aquí, pero echo de menos a mi familia.	*I like being here but I miss my family.*
Me gusta estar aquí, pero extraño a mi familia.	

Javier perdió tres clases. ⎫
Javier faltó a tres clases. ⎭ *Javier missed three classes.*

¡Apúrate o perderemos el tren! *Hurry up or we'll miss the train!*
Jorge pasó por alto los detalles *Jorge completely missed the details*
  del plan.   *of the plan.*

pay   pagarle   *give money to (for things or work)*
         prestarle atención a,   *pay attention to*
         hacerle caso a

En esta compañía nos pagan *At this company they pay us*
  al final del mes.   *at the end of the month.*
Debemos prestarle atención *We have to pay attention to*
  al director.   *the director.*

play   jugar   *participate in a game, gamble*
         tocar   *make music with an instrument*
         hacer/jugar un papel   *act a part in a play*

Van a jugar (al) fútbol después *They're going to play soccer after*
  de clase.   *class.*
¿Tocas un instrumento? *Do you play an instrument?*
Julián hace/juega el papel del *Julian is playing the part of the*
  padre en la pieza.   *father in the play.*

return   volver, regresar   *come/go back*
         devolver   *give/take something back*

Mariana regresa a su casa *Mariana is returning home*
  mañana.   *tomorrow.*
Debes devolver los libros a la *You have to return the books*
  biblioteca hoy.   *to the library today.*

ride   montar a caballo   *go on horseback*
         montar en bicicleta   *go on a bicycle*
         ir en coche/bus/tren/avión   *go by car/bus/train/airplane*

A Sonia le encanta montar *Sonia loves to ride horses.*
  a caballo.
Muchas personas montan en *A lot of people ride bicycles*
  bicicleta los fines de semana.   *on weekends.*
No quiero ir en tren. *I don't want to ride the train.*

spend   gastar   *use money*
         pasar tiempo   *use time*

Alfredo gasta todo el dinero que *Alfredo spends all the money*
  gana en regalos para su novia.   *he makes on presents for his*
      girlfriend.

Nos gustaría pasar un tiempo en Nicaragua. — *We would like to spend some time in Nicaragua.*

take	tomar	*grasp with the fingers, drink*
	sacar	*remove from, take (a photograph), make (a photocopy)*
	quitarle a uno	*take away from*
	quitarse	*take off (clothing)*
	cuidar	*take care of*
	dar una vuelta	*take a stroll/ride*

Ángeles tomó el diccionario del estante y buscó la palabra. — *Ángeles took the dictionary from the shelf and looked up the word.*

Los padres sacaron a los niños de la escuela. — *The parents took their children out of the school.*

Manuel siempre saca muchas fotos. — *Manuel always takes a lot of pictures.*

El policía le quitó la licencia de conducir. — *The policeman took his driver's license away from him.*

Los chicos deben quitarse la gorra al entrar en el salón de clase. — *The kids have to take off their caps when they enter the classroom.*

Norma se queda en casa para cuidar a sus niños. — *Norma stays home to take care of her children.*

Vamos a dar una vuelta por la ciudad. — *Let's take a ride around the city.*

| **take** and **bring** | llevar | *take (there)* |
| | traer | *bring (here)* |

Voy a tu casa y te llevo los documentos. — *I'm coming to your house and I'll bring you the papers.*

Carlos vino a mi casa y me trajo dos libros. — *Carlos came to my house and brought me two books.*

In English, you can "bring" something "there," when "there" means where the person you are speaking to is or expects to be at the time of your arrival. In Spanish, this is not possible.

AVOID THE *Blunder*

Do not use *traer*, unless you are already at your friend's house and mean, "I brought you the documents."

✗ Te traigo los documentos mañana.

try intentar hacer *make an effort to do something*
  tratar de hacer *act to do something*
  hacer un esfuerzo *make an effort*

Intenté hablar con él, pero no
  estaba en su casa cuando
  lo llamé.

*I tried to talk to him, but he
  wasn't at home when I called
  him.*

Susana trató de abrir la puerta
  con esta llave, pero no
  funcionó.

*Susana tried to open the door
  with this key, but it didn't
  work.*

Tienes que hacer un esfuerzo. *You have to try!*

used to acostumbrarse *get used to*
  estar acostumbrado *be accustomed to*

El niño tiene que acostumbrarse
  a seguir las instrucciones de
  la maestra.

*The child has to get used to
  following the teacher's
  instructions.*

Al principio me molestó el ruido
  de los aviones, pero ahora
  estoy acostumbrada.

*At first the airplane noise
  bothered me, but now I'm
  used to it.*

The imperfect tense of a verb is used to express "used to be" or "used to do" something regularly in the past.

The preterite tense of a verb is used to express "used to be" or "used to do" something, but not anymore.

Ana era muy flaca. Incluso
  intentaba ganar peso.

*Ana used to be really skinny. She
  even used to try to gain weight.*

Ella estuvo casada una vez. *She used to be married.*

watch ver *see, watch (television, a movie, a show, a game)*
  mirar *look at*

Las chicas vinieron a casa a ver
  la televisión.

The girls came home to watch TV.

Me gusta mirar a la gente andar
  por la calle.

*I like to watch people walking
  down the street.*

AVOID THE *Blunder*

In English one "watches" shows and games. In Spanish, *ver*, rather than *mirar*, is used to express this.

✗ Miro la televisión.
✗ Miramos el fútbol.

| **work** | trabajar | *do physical or mental labor* |
| | funcionar | *function* |

Trabajamos de lunes a viernes. / *We work from Monday to Friday.*
El lavaplatos no funciona. / *The dishwasher doesn't work.*

Adjectives and Adverbs

bad/badly   malo(-a)/mal

¿Cómo es ella? Es mala. / *What's she like? She's a bad girl.*
¿Cómo está ella? Está mal. / *How is she? She's in bad shape.*
Canta muy mal. / *She sings very badly.*

AVOID THE *Blunder*

Use *malo(-a)* after *ser*, and *mal* after *estar* or an action verb. *Mal* is an adverb, and its form does not change.

✗ Es mal.
✗ Está mala.
✗ Canto malo.

good/well   bueno(-a)/bien

¿Cómo es ella? Es buena. / *What's she like? She's a good girl.*
¿Cómo está ella? Está bien. / *How is she? She's well. /*
  / *She's in good shape.*
Habla español muy bien. / *She speaks Spanish very well.*

AVOID THE *Blunder*

Use *bueno(-a)* after *ser*, and *bien* after *estar* or an action verb. *Bien* is an adverb, and its form does not change.

✗ Ella es bien.
✗ Ella está bueno.
✗ Habla bueno.

little	pequeño(-a)	*small in size*
	poco(-a)	*a small amount, very little*
	un poco	*a small amount, some*

El apartamento es muy pequeño. / *The apartment is very little.*
Tenemos poco espacio. / *We have very little space.*
Nos gustaría tener un poco más / *We'd like to have a little more*
   de espacio. /   *space.*

| *right* | derecho(-a) | *opposite of left* |
| | a la derecha | *to the opposite of left* |

Cecilia escribe con la mano
derecha.

Cecilia writes with her right hand.

Dobla a la derecha en el segundo
semáforo.

Turn right at the second light.

Spanish Words with More Than One English Meaning

Following are some Spanish words that have noninterchangeable translations in English.

buscar   *look for, go get (a person or thing), pick up (a person to go somewhere)*

No sé dónde está el libro.
Voy a buscarlo.

*I don't know where the book is.
I'm going to look for it.*

El libro está arriba en el escritorio.
Voy a buscarlo.

*The book is upstairs on the desk.
I'll go get it.*

Vamos a buscarte a tu casa a las
ocho.

*We're going to pick you up at
your house at eight.*

ganar   *win, beat, earn, gain*

¡Ojalá que ganemos el partido!

I hope we win the game.

Les ganamos por dos puntos.

We beat them by two points.

Su marido gana suficiente dinero
para los dos.

*Her husband earns enough
money for both of them.*

Gané dos kilos durante mis
vacaciones.

*I gained two kilos during my
vacation.*

llevar   *wear, carry, take, have spent time*
llevarse con   *get along with*

Tu hermano siempre lleva ropa
muy elegante.

*Your brother always wears fine
clothes.*

Los bomberos sacaron al anciano
de la casa y lo llevaron al
hospital.

*The firemen got the old man out
of the house and took him to
the hospital.*

Horacio lleva veinte años
trabajando aquí.

*Horacio has been working here
for twenty years.*

María y Ana se llevan bien.
Patricia no se lleva bien con
María.

*María and Ana get along well.
Patricia doesn't get along well
with María.*

querer　　　*love, want*

> Juan quiere mucho a su hija.　　*Juan loves his daughter.*
> Juan quiere una casa nueva.　　*Juan wants a new house.*

AVOID THE *Blunder*

Querer means "love, care about" when it refers to people, and "want" when it refers to things.

tomar　　　*drink, take, grasp, pull*

> Miguel no toma café.　　*Miguel doesn't drink coffee.*
> Toma las pastillas después de comer.　　*Take the pills after eating.*
> Toma el vaso y ponlo en la mesa.　　*Take the glass and put it on the table.*
>
> ¡No me tomes el pelo!　　*Don't pull my hair! (Don't tease me!)*

Exercises

A Write the Spanish cognate of each of the following English nouns.

1. chocolate _____
2. solution _____
3. possibility _____
4. biology _____
5. patient _____

6. fragment _____
7. sentiment _____
8. arrogance _____
9. presence _____
10. feminist _____

B Write the English meaning of each of the following Spanish nouns.

1. arena _____
2. carpeta _____
3. compromiso _____
4. costumbre _____
5. decepción _____

6. discusión _____
7. fábrica _____
8. lectura _____
9. parientes _____
10. suceso _____

C *Write the Spanish that corresponds to each of the following English verbs. Give the infinitive form of the Spanish verb.*

1. warn _____
2. write down _____
3. pay attention to _____
4. argue _____
5. be unaware of _____

6. bother _____
7. remember _____
8. inform _____
9. apply (for school/job) _____
10. attend _____

D *Match the Spanish adjectives in the left column with the appropriate English adjectives in the right column.*

_____ 1. actual	a. sensitive
_____ 2. casual	b. unexpected
_____ 3. cómodo	c. pregnant
_____ 4. conveniente	d. advantageous
_____ 5. detallado	e. annoying
_____ 6. embarazada	f. royal
_____ 7. fastidioso	g. sensible
_____ 8. informal	h. casual
_____ 9. real	i. convenient
_____ 10. sensato	j. fastidious
_____ 11. sensible	k. current
_____ 12. verdadero	l. actual

E *Circle the expression that best completes each sentence.*

1. Llamé a mi amiga **dos tiempos | dos veces | dos horas**.
2. Ella me **pidió | preguntó | hizo una pregunta** dónde estaba el banco.
3. Su hermano **es | está | estaba** una persona muy simpática.
4. Su apartamento **es | está | fue** en el tercer piso.
5. Creo que la profesora **es | tiene | está** razón.
6. Tengo que **irse | ir | irme**.
7. **Vengo | Voy | Me voy** a tu casa mañana.
8. Él no **conoce | sabe | es** Nueva York.
9. Su abuelo es **bien | bueno | enfermo**.

CONSTRUCTIONS

Spanish and English use very different constructions for certain concepts. Following are some examples.

English to Spanish

since

- "after a time in the past when": *desde* (see pages 117 and 283)

Desde que tengo este coche, he gastado mucho dinero.	*Ever since I've had this car, I've spent a lot of money.*

- to indicate a period of time during which an event or activity has not occurred: *hace* (see page 116)

Hace años que no voy al teatro.	*It's been years since I've been to the theater.*

- "because": *como*

Como teníamos tanta hambre, fuimos a un restaurante.	*Since we were so hungry, we went to a restaurant.*

so

- to intensify the meaning of an adjective: *tan*

El profesor es tan exigente que me pone nervioso.	*The teacher is so strict that he makes me nervous.*

- to ask about recent news that's on the mind of both parties: *¿Y?* (see page 291)

  SITUATION The baby has just been born and the new father calls his parents.

MADRE	—¿Y...?	*"So ...?"*
HIJO	—¡Es una niña!	*"It's a girl!"*

- to introduce a consequence: *así que*

Tengo que trabajar el sábado, así que no voy a poder acompañarte al cine.	*I have to work on Saturday, so I won't be able to go to the movies with you.*

- to indicate "not good, not bad": *más o menos/regular*

—Hola Paco, ¿cómo van las cosas?	"*Hi, Paco. How are things?*"
—Pues, más o menos.	"*Oh, just so-so.*"

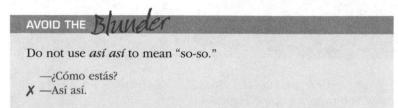

AVOID THE *Blunder*

Do not use *así así* to mean "so-so."

—¿Cómo estás?

✗ —Así así.

will

- to ask a favor: question using a verb in the present tense

¿Me ayudas con los paquetes?	*Will you help me with the packages?*
¿Me estacionas el coche?	*Will you park the car for me?*

- to accept a request: verb in the present tense

Te ayudo con mucho gusto.	*I'll gladly help you.*
Te estaciono el coche enseguida.	*I'll park the car for you right away.*

- to make a promise: verb in the present or future tense

La llamo esta tarde a las cinco. La llamaré esta tarde a las cinco.	*I'll call you this afternoon at five.*

- to predict the future: verb in the future tense

Su hijo será famoso.	*Your son will be famous.*
Tú viajarás por el mundo.	*You will travel throughout the world.*

- to indicate probability: verb in the future tense

—¿Qué vas a hacer?	"*What are you going to do?*"
—No sé. Me quedaré en casa y veré la televisión.	"*I don't know. I'll probably stay home and watch TV.*"

AVOID THE *Blunder*

Do not use the future tense in Spanish to translate all meanings of "will." Rather than translate words individually, think of the function of the Spanish equivalent for the entire expression.

✗ ¿Me ayudarás con los paquetes?

✗ ¿Me llamarás esta tarde?

wish

- to express a sentiment: indirect object pronoun + *desear*

Te deseo un feliz cumpleaños.	*I wish you a happy birthday.*
Les deseamos toda la felicidad del mundo.	*We wish you all the happiness in the world.*

- to express a wish that something were true: *ojalá* (*que*) + verb in imperfect subjunctive (see page 195)

Ojalá estuvieras aquí conmigo.	*I wish you were here with me.*
Ojalá tuviéramos más tiempo.	*I wish we had more time.*

- to wish that something were true or had not happened: *lamentar* + infinitive

Lamento no poder decírtelo.	*I wish I could tell you.*
Lamento no haber ido a verla.	*I wish I had gone to see her*

wonder

"I wonder" is best expressed in Spanish by using a question in the future tense or in the conditional (see pages 145 and 156). The future is used to express wonder about present time. The conditional is used to express wonder about past time.

¿Dónde estará mi hermano?	*I wonder where my brother is.*
¿Dónde estaría mi hermano?	*I wonder where my brother was.*

would

"Would" has several meanings in English. Each meaning uses a different expression in Spanish.

- "would rather": *preferir (ie, i)*

Preferimos quedarnos en casa.	*We would rather stay home.*

- past tense of "will"; to express refusal to act: "wouldn't," "refused to": *negarse a/no querer*

Se negó a ir al concierto. ⎫ No quiso ir al concierto. ⎭	*He wouldn't go to the concert./ He refused to go to the concert.*

- past habitual action: verb in imperfect tense (see pages 132–138)

Ella me decía sus secretos cuando éramos pequeñas.	*She would always tell me her secrets when we were little.*

- conditional action: verb in conditional (see pages 151–156)

Mi colega iría si pudiera.	*My colleague would come if she could.*

Ella estaría hablando contigo ahora si fuera posible.	*She would be talking to you right now if it were possible.*
Ya nos habríamos ido si no hubiéramos perdido tanto tiempo.	*We would have left by now if we hadn't wasted so much time.*

- to make a polite request: *poder* in conditional

¿Podría usted hacerme un favor?	*Would you do me a favor?*
¿Podrían ustedes ayudarnos?	*Would you all help us?*

- "would like": *gustarle a uno* in conditional; also, imperfect subjunctive of *querer, "quisiera"* + infinitive

¿Adónde te gustaría ir?	*Where would you like to go?*
Me gustaría comer afuera esta noche. Quisiera comer afuera esta noche.	*I would like to eat out tonight.*

- "would you mind if": *importarle a uno* in conditional

¿Te importaría si saliera temprano de la clase?	*Would you mind if I left class early?*

AVOID THE *Blunder*

Rather than translate "would" literally, think of the function of the Spanish equivalent for the entire expression.

Spanish to English

darle de alta   *release a patient*
darle de baja   *admit a patient*

A Marta le dieron de alta del hospital ayer.	*They released Marta from the hospital yesterday.*
A su papá le dieron de baja ayer.	*They admitted her father yesterday.*

darle la bienvenida a alquien   *welcome someone*

Vamos todos al aeropuerto para darles la bienvenida.	*We're all going to the airport to welcome them.*

desayunar, almorzar (ue), cenar   *eat breakfast, eat lunch, eat dinner*

No desayuno hasta las once.	*I don't eat breakfast until 11 o'clock.*
¿Quieres almorzar conmigo?	*Will you eat lunch with me?*
¿A qué hora cenan ustedes?	*What time do you all eat dinner?*

AVOID THE *Blunder*

In Spanish, you "breakfast," "lunch," and "dine." The nouns for meals, *el desayuno, el almuerzo,* and *la cena* are used with the verbs *preparar, cocinar,* and *servir.*

✗ No como el desayuno.
✗ ¿Quieres comer almuerzo?
✗ ¿A qué hora comen la cena?

despedirse de   *say good-bye to*

Tuvimos que despedirnos anoche.	*We had to say good-bye to each other last night.*

echarle la culpa a alguien   *blame someone*

Fue él quien lo hizo, pero a ella le echaron la culpa.	*He's the one who did it, but they blamed it on her.*

echarse a perder   *be ruined*

Ha llovido tanto que mis sandalias se han echado a perder.	*It has rained so much that my sandals are ruined.*

enamorarse de   *fall in love with*

Me temo que me estoy enamorando de él.	*I'm afraid I'm falling in love with him.*

estrenar   *use for the first time*

Esta noche va a estrenar su vestido nuevo.	*She's going to wear her new dress for the first time tonight.*

fijarse en   *notice, pay attention to*

Mi esposo ni se ha fijado en que me he cortado el pelo.	*My husband hasn't even noticed that I had my hair cut.*
¡Fíjate en cómo lo hacen los otros!	*Pay attention to how the others do it.*

soler   *usually (do)*

¿A qué hora suelen cenar?	*What time do you usually eat dinner?*
Solemos cenar a las ocho.	*We usually eat dinner at eight.*

tratarse de   *be about*

—¿De qué se trata la película?   *"What's the movie about?"*
—Se trata de la vida en un   *"It's about life in a small town."*
    pueblo pequeño.

Negative Constructions

In Spanish, as opposed to English, a negative clause must have *no* or another negative word before the verb.

■ Negative sentences are often expressed using a double negative, with *no* preceding the verb and another negative word following the verb.

—¿Tienes algo en la mano?   *"Do you have something in your*
                                        hand?"
—No, no tengo nada en la mano.   *"No, I don't have anything in*
                                        my hand."

—¿Está alguien en la casa?   *"Is anyone in the house?"*
—No, no está nadie.   *"No, no one is there."*

—¿Conoces a algún carpintero   *"Do you know a good carpenter?"*
    bueno?
—No, no conozco a ningún   *"No, I don't know a single*
    carpintero aquí.   *carpenter here."*

—¿Quieres ir a alguna parte?   *"Do you want to go anywhere?"*
—No, no quiero ir a ninguna   *"No, I don't want to go anywhere."*
    parte.

Algún día volverá.   *He'll come back one day.*
No volverá nunca.   *He'll never come back.*

Ella va al cine y yo también.   *She's going to the movies, and*
                                        so am I.

Ella no va a estudiar ni yo   *She's not going to study, and*
    tampoco.   *I'm not either.*

Él quiere cenar o ir al cine   *He wants to eat dinner and*
                                        go to the movies.

Ella no quiere ni cenar ni ir   *He doesn't want to eat dinner*
    al cine.   *or go to the movies.*

AVOID THE *Blunder*

✗ Tengo nada en la mano.
✗ Volverá nunca.

■ A negative word other than *no* sometimes precedes the verb, and the *no* is omitted.

Nada es más importante que la salud.	*Nothing is more important than health.*
Nadie está en la casa.	*No one is in the house.*
Ningún carpintero quiere hacer este proyecto.	*No carpenter wants to do this project.*
Nunca volverá.	*She'll never come back.*
No quiero ir al cine. Tampoco quiero quedarme aquí.	*I don't want to go to the movies. I don't want to stay here either.*
Ella no quiere hacer nada, ni quiere ir al cine.	*She doesn't want to do anything. She doesn't even want to go to the movies.*

AVOID THE *Blunder*

✗ No nadie está en casa.
✗ No nunca volverá.

Exercises

A *Express the following in Spanish.*

1. When are they going to release your grandmother from the hospital?

   _____

2. Are you going to wear your new shoes (for the first time)?

   _____

3. I want to be at the station to welcome you.

   _____

4. She went to Mexico and fell in love.

   _____

5. The dinner was ruined.

   _____

6. The girl didn't pay any attention to him at the party.

   _____

7. They blamed me.

   _____

8. They said goodbye this morning at the airport.

   _____

9. What is your paper about?

   _____

10. What time do you all eat breakfast?

   _____

B *Rewrite the following sentences, making them negative.*

1. Tengo que comprar algo.

   _____

2. Siempre viene a visitar los domingos.

   _____

3. Jorge va a estudiar, y yo también.

   _____

4. Alguien está en la oficina.

   _____

CATCH THE BLUNDERS

In the following paragraphs, each word printed in red contains at least one blunder. Correct all the blunders, referring to the English version when necessary, and fill in all the blanks. Then check your answers on pages 347–349.

A Soy en mi primero ano de colegio. Vivo en un dormitorio, que se llama "Jefferson Hall," con dos compañeras de cuarto, Mary y Jenna. Los dos están muy simpático y nos llevamos bien. Mary es bastante serio y ella estudia mucho. Jenna es buena estudianta, pero ella no estudia tan mucho que Mary. Nuestra dormitorio es no largo, pero lo es cómodo y bonito.

I'm a freshman in college. I live in a dorm, called "Jefferson Hall," with two roommates, Mary and Jenna. Both of them are very nice and we get along well. Mary is pretty serious and she studies a lot. Jenna is a good student, but she doesn't study as much as Mary. Our room isn't big, but it's comfortable and pretty.

B Desde quiero ser un médico, yo estudio biología y química, que yo me gusto mucho. Mis clases son en Lunes y en Miércoles son las diez en la mañana hasta _____ once y medio, a Washington Hall. Yo también tengo _____ estudiar ingles, historia, y espanol. _____ español es difícil por mi, pero yo me lo gusto y yo creo que está importante por mí carrera. La clase de inglés está en Martes y _____ Jueves son las nueve a Harrison Hall, la de historia son la mediadía en las mismas días y a el mismo edificio y la de español es de Lunes a Jueves desde las dos en la tarde a las tres, a Tyler Hall. No tengo que atender a clases en Viernes.

Since I want to be a doctor, I take Biology and Chemistry, which I like a lot. The classes are on Mondays and Wednesdays at 10 o'clock in the morning until 11:30, in Washington Hall. I also have to study English, History, and Spanish. Spanish is hard for me, but I like it and I think it is important for my career.

*My English class is on Tuesdays and Thursdays at 9 A.M. in Harrison Hall,
my History class is at noon on the same days and in the same building, and
my Spanish class is from Monday to Thursday from 2 P.M. until three, in Tyler
Hall. I don't have to attend classes on Fridays.*

C Entramos en un dormitorio de la universidad y vemos esté escena:

Hay ochos estudiantes sentado en el suelo preparandose por un exámen.

Están tratando _____ recordar todos los datos sobre de la Civil Guerra

de los Estados Unidos. Un chica tene una pizarra pequeña en el cual _____

escribando las importantes fechas. Un chico _____ esta explicando a su

amigo _____ que pasó al final de el guerra. Dos otros chicos está leiendo

sus libro de textos. Una estudiante está dormiendo y su amiga está tratando

a despertar a ella. Un muchacho está hablando en el celular a su novia. Nadie

está mirando _____ televisión. Todos los personos beben café y ellos

esperan la llegada de unas pizzas.

*We enter a college dorm room and see the following scene: There are eight
students sitting on the floor getting ready for a test. They're trying to remember
all the facts about the U.S. Civil War. One girl has a small blackboard on which
she is writing the important dates. A boy is explaining to his friend what
happened at the end of the war. Two other boys are reading their textbooks.
One student is sleeping, and her friend is trying to wake her up. A boy is talking
to his girlfriend on his cell phone. Nobody is watching TV. They are all drinking
coffee, and they're waiting for pizza to arrive.*

D En Viernes tengo una fiesta a la casa de un amigo. Yo voy _____

ir con dos otras chicas. Yo no sé qué van _____ llevar ellas, pero yo pienso

llevar mi nueva falda negra con una blusa rosada. Yo voy a usar unos zapatos

negros de tacón alto y unos pendientes platas. Mis amigas vienen a buscarme

son las siete, así que voy a tener que cambiar mis ropas rápido porque mi

pasada clase no termina hasta las 5:30. Estoy segura de que vamos a tener

un tiempo muy bueno.

*On Friday I'm going to a party at a friend's house. I'm going to go with two other
girls. I don't know what they're going to wear, but I plan to wear my new black
skirt with a pink blouse. I'm going to wear my black high heels and some silver
earrings. My friends are coming to get me at seven, so I'm going to have to
change my clothes fast because my last class doesn't end until 5:30. I'm sure
we're going to have a good time.*

E Cuando estaba joven, viví en la ciudad con mis padres y _____ mis hermanos. Todos los domingos fuimos a el pueblo para comer almuerzo a la casa de mis abuelos. También fueron mis tíos con sus hijos, y a veces invitábamos _____ alguno amigo. En fin, era muchas gentes que comerían y tendrían un buen tiempo en esa casa en domingos. Mi abuela, la mejor cocinera en el mundo, preparó una grande comida, con por lo menos dos tipos de carne, varios platos de verduras, dos o tres ensaladas, y frutas. Nunca faltaba el pan especial hecho por mano por mi abuela. Luego se servía un pastel o una torta de postre. _____ Todo el mundo _____ gustaban a comer en casa de mi abuela. Yo me gustaba a jugar con mis primos, pero lo que yo me gustaba más era sentando en la mesa con los viejos y escuchando a sus cuentos.

When I was young I lived in the city with my parents and my brothers and sisters. Every Sunday we went to the country to eat lunch at my grandparents' house. My aunts and uncles and their kids always went too, and sometimes we invited a friend as well. So there were always a lot of people who would eat and have fun at that house on Sundays. My grandmother, the best cook in the whole world, used to prepare a huge meal, always with at least two kinds of meat, several platters of vegetables, two or three salads, and fruit. There were always my grandmother's homemade biscuits. Later a pie or cake was served for dessert. Everybody liked to eat at my grandmother's house. I liked to play with my cousins, but what I liked best was sitting at the table with the old people and listening to their stories.

F Uno domingo cuando estuvimos en mis abuelos' casa, mi hermano se caió fuera de un árbol, donde estaba jugando con nuestros primo. Todos estábamos muy preocupado. Alguien llamaba _____ la ambulancia. Mientras esperábamos para ayuda, mi mamá trataba a calmar _____ mi hermano, que fue agitado. Él no lloraba, aunque estaba muy herido. Yo trataba a calmar _____ mi hermanita, que sí lloraba por lo ocurrido. Por fin llegaba la ambulancia. Los paramédicos examinaban _____ mi hermano y llevaron lo a el hospital, donde determinaron que rompió su clavícula. Le ponían algunas vendas, le daron un calmante y luego llevábamos lo a casa.

One Sunday when we were at my grandparents' house, my brother fell out of a tree, where he was playing with our cousin. We were all really worried. Somebody called an ambulance. While we were waiting for help, my mother tried to soothe my brother, who was upset. He didn't cry, even though he was badly hurt. I tried to soothe my little sister, who cried because of what happened. Finally the ambulance arrived. The paramedics examined my brother and took him to the hospital, where they determined that he had broken his collarbone. They put some bandages on him, gave him a tranquilizer, and then we took him home.

G Un español clase es planeando tener una fiesta _____ celebrar el final de semestre. El profesor quiere que los estudiantes traen platos auténticos de la cocina hispana. _____ dice a tres chicas a preparar arroz con pollo en el estilo colombiano. _____ sugiere a dos otras a seguir una receta por unas papas en el estilo peruano. A uno chico _____ recomienda a hacer una española tortilla, y a un otro chico a preparar uno flan. El profesor _____ da recetas por todos estes platos. Los estudiantes salgan entusiasmados, piensando de su fiesta y _____ la comida rica que van _____ cocinar.

A Spanish class is planning to have a party to celebrate the end of the semester. The teacher wants the students to bring authentic Hispanic dishes. He tells three girls to prepare chicken and rice, Colombian style. He suggests to two others that they follow a recipe for Peruvian-style potatoes. He recommends to one boy that he make a Spanish tortilla, and to another that he make a flan. The teacher gives them recipes for all these dishes. The students leave excitedly, thinking about their party and the delicious food they're going to cook.

H Una clase de español **era** planeando **tener** una fiesta para celebrar el final del semestre. El profesor **quiso** _____ los estudiantes **a traer** platos auténticos de la cocina hispana. _____ **dijó** a tres chicas **a preparar** arroz con pollo al estilo colombiano. _____ **sugieró** a otras dos **a seguir** una receta para unas papas al estilo peruano. _____ un chico _____ **recomendió a hacer** una tortilla española, y a **uno otro chico a preparar** un flan. El profesor _____ **dó** recetas para todos estos platos. Los estudiantes **salgaron** entusiasmados, pensando **de** su fiesta y _____ la comida rica que **fueron** _____ cocinan.

A Spanish class was planning to have a party to celebrate the end of the semester. The teacher wanted the students to bring authentic Hispanic dishes. He told three girls to prepare Colombian-style chicken with rice. He suggested to two others that they follow a recipe for Peruvian-style potatoes. He recommended to one boy that he make a Spanish tortilla, and to another that he make a flan. The teacher gave them recipes for all these dishes. The students left excitedly, thinking about their party and the delicious food they were going to cook.

I "¿Qué van a hacer ustedes cuando _____ graduan?" pidió la señora

que visitaba la universidad con sus hija. Una chica contestó, "voy a estudiar

medicina y algún día seré médico." Otra dijó, "tomaré un viaje alrededor el

mundo y no vuelveré hasta _____ me canso de la aventura." Otras dijierón

que no supieron que van _____ hacer. Algunas fueron seguros de que

quisieron conseguir casados y tener hijos algún día, sino otras no.

"What are you all going to do when you graduate?" asked the woman who was
visiting the university with her daughter. One girl answered, "I'm going to study
medicine and one day I'll be a doctor." Another said, "I'll take a trip around the
world and I won't come back until I get tired of the adventure." Others said they
didn't know what they were going to do. Some were sure that they wanted
to get married and have children one day, but others weren't.

J Para el año 2050, todos nosotros seremos viejo y habremos hacido muchas

cosas. Mi hermano dice _____ se habrá jubilado después que ha trabajado

cuarenta años. Se habrá casado _____ su novia corriente y tendrán tres

hijos. Los niños ya habrán terminados sus carreras y ellos vivirán en varias

partes del mundo. Mi hermano piensa _____ se reunirán todos por lo menos

cuatro veces un año. Su novia dice que ella también se habrá jubilada y que sí,

se habrá casado a mi hermano. Pero ella dice que no tendrán tres hijos, pero

dos, y que los dos vivirán cerca _____ sus padres cuando son grandes.

By the year 2050, we'll all be old and we will have done a lot of things.
My brother says that he will have retired after working forty years. He will have
married his present girlfriend and they will have three children. The children will
have already finished their education and will be living in different parts of the
world. My brother thinks they will all get together at least four times a year. His
girlfriend says that she will have retired too, and that, yes, she will have married
my brother. But she says they won't have three children, but two, and that both
of them will live near their parents when they are grown.

K Si yo ganaba "el gordo" de la lotería, o si alguien me dio diez millon dólares,

antes que yo hice otra cosa, yo contrataría a alguien quien serviría como mi

gerente personal, que manejaría el dinero, que lo invertiría bien, que me ayudaría

en elegir proyectos filantrópicos y que aseguraría que no perdería el dinero tan

rápido que lo habría ganado. Luego dejaría trabajando y pensaría de la mejor

manera de disfrutar de la vida. Yo creo que buscaría una casa elegante, sino que no muy grande, y que también yo compraría una casa nueva para mis padres. Yo compraría un coche de lujo. Yo tomaría viajes a los países que me parecieron interesantes, pero antes que yo tomaba cada viaje, yo estudiaría el idioma y la cultura del lugar. Yo leería mucho para aprender más del mundo. Claro, yo también tendría muchas fiestas en la nueva casa y invitaría _____ todos mis amigos.

If I won the lottery jackpot, or if someone gave me ten million dollars, before I did anything else, I would hire someone to be my personal manager, to take care of the money, to invest it well, to help me to choose charitable projects, and to make sure that I didn't lose the money as fast as I had gotten it. Then I would stop working and would think about the best way to enjoy life. I think I would look for an elegant house, but not a big one, and I would also buy a new house for my parents. I would buy a luxury car. I would take trips to the countries that seemed interesting, but before taking each trip, I would study the language and the culture of the place. I would read a lot, to learn more about the world. Of course I would also have a lot of parties at the new house, and I would invite all my friends.

L Mi tío ya es viejo y él dice él ha vivido bien. Claro, hay cosas que habría cambiado si había tenido la oportunidad, pero en general está contento. El más triste tiempo de su vida fue diez años pasados, cuando mi tía morió de cáncer. Durante estos diez años, mi tío _____ ha sentido muy sólo. Él habría gustado mucho disfrutar de sus esposa's compania. Sin embargo, sus dos hijas visitan a él todos los días, y si necesita cualquiera cosa, sólo tiene que decirlo y se cumple el deseo en seguida. _____ siente dichoso y muy orgulloso de su familia, pues no conoce _____ ninguno otro anciano que tiene hijos tan atentos. También es muy agradecido de haber gozado de bien salud todos estos años.

My uncle is old now, and he says he has lived well. Of course, there are things he would have changed if he had had the chance, but in general he's happy. The saddest time of his life was ten years ago, when my aunt died of cancer. For these ten years, my uncle has been lonely. He would have liked to have had his wife by his side. Still, his two daughters visit him every day, and if he needs anything, he only has to mention it and it's done. He feels lucky and proud of his family—he doesn't know anybody else his age who has such attentive children. He's also very grateful to have been in good health all these years.

ANSWER KEY

Spelling (page 16)

A
1. ca, que, qui, co, cu
2. ga, gue, gui, go, gu
3. za, ce, ci, zo, zu
4. cua, cue, cui, cuo
5. gua, güe, güi, guo
6. ja, je/ge, ji/gi, jo, ju

B
1. Mi hermano no vino a clase porque no hizo la tarea. Ahora está en casa.
2. ¿Quiénes van al cine esta tarde? ¿Vas tú? ¿Va tu hermano?
3. Sí, mi hermano va, pero sólo si hace la tarea primero.

C
1. 5
2. 2
3. 3
4. 0
5. 4

Capitalization (page 19)

A
1. D.
2. Sra.
3. Ud.
4. Sres.

B
1. septiembre
4. inglés
6. católico
8. miércoles
9. argentino

Punctuation (page 21)

A
1. Maria, ¿vas a estudiar conmigo hoy?
2. No, no puedo.
3. ¿Me llamas más tarde?
4. Sí, te llamo a las ocho.
5. "Te voy a extrañar", dijo Paco.
6. Fueron a Guatemala, El Salvador, Honduras y Nicaragua.

Nouns (page 37)

A
1. la hermana
2. el profesor
3. la médico
4. el especialista
5. la paciente
6. el amigo
7. la miembro
8. el jefe
9. la mujer

337

B 1. el
2. la
3. el
4. el
5. la
6. el
7. la
8. la
9. el
10. el
11. la
12. la

C 1. casas
2. libros
3. esquíes
4. ladrones
5. ciudades
6. lápices
7. órdenes
8. lunes
9. domingos
10. los Sres. Pérez / los Pérez

Numbers (page 52)

A 1. dos
2. diez
3. catorce
4. veintidós
5. treinta y nueve
6. ciento cuarenta y seis
7. cuatrocientos setenta y tres
8. quinientos once
9. mil novecientos ochenta y cuatro
10. dos mil siete

B 1. el primer libro, la primera novela
2. el segundo piso, la segunda vez
3. el tercer edificio, la tercera casa
4. el cuarto año, la cuarta calle
5. el quinto día, la quinta persona

C 1. veintiún chicos
2. veintiuna chicas
3. cien libros
4. doscientos tres niños
5. dos millones de dólares
6. el dos de octubre de mil novecientos setenta y siete
7. dos cero dos, cuatro noventa, treinta y tres, sesenta y uno
8. las diez y media de la mañana
9. medio kilo
10. dos kilos y medio

Noun Determiners (pages 78–79)

A 1. el águila
2. estos libros
3. la lección
4. las aguas
5. aquel día
6. aquellas personas
7. algún chico
8. unos libros

B 1. el
2. los
3. en el
4. en el
5. al
6. el
7. X
8. X
9. otra
10. otras dos
11. ninguna
12. X
13. un
14. X
15. las
16. la
17. X

C 1. g
2. b
3. f
4. h
5. d

6. a
7. c
8. i
9. e

D 1. Ese hombre
2. libro cualquiera
3. cualquier libro
4. propio negocio

5. negocio propio
6. única mujer
7. mujer única
8. cierto problema

Descriptive Adjectives (pages 94–95)

A 1. la chica interesante
2. el hombre optimista
3. las jóvenes encantadoras

4. los niños felices
5. el muchacho alto

B 1. la casa pequeña y hermosa
2. la blusa y falda nuevas

3. los zapatos azules y bonitos
4. las blusas roja y blanca

C 1. nuevo coche
2. gran hombre
3. antigua ciudad

4. familia pobre
5. viejo amigo

D 1. el verde
2. los grandes
3. lo bueno

4. lo interesante
5. los interesantes

E 1. es
2. está
3. es
4. es

5. es
6. está
7. está
8. es

F 1. muy
2. un poco
3. demasiado / bien / sumamente /
extremadamente / requete
4. ísimo

5. el chico más alto de la clase
6. más enérgica que Esteban
7. ísima
8. la chica más seria de la escuela

The Infinitive (page 101)

A 1. Tenemos que estudiar más.
2. Volvió a escribir el ejercicio.
3. Quieren dejar de fumar.
4. Nos encanta ir de compras.
5. Vi salir al jefe.
6. Ella me hizo trabajar.

7. (El) saber montar en bicicleta
es importante en esta ciudad.
8. Acaba de llegar.
9. Es difícil estudiar aquí.
10. Estos libros son fáciles de
entender.

Types of Verbs (page 109)

A
1. sales, a
2. levanto, b
3. caminan, a
4. llama, c
5. cuenta, d
6. queja, b
7. envía, d
8. pierden, g
9. encantan, e
10. da, d
11. olvida, g
12. visita, c
13. dice, f
14. acaba, g
15. fascina, e
16. lastiman, b
17. gusta, e
18. aconsejo, f
19. sugiere, f
20. quiero, c
21. vamos, a

The Present Tense (page 121)

A
1. hacen
2. leyendo
3. tenemos
4. estudias
5. hablo
6. está
7. ir
8. voy a estudiar
9. se cae
10. canta en público

B
1. Construyen/Están construyendo una casa nueva.
2. Llevamos diez años viviendo en esta ciudad./Hace diez años que vivimos en esta ciudad./Vivimos en esta ciudad desde hace diez años.
3. Esta es la primera vez que como mole.
4. (Ella) acaba de leer esa novela.
5. ¿Te llevamos a tu casa?
6. Casi/Por poco tienen un accidente.
7. Si me llamas, te ayudo.
8. Nos vamos a las seis y la película empieza a las siete.
9. ¿Vas a salir con tus amigos mañana por la noche?
10. ¿Me ayudas?

The Preterite Perfect Tense (page 126)

A
1. Mis padres han comido.
2. ¿Qué has hecho?
3. He terminado con mis exámenes.
4. Ana ha recibido un mensaje.

B
1. Acaban de llegar.
2. Ya hemos escrito las cartas.
3. No ha enviado su solicitud todavía.
4. Abrió la ventana hace unos minutos.
5. ¿Cuántas veces han visto ustedes esa película?

The Preterite Tense (page 131)

A
1. jugué
2. almorzó
3. fuimos
4. tuve
5. corrió
6. hicieron
7. estuvo
8. estudié
9. volvió
10. dormí
11. hizo
12. comí
13. pudo
14. oíste
15. leyó
16. dio
17. vi
18. buscó
19. escribí
20. visitó
21. leí
22. fui
23. sintió
24. supe

B
1. Yo siempre pagué las cuentas.
2. Jorge bailó bien.
3. Fuimos al cine el sábado.
4. No hicimos nada el jueves.
5. ¿Adónde fuiste?
6. Nuestro equipo jugó bien.
7. Los niños durmieron toda la noche.
8. A Beatriz no le gustó la película.
9. Me dio mucho gusto conocerlo.
10. Estuvo muy cansado.

The Imperfect Tense (pages 138–139)

A
1. Era pequeña y un poco seria.
2. Tenía un perro y me gustaba jugar con él.
3. Iba al cine con mis amigas todos los miércoles.
4. Mi familia y yo comíamos en la casa de mi abuela los domingos por la tarde.
5. Escribía mis tareas en la tarde después de las clases.
6. Mis hermanas y yo ayudábamos en la casa.
7. Mis amigos iban a la playa en el verano y a veces yo los acompañaba.
8. La actividad que me gustaba más era leer.

B
1. cocinaba, veía
2. entré, jugaban (estaban jugando)
3. estábamos, apagó
4. llamaste, estaba
5. quería
6. podía, tenía que, fui

The Pluperfect Tense (page 142)

A
1. había leído el periódico
2. ya había comido
3. no había estudiado

The Future Tense (page 148)

A 1. tendré
2. encontrarás
3. vivirá
4. vendrá

B 1. regrese
2. estudie
3. estén
4. comes
5. tenga

The Future Perfect Tense (page 150)

A 1. habrán
2. habrá
3. habremos
4. habré.... (*Answer will vary.*)

The Simple Conditional (page 154)

A 1. Tendrías frío.
2. Estaría enferma.
3. Si yo fuera tú (usted), no saldría.
4. Si tuviera más dinero, compraría una casa.
5. ¿Qué harías tú?/¿Qué haría usted?

The Conditional Perfect (page 157)

A 1. ¿Qué habríamos hecho?
2. Si hubiera tenido tiempo, te habría llamado.
3. Si hubiera estado allí tu hermano, no habrías hecho eso.
4. Si hubiéramos sabido la verdad, no habríamos trabajado aquí.

The Present Subjunctive (pages 175–176)

A 1. tenga
2. habla
3. guste
4. escribamos
5. llames
6. llegue
7. vienen
8. acepten
9. ir
10. vayan

B 1. No hay nadie que cocine como mi mamá.
2. Buscamos un gerente que hable español.
3. Espero que vengas a la fiesta.
4. Ella te aconseja que trabajes más.
5. ¡Es maravilloso que estés aquí!
6. Él duda que yo lo pueda hacer.
7. Te llamo en cuanto/tan pronto como/cuando sepa las noticias.
8. Te recojo a menos que tenga que trabajar.
9. Ella sale sin que él lo sepa.
10. Ahorrarán dinero para poder viajar.

C 1. Ven conmigo.
2. Siéntese, por favor.

3. Levántense.
4. ¡Vamos al cine!

D 1. No vengas conmigo.
2. No se sienten, por favor.

3. No se levanten.
4. No vayamos al cine.

The Preterite Perfect Subjunctive (page 183)

A 1. haya estudiado
2. haya terminado
3. hayas podido

4. haber podido
5. haya pagado

The Imperfect Subjunctive (page 196)

A 1. tuviera
2. acompañaran

3. solicitara
4. llamara

B 1. estudiara
2. ver
3. leyeras

C 1. Si lo quisiera, me casaría con él.
2. Si él me llamara todas las noches, no contestaría el teléfono.
3. Si quisieras tocar el piano, practicarías todos los días.
4. Si mi papá estuviera aquí, me ayudaría.

The Pluperfect Subjunctive (page 199)

A 1. Si lo hubiera querido, me habría casado con él.
2. Si él me hubiera llamado todas las noches, no habría contestado el teléfono.
3. Si hubieras querido tocar el piano, habrías practicado todos los días.
4. Si mi papá hubiera estado aquí, me habría ayudado.

Reported Speech (page 203)

A 1. quiere ir al cine, quería ir al cine
2. fueron al cine ayer, habían ido al cine ayer
3. le ayude con la computadora, le ayudara con la computadora
4. va a estar en su casa esta tarde, iba a estar en su casa esta tarde

Subjects, Objects, and Their Pronouns (pages 228–230)

A 1. -tigo
2. -sigo
3. usted
4. mí

5. mí
6. ti
7. nosotros
8. él

B 1. nos
2. se
3. Me

4. se
5. -se
6. -te

C 1. se aprovechó   4. me siento
    2. quedaron   5. Despedimos
    3. se quedó

D 1. Juan no la llamó esta tarde.
    2. Susana las dejó en el mercado.
    3. Los queremos mucho.

E 1. me   3. nos
    2. les   4. Te

F 1. Me la va a enviar la próxima semana.
    2. Ángela se las dará muy pronto.
    3. ¿Te lo dijo Jorge?

G 1. A Victoria le interesan las películas. Le encantan.
    2. A Roberto le fastidia el tráfico. Le molesta mucho.
    3. A Juan le gusta Inés. Ella le fascina (a él)./ Le fascina.

H 1. A Mario se le quedaron las llaves en el coche.
    2. Se nos cayeron los libros.
    3. Se les olvidó la tarea.

I 1. habla   3. venden
    2. enseñan   4. sirve

J 1. Lo bueno   3. el cual
    2. lo difícil   4. de las cuales

Adverbs and Prepositions with Adverbial Functions
(pages 254–256)

A 1. pasada   7. buen tiempo
    2. anoche   8. veces
    3. última, hace dos semanas   9. ¿Te divertiste?/¿Lo pasaste bien?
    4. últimas   10. tiempo
    5. siguiente   11. otra vez/una vez más
    6. próximo   12. A veces

B 1. leer   3. vuelvan
    2. regrese   4. vestirse

C 1. los lunes   4. más de
    2. el lunes   5. en
    3. Siempre

D 1. delante de   3. dentro de
    2. afuera   4. abajo

E 1. suave y dulcemente   3. con calma
    2. recién   4. despacio/lento/lentamente

F 1. b 4. a
2. e 5. d
3. c

G 1. ¿Adónde vas? / ¿Adónde va usted?
2. ¿De qué hablan ustedes? / ¿De qué habláis?
3. ¿Con quién vas al cine? / ¿Con quién va usted al cine?
4. ¿Cuándo regresan/vuelven ustedes? / ¿Cuándo regresáis/volváis?

H 1. No voy a ninguna parte.
2. No hablamos de nada.
3. No voy al cine con nadie.
4. No regresamos nunca. / No volvemos nunca.

I 1. d 5. a
2. g 6. c
3. f 7. b
4. e

Other Prepositions (pages 288–289)

A 1. tú y yo 4. ella
2. -tigo 5. ella y por él
3. a la

B 1. ¿En qué piensas? / ¿En qué estás pensando?
2. ¿A quién busca? / ¿A quién está buscando?
3. ¿Con quién va?
4. ¿Qué esperamos? / ¿Qué estamos esperando?
5. ¿Qué miras? / ¿Qué estás mirando?
6. ¿De quién es la carta?
7. ¿Desde cuándo estás aquí? / ¿Hace cuánto tiempo que estás aquí?
8. ¿Con qué frecuencia visitas a tu abuela?

C 1. a 6. de
2. a 7. de
3. con 8. de
4. con 9. por
5. en 10. en

D 1. por 6. para
2. para 7. para
3. por 8. por
4. para 9. por
5. Para

Conjunctions (page 296)

A
1. e
2. sino
3. y
4. ni
5. o

6. pues
7. Tanto, como
8. O, o
9. u
10. ni / ni siquiera

Words (pages 321–322)

A
1. chocolate
2. solución
3. posibilidad
4. biología
5. paciente

6. fragmento
7. sentimiento
8. arrogancia
9. presencia
10. feminista

B
1. sand
2. folder
3. commitment
4. custom
5. disappointment

6. argument
7. factory
8. reading
9. relatives
10. event

C
1. advertir
2. notar
3. atender
4. discutir
5. ignorar

6. molestar
7. recordar
8. avisar
9. solicitar
10. asistir

D
1. k
2. b
3. i
4. d
5. j
6. c

7. e
8. h
9. f
10. g
11. a
12. l

E
1. dos veces
2. preguntó
3. es
4. está
5. tiene

6. irme
7. Voy
8. conoce
9. bueno

Constructions (page 330)

A 1. ¿Cuándo van a darle de alta a tu abuela? / ¿Cuándo le van a dar de alta a tu abuela?
2. ¿Vas a estrenar tus nuevos zapatos?
3. Quiero estar en la estación para darte la bienvenida.
4. Ella fue a México y se enamoró.
5. La cena se echó a perder.
6. La chica no se fijó en él durante la fiesta.
7. Me echaron la culpa (a mí).
8. Se despidieron esta mañana en el aeropuerto.
9. ¿De qué se trata tu trabajo?
10. ¿A qué hora desayunan ustedes? / ¿A qué hora desayunáis?

B 1. No tengo que comprar nada.
2. Nunca viene a visitar los domingos.
3. Jorge no va a estudiar, ni yo tampoco.
4. Nadie está en la oficina.

Catch the Blunders (pages 331-336)

A Estoy en mi primer año de la universidad. Vivo en una residencia, que se llama "Jefferson Hall", con dos compañeras de cuarto, Mary y Jenna. Las dos son muy simpáticas y nos llevamos bien. Mary es bastante seria y estudia mucho. Jenna es buena estudiante, pero no estudia tanto como Mary. Nuestro dormitorio no es grande, pero es cómodo y bonito.

B Como quiero ser médico, estudio biología y química, que me gustan mucho. Mis clases son los lunes y los miércoles desde las diez de la mañana hasta las once y media, en Washington Hall. También tengo que estudiar inglés, historia y español. El español es difícil para mí, pero me gusta y creo que es importante para mi carrera. La clase de inglés es los martes y los jueves a las nueve en Harrison Hall, la de historia es a mediodía los mismos días y en el mismo edificio y la de español es de lunes a jueves desde las dos de la tarde hasta las tres, en Tyler Hall. No tengo que asistir a clases los viernes.

C Entramos en un dormitorio de la universidad y vemos esta escena: Hay ocho estudiantes sentados en el suelo preparándose para un examen. Están tratando de recordar todos los datos sobre la Guerra Civil de los Estados Unidos. Una chica tiene una pizarra pequeña en la cual está escribiendo las fechas importantes. Un chico le está explicando a su amigo lo que pasó al final de la guerra. Otros dos chicos están leyendo sus libros de texto. Una estudiante está durmiendo y su amiga está tratando de despertarla. Un muchacho está hablando por celular con su novia. Nadie está viendo la televisión. Todos beben café y esperan la llegada de unas pizzas.

D El viernes tengo una fiesta en la casa de un amigo. Voy a ir con otras dos chicas. No sé qué van a llevar ellas, pero yo pienso llevar mi nueva falda negra con una blusa rosada. Voy a usar unos zapatos negros de tacón alto y unos pendientes de plata. Mis amigas vienen a buscarme a las siete, así que voy a tener que cambiarme de ropa rápido porque mi última clase no termina hasta las 5:30. Estoy segura de que vamos a divertirnos mucho.

E Cuando era joven, vivía en la ciudad con mis padres y con mis hermanos. Todos los domingos íbamos al pueblo para almorzar a la casa de mis abuelos. También iban mis tíos con sus hijos, y a veces invitábamos a algún amigo. En fin, había mucha gente que comía y se divertía en esa casa los domingos. Mi abuela, la mejor cocinera del mundo, preparaba una gran comida, con por lo menos dos tipos de carne, varios platos de verduras, dos o tres ensaladas y frutas. Nunca faltaba el pan especial hecho a mano por mi abuela. Luego se servía un pastel o una torta de postre. A todo el mundo le gustaba comer en casa de mi abuela. A mí me gustaba jugar con mis primos, pero lo que me gustaba más era sentarme en la mesa con los viejos y escuchar sus cuentos.

F Un domingo cuando estábamos en la casa de mis abuelos, mi hermano se cayó de un árbol, donde estaba jugando con nuestro primo. Todos estábamos muy preocupados. Alguien llamó a la ambulancia. Mientras esperábamos ayuda, mi mamá trataba de calmar a mi hermano, que estaba agitado. Él no lloraba, aunque estaba muy herido. Yo trataba de calmar a mi hermanita, que sí lloraba por lo ocurrido. Por fin llegó la ambulancia. Los paramédicos examinaron a mi hermano y lo llevaron al hospital, donde determinaron que se le había roto la clavícula. Le pusieron algunas vendas, le dieron un calmante y luego lo llevamos a casa.

G Una clase de español está planeando hacer una fiesta para celebrar el final del semestre. El profesor quiere que los estudiantes traigan platos auténticos de la cocina hispana. Les dice a tres chicas que preparen arroz con pollo al estilo colombiano. Les sugiere a otras dos que sigan una receta para unas papas al estilo peruano. A un chico le recomienda que haga una tortilla española, y a otro que prepare un flan. El profesor les da recetas para todos estos platos. Los estudiantes salen entusiasmados, pensando en su fiesta y en la comida rica que van a cocinar.

H Una clase de español estaba planeando hacer una fiesta para celebrar el final del semestre. El profesor quería que los estudiantes trajeran platos auténticos de la cocina hispana. Les dijo a tres chicas que prepararan arroz con pollo al estilo colombiano. Les sugirió a otras dos que siguieran una receta para unas papas al estilo peruano. A un chico le recomendó que hiciera una tortilla española, y a otro que preparara un flan. El profesor les dio recetas para todos estos platos. Los estudiantes salieron entusiasmados, pensando en su fiesta y en la comida rica que iban a cocinar.

I "¿Qué van a hacer ustedes cuando se gradúen?" preguntó la señora que visitaba la universidad con su hija. Una chica contestó, "voy a estudiar medicina y algún día seré médico". Otra dijo, "haré un viaje alrededor del mundo y no volveré hasta que me canse de la aventura". Otras dijeron que no sabían qué iban a hacer. Algunas estaban seguras de que querían casarse y tener hijos algún día, pero otras no.

J Para el año 2050, todos nosotros seremos viejos y habremos hecho muchas cosas. Mi hermano dice que se habrá jubilado después de haber trabajado cuarenta años. Se habrá casado con su novia actual y tendrán tres hijos. Los hijos ya habrán terminado sus carreras y vivirán en varias partes del mundo. Mi hermano piensa que se reunirán todos por lo menos cuatro veces al año. Su novia dice que ella también se habrá jubilado y que sí, se habrá casado con mi hermano. Pero ella dice que no tendrán tres hijos, sino dos, y que los dos vivirán cerca de sus padres cuando sean grandes.

K Si yo ganara "el gordo" de la lotería, o si alguien me diera diez millones de dólares, antes de hacer otra cosa, contrataría a alguien que sirviera como mi gerente personal, que manejara el dinero, que lo invirtiera bien, que me ayudara en elegir proyectos filantrópicos y que asegurara que no perdiera el dinero tan rápido como lo hubiera ganado. Luego dejaría de trabajar y pensaría en la mejor manera de disfrutar de la vida. Creo que buscaría una casa elegante, pero no muy grande, y que también compraría una casa nueva para mis padres. Compraría un coche de lujo. Haría viajes a los países que me parecieran interesantes, pero antes de hacer cada viaje, estudiaría el idioma y la cultura del lugar. Leería mucho para aprender más del mundo. Claro, también haría muchas fiestas en la nueva casa e invitaría a todos mis amigos.

L Mi tío ya es viejo y dice que ha vivido bien. Claro, hay cosas que habría cambiado si hubiera tenido la oportunidad, pero en general está contento. La época más triste de su vida fue hace diez años, cuando mi tía murió de cáncer. Durante estos diez años, mi tío se ha sentido muy solo. Le habría gustado mucho disfrutar de la compañía de su esposa. Sin embargo, sus dos hijas lo visitan todos los días, y si necesita cualquier cosa, sólo tiene que decirlo y se cumple el deseo en seguida. Se siente dichoso y muy orgulloso de su familia, pues no conoce a ningún otro anciano que tenga hijos tan atentos. También está muy agradecido de haber gozado de buena salud todos estos años.

INDEX OF SPANISH WORDS AND EXPRESSIONS

SUBJECT INDEX